Transfiguring
LOSS

Transfiguring LOSS

Julian of Norwich
as a Guide for Survivors
of Traumatic Grief

JANE F. MAYNARD

"all shall be well"

Jane Maynard

THE
PILGRIM
PRESS
Cleveland

This book is dedicated

to those around the world
who are living with AIDS and HIV disease

in loving memory of those who have died from AIDS,
particularly the Rev. Ted Boya, my mentor and friend,

in thanksgiving for the generous love
of the men and women of All Saints Church, San Francisco,
who have taught me so much about death and resurrection,

and to The Rt. Rev. William Swing, Episcopal Bishop of California,
who provided courageous leadership in the early days
of the AIDS pandemic

The Pilgrim Press
700 Prospect Avenue
Cleveland, Ohio 44115-1100
thepilgrimpress.com

© 2006 by Jane F. Maynard

Printed in the United States of America on acid-free paper

10 09 08 07 06   5 4 3 2 1

Library of Congress Cataloging-in-Publication Data

Maynard, Jane Frances.
   Transfiguring loss : Julian of Norwich as a guide for survivors of traumatic grief /
Jane F. Maynard.
     p. cm.
   Includes bibliographical references.
   ISBN-13: 978-0-8298-1601-3 (alk. paper)
   1. Julian, of Norwich, b. 1343. 2. Suffering – Religious aspects – Christianity.
3. Bereavement – Religious aspects – Christianity. I. Title.
BV5095.J84M39 2006
248.8′66 – dc22

                                2006012486

ISBN-13: 978-0-8298-1601-3
ISBN-10: 0-8298-1601-1

Contents

Preface

Slightly over six hundred years ago, in a sickroom in Norwich, England, a young woman lay poised between life and death. After nearly a week of serious illness and pain, and despite a desire to continue living for the sake of God's love, she embraced the gravity of her illness and consented to die. Fixing her eyes on a crucifix placed before her, she felt her life slipping away and her sight beginning to fail. She truly believed that she was at the point of death, yet somehow, paradoxically, in consenting to die, all pain left her and she felt completely well.

Puzzled, yet still expecting to die, she recalled how earlier in her life she had prayed for the ability to suffer with Christ in his passion. She wanted to feel his pains and share his suffering as if she were an eyewitness to his death. Hardly had this thought passed than she became vividly aware of red blood trickling from under the crown of thorns on Christ's head. It soon became a copious flow of blood. In that instant, Julian entered into a lively series of visions that would continue for the next eleven hours, concluding with one definitive "shewing" the following evening. These visions would transform her psychologically and spiritually, healing her from the pain of earlier traumatic loss and bringing to birth within her a vibrant love of God and a passionate and warm-hearted acceptance of her "even Christians."[1]

Although she lived many centuries ago, the theological and spiritual insights of Julian of Norwich still speak with power and promise to survivors of traumatic loss. Her optimistic view of creation, the immediacy of her encounter with a "courteous" God, and her balanced appraisal of the human potential for loving service, even amid limitations of vision and strength, provide grounds for hope and optimism.

This book explores the contributions that Julian's theology and spirituality may offer to survivors of traumatic loss. For Julian may be understood as a survivor of traumatic loss arising from the plague, and here I explore particular ways in which her survival of at least three epidemics of the Black Death pandemic of the mid-fourteenth to early fifteenth centuries shaped her social, religious, and psychological experience. Surviving the plague primed her for the experience of compassionate suffering she sought and achieved through her visions. She experienced both intense pain and healing through her visions, and her experience as a survivor contributed to her focused theological reflection upon the content of her visions and her passion to communicate the insights they generated to her fellow Christians. In the words of the psychiatrist Robert J. Lifton, Julian's text constituted her "survivor mission," and it continues to inspire and intrigue fellow seekers to this day.[2]

I first identified Julian's theology as a resource in my own search for meaning. Fresh from two years of AIDS ministry in San Francisco, I encountered these words in Julian of Norwich's *Revelation of Love*, words Julian uttered during a vision of Christ's suffering and death on the cross:

> But of all the pains that lead to salvation, this pain is the most: to see your love suffer. How might any pain be more to me than to see him who is my whole life, my bliss and all my joy suffer? Here I truly felt that I loved Christ so much above myself that there was no worse pain I might suffer than to see him in pain.[3]

I was galvanized. Her words vividly reminded me of sentiments expressed by partners, family members, and friends of
those who died with AIDS. Further, they brought to mind my
own pain in witnessing AIDS deaths. In short, they articulated
the perspective of a survivor. I knew upon reading them that
Julian was acquainted with death, and in that moment I became curious about her. Who was she and how had she come
to express this compassion for suffering so clearly? My questions were the beginning of a search that led finally to the
understanding of Julian and her context that I shall elaborate
in this book.

In my work as an AIDS chaplain in the early nineties in
San Francisco, I experienced what Lifton has called "death in
life": a loss of vitality and hope accompanied by the sickening
sense that life itself is dying amid the encounter with relentless
death.[4] I have since learned that similar psychological dynamics
arise in situations of traumatic loss, regardless of the cause of
death. Whether arising from pandemics such as AIDS, from
natural disasters such as earthquakes, tsunamis, tornadoes, or
hurricanes, from accidents, or from terrorist activity, traumatic
loss raises fundamental questions about the fragility of life, the
meaning of safety, human limitation, the trustworthiness of
creation, and death and the afterlife.

In Julian's writings, I found a spiritual and theological
framework compassionate enough to soothe my own painful
experiences of suffering and loss and large enough to embrace
the perplexing questions arising from this trauma. Strengthened by my encounter with her hopeful vision, I continued to
work with AIDS survivors in the nineties. Reading Julian taught
me that a transcendent experience of love offers hope in the
midst of loss. My continuing work with AIDS survivors con-
firmed this insight. Rebecca Chopp has described how theology
shaped in response to the moral summons of testimony reveals

transcendence as the power and spirit of transfiguration. Following Chopp, I now believe that transcendence transfigures loss. That is, loss is transfigured when it becomes an encounter with God's transcendent love, love that offers hope and the promise of liberation.[5]

Far too many people have died from HIV disease in deaths that could have been prevented. The global consequence of AIDS loss is unprecedented suffering. When one adds to this suffering the effects of other traumatic losses in our time, whether from genocide, war, violence, terrorism, or natural disaster, the overwhelming burden of loss threatens to crush us. My study of Julian and other survivors, however, has convinced me of the Spirit's ability to transfigure the experiences and memories of suffering so that they may empower the creation of a new and more just world. Like Chopp, I affirm the presence of God, not only in transcendent love amid loss, but also in the acts of remembering beloved dead, in shaping a new life among survivors, in critiquing the present, and in creatively naming possibilities for a more just world.[6]

Through my research on traumatic loss, I have learned that hope may be found in a self-giving love that transcends death. The fruit of hope in the face of traumatic death is resurrection life, a life of justice empowered by the dangerous memories of love to which survivors testify.

I began the ministry that gave rise to this book sixteen years ago, and many friends and colleagues have influenced my formation as a pastoral theologian in that time. I offer particular thanks to Dr. Tim Greene, my clinical supervisor at San Francisco General Hospital, who first encouraged me in the AIDS chaplaincy that stimulated my interest in traumatic loss. Friends and colleagues at Grace Cathedral, including Alan Jones, Frances Tornquist, and Sue Singer, supported my growing efforts in theological reflection on loss, and I drew strength from the Cathedral Community's inspiring response to the AIDS pandemic. The parishioners and clergy at All Saints Church in San Francisco allowed me to share their lives, and they opened their hearts in stimulating and moving conversations about their experiences with HIV/AIDS. It is through their fellowship and rich liturgical life that I began to experience concretely the presence of God in transfiguring loss. I am very grateful to all of them, but especially to Kenneth Schmidt, their gifted and caring rector.

Karen Torjesen encouraged my early exploration of the parallels between Julian's experience and the experience of AIDS survivors. Mary Elizabeth Mullino Moore, Kathleen Greider, and William Clements guided the dissertation research and writing that laid the foundation for this work. The faculty of the Church Divinity School of the Pacific in Berkeley, California, offered encouragement, and I am particularly grateful to Arthur Holder and Donn Morgan for their support as the book first began to take shape. The parishioners at Good Samaritan Episcopal Church in Sammamish, Washington, showed genuine enthusiasm for this work, and their healthy curiosity about the subject matter and my progress encouraged my persistence. Durward James Hindle III, the senior warden, helped me to maintain the focus required to bring this project to completion. Colleagues in the Society for Pastoral Theology have also been a tremendous help. I offer particular thanks to Charles Scalise and Sharon Thornton for their friendship and belief that I could find a way to combine the ministries of scholar and parish priest. My editor at The Pilgrim Press, Ulrike Guthrie, read the text with a careful and critical eye, and the book has been vastly improved through her efforts. I offer sincere thanks to the personnel at the Julian Centre, to the sisters at All Hallows, and to Father Robert Llewelyn in Norwich for their hospitality during my two visits.

Finally, I am grateful to family and friends who give my life depth and whose love has sustained me during the investigation of this demanding topic. My parents, Paul and Rita Maynard, offered unflagging support. Tom Menten made many sacrifices to bring this work to fruition. My children, Beckie and Dan Menten, have encouraged me to care for the world and its future. Finally, my husband, Jim Treyens, patiently lived with the ups and downs of the writing life, offering love, perspective, and pleasant diversions at just the right moments. I am grateful to him for believing in me and in my dreams for a more whole world.

In closing, I offer the present work, as one empowered and enriched in part by the memories of love I have shared with dear departed friends. I pray that it will contribute to the transfiguration of loss for the healing of the world.

Acknowledgment is gratefully given for permission to quote from the following:

Julian of Norwich, *Revelation of Love,* ed. and trans. John Skinner (Evesham, Worcestershire: Arthur James, 1996; New York: Doubleday, 1997). Quoted by permission of John Hunt Publishing.

Julia Gatta, *The Pastoral Art of the English Mystics: Julian of Norwich, The Cloud of Unknowing, Walter Hilton* (Eugene, Ore.: Wipf & Stock, 2004). Reprinted by permission of Wipf & Stock.

Rosemary Horrox, ed. and trans., *The Black Death,* Manchester Medieval Series (Manchester: Manchester University Press, 1994). Reprinted by permission of Manchester University Press.

"Tsunami Afterward: The One Face of Grief," *New York Times,* December 30, 2004, © 2004 by The New York Times Co. Adam Nossiter, "Hurricane Takes a Further Toll: Suicides Up in New Orleans," *New York Times,* December 27, 2005, © 2005 by The New York Times Co. Jennifer Medina, "Storm and Crisis: Returnees, in Those Largely Spared, a Stubborn Sense of Guilt," *New York Times,* October 18, 2005, © 2005 by The New York Times Co. Reprinted with permission.

ONE

The Experience of
Traumatic Loss

Grief is love's alter ego, after all, yin to its yang, the necessary other; like night, grief has its own dark beauty. How may
we know light without knowledge of dark? How may we know
love without sorrow? "The disorientation following... loss can
be terrible... but grief gives the full measure of love, and it is
somehow reassuring to learn, even by suffering, how large and
powerful love is."   — Fenton Johnson, *Geography of the Heart*[1]

Setting the Stage: Stories of Traumatic Loss

JW is a gay man in the San Francisco Bay Area who lost at least
thirty close friends and lovers and hundreds of acquaintances
to AIDS. JW's most significant experience with AIDS loss came
through an AA group that for nearly eight years he attended
in the Castro, a predominantly gay and lesbian neighborhood
in San Francisco. Many members of this group died, and JW
still remembers the emotions of wondering before each meeting
who would not be attending because they were in the hospital, who might be looking worse, and who might be starting
to look better. He recalls his own fear at the height of the epidemic — his sense of being totally overwhelmed, totally crushed
by the weight of the loss. JW describes becoming numb after a
while to loss — his barber died, and then his second barber died,
then his dermatologist, whom he really liked, and the man who

worked at the grocery store around the corner, as well as half of a ragtime band to which he belonged — and still the losses relentlessly piled up. Some time ago, he went with another friend to the Castro Street Fair — he hadn't been in years — and he remarked to his friend that there really weren't many men his age there. His friend, Andrew, said, "Of course not; they are all dead." And it really sunk in to JW that almost an entire generation had died — his generation.[2]

AJ, an eye-care consultant from Florida, found herself at the Mall Level of the World Trade Center on the morning of September 11, 2001, after the first plane hit. Along with thousands of others, she followed the directions of a New York City police officer, seeking safety, walking away from the tower. She recalls looking up and seeing the hole in the tower with smoke roaring out and small bits of something floating in the air giving the impression that she might be in a ticker tape parade showered with confetti. All she could hear was the sound of thousands with her walking away from the tower. Having crossed the street, she stopped momentarily to consider how to proceed when she heard the deafening sound of an airplane engine. It vibrated her spirit, soul, and body. It was a second plane, laboring fully burdened with fuel, passengers, and massive metal not far above. The sound ended when it hit Tower Two. There was so much to hear and so much to feel. AJ remembers the smell of cremation: burning body fat, skin, hair, wires, fuel, too many things flying everywhere and her question, "Oh, GOD, how can I be here?, I am only a little mama, a little girl lost in your hand." She also recalls how, with a singular, swift motion, she was swept into the doorway of a building, deep and dark, with stairs that held others. She was sheltered there from the rain of body parts and airplane parts and car parts. The smell made her want to drop to her knees to protect herself from invasion, yet she could not do it, as there were too many inhabitants in this now sacred space. She says, "A Chinese man allowed me to lean on him, and I was grateful for the warmth of his body for the moment. A small woman wanted to lean on me, and I cherished it." She recounts, also, the cry of her plaintive, inner voice, which asked, "How long will I wait in here? I want to leave before the whole building explodes, but where is North, where is Manhattan from here?"[3]

PV, an Indian relief volunteer, arrived at Kameshwaram, a fishing village in southern Tamil Nadu, several days after the 2004 tsunami hit. When he arrived, he found that one hundred of the village's two hundred families were wiped out in the tsunami. Bulldozers were clearing the top of a hut. His nostrils were assailed by the foul smell of rotting flesh. He saw a young girl's body being dug out from the mud seven days after her death. The physical devastation was enormous: fishing nets, the prime source of livelihood for the villagers, were hopelessly tangled; boats were toppled, and many were broken beyond repair; and most of the village's homes were completely destroyed. One woman began talking to PV without looking at him, saying, "I lost my husband and two kids." She then turned toward a ruined hut that he assumed to be her residence. When he mumbled, "We're here to help you. God will...," she said, "I lost six goats." She seemed not to hear his response. She didn't seem even to acknowledge his presence. Another woman was weeping and said, "I want to see my daughter's face. That's all I want." PV decided it was better not to waste his words of hope and future because no one was listening. He concluded, "There were many survival stories and many death stories. They all sounded the same and, somehow, each one was different, as if every single death and every single survival had its own personal tsunami."[4]

JH, a musician and resident of a housing project in New Orleans, rode out Hurricane Katrina at his house on the corner of Orleans and Claiborne. Thankfully, JH says, not one window in his house broke, "even though the trees outside were falling like bowling pins and the waters kept rising." Throughout the day, water continued to rise until by evening it was six or seven feet deep. Finally, a day later, when the water to his home was shut off, he and his family evacuated. JH and his wife put their children on their shoulders and walked up the ramp to the Interstate leading to the New Orleans Convention Center. They stayed there two and a half days. JH said, "It was the worst thing I've ever been through in my life. I wouldn't wish that on my worst enemy." They saw no police officers in the Convention Center. He and his wife took over a corner and guarded their children. There was no running water, no lights, and it was hot. There were tens of thousands of people and all kinds of things happening that he doesn't care to remember. He said, "Old people were dropping dead right next to us. We saw people dragging out bodies in garbage bags." The hardest thing was the uncertainty and the questions: What would happen next? Would we have food or water? JH reports that the National Guard lied to those inside the Center about the availability of supplies. He kept thinking, "How am I going to get out of this alive with my wife and kids? How are my children going to survive if anything happens to me?" The only thing he could focus on was staying alive in the midst of the fighting around him. Fortunately, he and his family took shelter in a large room in the back that he knew about through his work as a musician. On Friday, when he heard that two young children had been murdered, he and his wife and children took off in the rain, walking blindly. Suddenly they saw a city transit bus and the driver was nice enough to pick them up. After the bus missed the turn to Baton Rouge, it traveled all the way to Lafayette, where JH and his family spent two and a half days more at a shelter. Finally, they connected with his sister, and folks from her congregation drove to Lafayette and picked them up. He hopes to get back to New Orleans if it becomes an adequate place to live. If not, he knows he'll have to start his life somewhere else. But his main goal is to return to New Orleans.[5]

These stories, drawn from different continents and tragedies, describe the pain of overwhelming loss. Taken together, they capture certain emotional dynamics associated with traumatic bereavement. These include the helplessness that comes from confronting a massive quantity of loss; the numbness that survivors and their helpers experience; and the vivid sensory memories associated with the experience of traumatic loss, including sights, sounds, and smells that mark the experience. We learn also of the deep sense of connection to others that those undergoing the trauma may find in it, as well as the sense of disorientation that may follow the traumatic event. Some survivors may experience an intense focus upon personal loss, while others may experience the paradox that PV describes: the sense of being caught at the same time between the uniqueness of each loss and the sameness of them, too. Clearly, the experience of traumatic loss is complex and multifaceted.

In this chapter, I provide an overview of the emotional, psychological, and spiritual dynamics associated with traumatic loss and exemplified in these opening stories, and introduce factors contributing to healing. This summary lays the groundwork for considering Julian as a survivor and describes pathways to healing from traumatic loss for contemporary survivors.

Understanding Traumatic Loss

Kathleen R. Gilbert has offered a useful definition of traumatic loss that helps to bring into focus experiences like those I have just described. She defines a traumatic loss as "one that over-whelms the resources of the bereaved, leaving them feeling helpless with their view of the world shattered."[6] Her definition articulates three aspects of the experience of traumatic loss that we shall consider in greater detail: its character as trauma, the psychological effects of the experience on the bereaved, and the implications of the loss for the bereaved person's worldview and sense of self.[7]

The Traumatic Nature of Loss

In recent years, thanatologists and traumatologists have begun to work together to describe and treat the traumatic aspects of loss.[8] Certain early studies, such as Lindemann's work with survivors of the Coconut Grove Fire in Boston and Horowitz's work on traumatic stressors, considered the effects of grief complicated by trauma.[9] Yet researchers in each field paid relatively little attention to the dual nature of death as loss *and* trauma. However, in the 1980s, thanatologists began to describe variations in the grief process in greater detail.[10] A much more nuanced understanding of bereavement, including the effects of the traumatic nature of certain types and contexts of death, emerged from the research of key pioneers in this area, such as Therese Rando, Beverly Raphael, and Colin Parkes and his associates.[11]

Researchers describe several helpful distinctions related to traumatic loss. On the one hand, they note that all loss is subjectively traumatic and places tremendous demands upon those who experience it. On the other hand, some forms of loss are objectively traumatic and offer additional challenges to those facing them. For example, Rando describes six factors that make any death traumatic.[12] The presence of any one of these factors increases the risk that those enduring them may display symptoms of post-traumatic stress in addition to grief. They include:

(1) sudden death occurring without anticipation; (2) death involving violence, mutilation, and destruction; (3) death that is viewed as random or preventable; (4) the loss of a child; (5) multiple death; and (6) a personal encounter with death that involves a significant threat to survival and/or a massive and shocking confrontation with the death and mutilation of others. We have already noted the presence of these factors in our opening stories.

Colin Parkes has also considered the relationship between trauma and grief.[13] Like Rando, he has described aspects of death that increase the propensity to trauma. His description of traumatic loss includes experiencing sudden, unexpected, and untimely bereavements; witnessing horrific events; sustaining possible personal culpability for a death; experiencing death by suicide, murder, or manslaughter; witnessing multiple losses; or experiencing the death of a person for whom one has provided personal long-term care. Thus, there are both commonalities and differences in these two sets of descriptors of traumatic loss. Taken together, they present a more complete description of the experience. Kathleen Gilbert notes, further, that deaths resulting from human-made versus natural disasters also have increased traumatic potential,[14] a finding that Robert J. Lifton highlights in his analyses of Hiroshima and 9/11.[15] A final criterion frequently associated with traumatic loss includes stigmatized death, such as death associated with AIDS.[16]

Other grief stressors besides those associated with the nature of the loss per se are known to complicate the process of mourning. The presence of these stressors may also affect those mourning deaths that are less objectively traumatic. They include characteristics of the bereaved person's relationship with the deceased; particular vulnerabilities of the survivor, including past experiences of unresolved grief and mental health concerns; previous experience with trauma; lack of support for the bereaved in the family or social network; and other crises that may arise subsequent to a loss, including financial or role-related difficulties.[17] As Ambrose notes, the presence of these complicating factors, in addition to trauma, may seriously challenge a bereaved person's ability to cope, and thus clinicians must assess for their presence when assisting those who have sustained serious losses.[18] Clearly, in the case of traumatic loss, their presence may further complicate both treatment and recovery.

Perhaps the most important reason for differentiating trauma and grief arises from implications of this distinction for treatment. Individuals who have sustained a traumatic loss are at high risk for developing complicated bereavement.[19] Therefore, they tend to require treatment that addresses the traumatic aspects of the loss in addition to grief. For example, Green, Grace, and Leser studied survivors of the Beverly Hills Supper Club fire.[20] They found that the effects of the trauma and grief operated separately. In order to address the grief issues present, it was first necessary to treat the traumatic stress. Rando also notes that treating traumatic symptoms is a priority when a significant overlay of post-traumatic stress is present following a loss. When post-traumatic stress symptoms are less urgent, however, techniques for working through post-traumatic symptoms may be incorporated into an overall program designed to address grief and mourning. Thus, in the latter case, both grief and trauma issues may be addressed either simultaneously or intermittently.[21]

Ambrose provides a helpful analysis of the crippling effects of trauma on grief work. She notes that the experience of trauma continually intrudes on the recollection of the death. Further, she hypothesizes that the alternating cycle of denial and intrusion that characterizes trauma in particular may interfere with the bereaved person's ability to address the first task of grief, namely, recognizing and accepting the reality of the loss. When the loss itself has been traumatic, the reality of it may simply be "too terrible to bear."[22]

The body of research on traumatic loss clearly indicates that individual variation characterizes survivors' reactions. Robert A. Neimeyer notes that many survivors of apparently traumatic loss do not develop traumatic grief symptoms, whereas approximately 15 percent of non-traumatically bereaved persons do.[23] Thus, establishing a diagnosis of traumatic grief requires assessment of the bereaved person's subjective experience of the loss. One should not automatically assume that the objective circumstances of the death define the consequences of it. In fact, Neimeyer notes that even individuals experiencing more "normative" deaths such as the death of a parent in midlife or the death of a spouse in later life may respond with symptoms of trauma and grief, particularly if the loss reopens old wounds or touches on other predisposing factors associated with complicated mourning.[24]

Psychological Effects of Traumatic Loss

Psychologists and other helpers struggling to assess and treat traumatic loss have searched for adequate diagnostic criteria to distinguish traumatic loss from other forms of grief. The psychologist Holly Prigerson and her colleagues have identified a cluster of symptoms that define traumatic grief. They include yearning for the deceased, extreme loneliness, intrusive thoughts about the death, feelings of numbness and disbelief, and a fragmented sense of security and trust, associated with impaired functioning, sleep disturbance, and decreased self-esteem.[25] In contrast to these signs of traumatic grief, Neimeyer's diagnostic criteria for traumatic grief are more extensive. The first criterion involves the death of a significant other along with intrusive, distressing preoccupation with the deceased. The second criterion includes a cluster of symptoms that must be marked and persistent. Among these are classic symptoms of post-traumatic stress, including efforts to avoid reminders of the loss; numbness and lack of emotional responsiveness; and irritability, bitterness, and anger. However, they also include a range of symptoms arising from the difficulties the traumatically bereaved experience in making meaning from the trauma they have sustained. These include such factors as a sense of purposelessness and futility about the future, a feeling that life is empty and meaningless, and a shattered worldview. The third criterion, describing the duration of distress, requires that the symptoms endure for some time. Persistence of symptoms for a minimum of two months is required, while a six-month duration of symptoms provides a more clearcut diagnosis. Finally, significant impairment in social, occupational, or other functioning must be present.[26] While Neimeyer's criteria are comprehensive and helpful, they do seem to require the death of a significant other. Indeed, as we have observed, many traumatic losses such as those sustained with 9/11, may involve exposure to the death of many strangers rather than the death of a family member or close friend.

Like Neimeyer, Andrew Weaver and his associates describe psychological symptoms that may be present in traumatic bereavement. They include serious depressive symptoms, such as a loss of vitality, fatigue, feelings of hopelessness, and suicidal ideas.[27] In our opening accounts of survivors' experiences we observed how survivors of traumatic loss feel a sense of sadness as their sources of companionship and livelihood are stripped away. A strong sense of helplessness is often present in those who have experienced traumatic loss, and it may be related to what Lifton has described as "failed enactment." He defines it as an "inability at the moment of the disaster to act in the way one would have expected of oneself (saving people or resisting the perpetrators) or even to have experienced the acceptable and appropriate emotions (strong compassion for victims and rage toward perpetrators.)"[28] Survivors of traumatic bereavement may also have strong concerns about their own personal vulnerability and overwhelming anxiety. David Baldwin identifies a concern with safety as the core issue among survivors of trauma, whatever the cause.[29] Survivors' feelings of decreased safety within Manhattan following 9/11 may explain why a number of them have moved away from New York City to begin new lives elsewhere.

A final psychological effect of trauma that most complicates recovery is the vivid memories it creates in survivors. As Neimeyer notes, exposure to traumatic events floods the brain with neurotransmitters, and thus vivid sensory memories of the event become permanently "stamped in." Further, these atypical memories frequently take the form of fragmented or dissociated images, sensations, or emotions — such as the smell of burning flesh, the sight of the wasting associated with chronic illness, or the sound of gunfire. These images reside at the level of the amygdala of the brain and resist the conscious control of higher brain centers. As Neimeyer explains, the propensity for an entire complex of traumatic memories to be triggered by exposure to subsequent stimuli is adaptive in an evolutionary sense. However, when events bearing only a slight relationship to the original trauma trigger their recall, trauma survivors may find themselves in a chronically aroused state, alternating between memory intrusion and avoidance.[30] As we shall consider below, the unique and disturbing nature in which memories are created in traumatic situations challenges survivors' attempts to recall the events experienced and to make meaning of them.

Bereavement Overload
and Its Effects Upon Survivors:
The Work of Robert J. Lifton

Robert J. Lifton's psychology of the survivor offers invaluable resources in developing an understanding of traumatic loss. His theory, shaped in situations of overwhelming loss, seems particularly well suited to describe the joint effects of grief and trauma. It also provides a helpful paradigm for describing the healing effects of Julian's vision following her experience of plague loss.

Lifton has spent many years working with survivors of various traumas. His research in this field began in the 1960s with his monumental work *Death in Life: Survivors of Hiroshima.* Since that time, he has worked with Vietnam war veterans, survivors of the Buffalo Creek flood in West Virginia, Nazi doctors, and members of a terrorist sect in Japan. In his research on massive death, Lifton has identified certain common psychological patterns that appear to be present in survivors of traumatic death, regardless of the particular cause of the death exposure.

Lifton begins by offering a definition of the survivor. In his words, a survivor is "one who has encountered, been exposed to, or witnessed death and has himself or herself remained alive."[31] Lifton suggests that survivors normally pursue one of two options. Either they confront the immersion in situations of massive and overwhelming death they have experienced and seek insight and healing, or they confront the death immersion and respond with cessation of feeling or psychic numbing, a reduction in their ability to create symbols for and thus integrate the experience of loss. He notes that, on the one hand, the pattern of response characteristic of survivors of death immersions is distinctive to that experience. On the other hand, in understanding this experience, it is possible to draw on other developmental phenomena such as separation, stasis, and disintegration. The power of survivors' emotional experience derives from the psychological wedding of these two phenomena, namely, trauma from massive death and painful experiences in development.

Lifton believes that five distinctive psychological themes characterize the psyche of survivors. The first is the presence of the *death imprint and associated death anxiety*. The death imprint consists of "indelible images not just of death but of grotesque and absurd (that is, totally unacceptable) forms of death."[32] According to Lifton, the death imprint is recalled with great clarity and immediacy many years after the original event. Survivors may have a sense of being bound by it and of seeing all subsequent experiences through its lens. Thus, for example, some survivors of 9/11 remember with stunning clarity images of victims leaping to their deaths from the upper floors of the Twin Towers. The death imprint derives psychological force from the convergence of two phenomena: the association of its constitutive imagery with prior experiences of separation, breakdown, and stasis and its association with the fear of death. It derives further force from feelings of guilt and self-blame that are often attached to it. As Lifton notes, in situations of overwhelming death, "one feels responsible for what one has not done, for what one has not felt and above all, for the gap between the physical and psychic inactivation and what one felt called upon (by the beginning image-formation) to do and feel."[33]

The term "inactivation" refers to the fact that there is an element of frustrated enactment associated with the death imprint: survivors may feel tremendous helplessness and are haunted by a desire to replay the scenario of death in a way that would bring it to a more acceptable conclusion. This may involve "preventing others from dying, taking bolder action of any kind, experiencing stronger compassion or pity or perhaps suffering or dying in place of the other or others. In that way, the hope is to be relieved of the burden of self blame."[34] Thus, many parents who lost children in the tsunami may endlessly replay images of the waves' onset, wondering if there is something they might have done differently in those few moments of anticipation to prevent their child's death. However, as Lifton notes rather ironically, actual recovery and relief from guilt depend much more upon survivors' understanding and acceptance of their inability to respond more actively in times of traumatic loss.

The second distinctive psychological theme that characterizes the survivor is *death guilt.* Death guilt is epitomized by the survivor's question: Why did I survive while others died? This guilt is directly related to the failed enactment described above. Survivors feel a responsibility and debt toward the dead because of their inability either to act in a way they would ordinarily have thought appropriate in a death situation or to feel the feelings they ought to have felt for the dying and the dead. Frequently, this guilt is also accompanied by a sense of shame for these failures. As Lifton poignantly puts it: "One could define the traumatic syndrome as the state of being haunted by images that can neither be enacted nor cast aside. Suffering is associated with being 'stuck.'"[35] In the case of 9/11, for example, surviving New York firefighters may be haunted by guilt and shame because they were unable to prevent the deaths of their colleagues who were buried in rubble following the collapse of the World Trade Center towers.

Those experiencing death guilt are often haunted both by unwanted dreams and intrusive waking images of "ultimate horror": by a particular picture that summarizes, as it were, the horror and brutality of the death scenes they have witnessed. Again, survivors may experience two different results: they can remain "stuck," doomed to replay these images and their associated guilt, or they can experience transformation around the image. Lifton notes that one form of transformation of the guilt feelings occurs through "religious visions of realization and moral growth through suffering."[36] Unfortunately, survivors often feel guilt about their joy at having survived. As Lifton notes, there is an ethical quality to this pain. The existence of survivor guilt sensitizes us to the often unconscious feelings of responsibility we hold for our fellow human beings and our desire for their survival.

The third psychological theme characteristic of survivors' experience is *psychic numbing*. This is a diminished capacity to feel that emerges in situations of trauma. Psychic numbing is a necessary psychological defense against overwhelming images and stimuli. It may be understood as a disconnection between cognitive images and the emotions that would normally accompany them. In essence, it constitutes an impairment of the ability to create symbols. In psychic numbing:

> the self is severed from its own history, from its grounding in such psychic forms as compassion for others, communal involvement and other ultimate values. That is what is meant by the mind being severed from its own forms. And that severance, in turn, results in the failed enactment and guilt we spoke of before.[37]

In short, psychic numbing constitutes a dissociative phenomenon in which crucial components of the self are simply unavailable to the ego. For survivors, one particularly crucial challenge is to "hit upon" the right degree of psychic numbing: too much, and it is as if one is already dead; too little, and one continues to be overwhelmed by pain. Recovery from psychic numbing involves developing the capacity to feel again. In a subsequent chapter, we shall see how psychic numbing following 9/11 may have contributed to U.S. policymakers' tendency to minimize the potential of casualties when moving toward war in Afghanistan and Iraq.

The fourth psychological theme characterizing survivors is, in many ways, the most complex. Lifton describes it as *the suspicion of counterfeit nurturance,* and this term describes the conflicted feelings survivors hold about interpersonal relationships. On the one hand, survivors struggle with issues of autonomy. They feel the effects of their ordeal but are often reluctant to receive support. To do so is to acknowledge the impact of the trauma they have experienced. A second issue is contagion, and this has two aspects. First, survivors feel themselves marked by their experiences. Second, survivors are aware that others perceive them as tainted. These feelings may lead survivors to patterns of mistrust in relationships and to mutual antagonism and even avoidance of others. For example, persons living with HIV disease may feel contaminated through the presence of the virus in their bodies. As a result, they may fear rejection and hide their illness from others even as they need help in coping. Alternatively, they may accept help, but question the motives and compassion of their caregivers in an attempt to preserve a sense of their own autonomy and integrity.

Trauma affects survivors' perceptions of the nature of day-to-day life. Survivors may have a sense after trauma that the everyday world is counterfeit because it is a "moral inversion" of the traumatic world in which they have lived. Survivors may feel that they have come from a world in which living and dying "were divested of moral structure and lost all logic."[38] Living in such a world, survivors must decide either to reject it as counterfeit or to adapt to its inverted logic and survive. For example, survivors of 9/11 struggle particularly because the violence they experienced was perpetrated in the name of God.

This awareness may catapult them into a moral or spiritual crisis. As Lifton notes, survivors can become paralyzed by these
conflictual dynamics, or "alternatively, survivors can transcend
these conflicts and achieve an enhanced sensitivity to falseness,
to counterfeit behavior of any kind, and an equally enhanced appreciation of what is authentic and fundamental in relationship
to living and dying."[39] In other words, survivors can come away
from trauma with a deepened sense of what is authentic and
inauthentic in both life and death.

The phenomenon of counterfeit nurturance is frequently associated with emotions of anger, even rage, and with such
psychological phenomena as blaming scapegoats and identifying with aggressors. Lifton understands these emotions as
survivors' desperate attempts to maintain vitality, particularly
when they feel that they are living among the annihilated.
For example, the political antics of ACT-UP, an AIDS ac-
tivist organization, may exemplify the expression of vitality
and meaning through angry protest. He notes that feelings of
anger can help to displace guilt and anxiety and can be a useful psychic lifeline for those who feel overwhelmed by images
of death.

Lifton describes the final psychological dynamic characteristic of survivors as *formulation*. This term describes survivors'
struggles for meaning and sense of inner form in the face of the
trauma they have experienced. There may be several aspects
to this search: some survivors become "collectors of justice,"
seeking some acknowledgment of the crimes committed against
them. They seek to reestablish a sense of a moral universe. For
example, such feelings may have motivated the heightened en-
listment of young people in the U.S. military following 9/11.
Other survivors feel compelled to bear witness, to develop a survivor "mission" related to the injustices they have experienced.
This phenomenon is reflected, for example, in the efforts of

Hiroshima survivors in the peace movement and in concentration camp survivors' involvement in the creation of the state of Israel.

The essential task of the survivor is to find meaning in the trauma, to recover the capacity to create symbols that is lost in the process of surviving. One of the most frequent ways to recover meaning is through biological reproduction, which allows the survivor to contribute concretely to the continuance of life, a symbolic mode of immortality. *The key to survival is to find ways to assert the continuity of life and the integrity of the self that are also true to the experience of death one has known.* Survivors must find a way to grieve the losses they have experienced and to give form and significance to the death immersion, or else they risk stasis and entrapment in the mourning process. Typically, attempts to find meaning after death immersion require three elements: first, developing *a sense of connection,* of relationship both with people and with other aspects of the environment and psyche; second, developing *a sense of the symbolic integrity of one's life,* a sense that all of one's life, including the death immersion, has meaning; and third, developing *a sense of movement,* of development and change rather than of stasis.[40] The efforts of the September 11th Families for Peaceful Tomorrows, dedicated to finding alternatives to war following 9/11, provide an example of a well-integrated response to the death immersion they experienced following the terrorist attacks.

This summary of Lifton's theory captures the essential aspects of his survivor psychology, which he crafted through his studies of historical and contemporary death immersions. Let us now explore how Lifton and other theorists have described the movement toward wholeness and healing in survivors of traumatic loss.

Finding Solace, Meaning, and Hope in Traumatic Loss

In his analysis of trauma, the psychologist David Baldwin states that "the essential feature of a traumatic event is that it raises concerns about death, safety, or security."[41] In practice, experiences of traumatic loss may encompass all three of these concerns simultaneously. The experience of loss, as Thomas Attig reminds us, is an experience of suffering in which our sense of wholeness is impaired. This impairment, while present in all forms of loss, is most certainly evident in traumatic loss, as the bereaved suffer a loss of connection, a loss of integrity, and a loss of personal power. These losses compound the loss of safety or security at the core of the experience of trauma.[42]

As Lifton has clearly indicated, the most jarring aspect of the encounter with massive death, regardless of the source of the death, is that it brings one face to face with the inevitability of *one's own death.* This is the greatest threat imaginable to the integrity of the self, and in situations of massive death, the discontinuity between past and present associated with this realization may be particularly marked.

In the face of the trauma they have sustained, survivors face three great needs. First, they must find relief from the symptoms of anxiety that continue to plague them following the trauma. Second, they must reconstruct meaning and their identities in a manner that is true to the suffering that they have experienced. Finally, they must seek spiritual wholeness. Here again, there are three important tasks: First, they must recover a meaningful sense of purpose and life-integration through self-transcendence toward an ultimate value.[43] Second, they must move toward compassionate community. And third, they must move toward healthy self-acceptance. A more detailed exploration of these aspects of emotional, cognitive, and spiritual healing from trauma follows.

Symptom Relief, Soothing, and Solace

Survivors of traumatic loss may be plagued by physiological symptoms of anxiety and intrusive memories of the traumatic events that they have witnessed. These symptoms may be intense in light of the vivid multimodal memory traces that arise in trauma, such as those we witnessed in our opening vignettes. As Kenneth Sewell and Amy Williams remind us, an important first step on the road to recovery is symptom management.[44] Efforts to ease distressing symptoms help to instill hope in the survivor. They also allow therapists and other helpers to join with the survivor in his or her pain, thus enabling the survivor to feel less alone in the struggle to wrest meaning and relief from the trauma. Inviting survivors to examine the present pain they are experiencing in order to find ways to address and alleviate it is an important first step in healing. Sewell and Williams indicate that a variety of techniques may be used to assist with this pain, including cognitive and behavioral therapies, such as relaxation, thought-stopping, self-talk modification and disputation, and breathing retraining. Other techniques that may assist in healing include grounding techniques and interpersonal skills training. Medications may also help to relieve the sleep disturbances and depression that often trouble survivors. Finally, as Sewell and Williams note, it is also critical to assess for the presence of substance abuse, as survivors may rely on self-medication to cope with the overwhelming and frightening symptoms they experience.

While therapeutic work may be necessary for many trauma survivors, others experience hope through participation in a supportive community. In his work with a local chapter of Compassionate Friends, Dennis Klass describes ways in which parents who have lost a child may experience a soothing of their loss through developing solace.[45] Bereaved parents experienced solace through their relationship to their dead children in four ways: through linking objects connected with the child to evoke the child's presence; through connecting with the child through numinous experiences such as prayer, a sense of the uncanny, or a belief in immortality; through reflecting on memories of their beloved child; and through merging their inner representation of their child into their own self-representation. Solace provides soothing from symptoms of anxiety accompanying grief. It also provides a symbolic form of immortality that offers comfort to those experiencing the tragic loss of a child, who are able through solace to feel a continuing sense of connection to their departed offspring. Finally, the compassionate support of other survivors of child loss certainly plays a key part in the resolution of grief experienced by the parents Klass studied.

The Reconstruction of Meaning: Recovering Integrity

In his work with the bereaved, psychologist Robert Neimeyer believes that "meaning reconstruction is the central process in what we conventionally refer to as grieving."[46] His work has helped to supplement older, emotionally focused work on grief recovery, as he has attended to the *cognitive* tasks survivors face. Neimeyer and other theorists represent what is known as a "constructivist shift" in grief recovery; they emphasize the human tendency to shape narratives to make sense of the troubling transitions that we encounter in our lives. Cognitive theorists such as Neimeyer recognize the discontinuity in identity that Lifton describes so vividly in survivors of massive death. They emphasize that traumatic loss may frequently involve the loss of daily and long-range goals, basic self-definition, and the plot of life narratives. Healing requires that the bereaved

"relearn" the self and the world in the wake of loss.[47] Some theorists, such as Ronnie Janoff-Bulman and Colin Parkes, speak
of the loss of an *assumptive world,* while others, such as P. Marris, talk of loss of the world of meaning, while yet others, such
as Neimeyer and his colleagues, describe the loss of a personal
construct. However the task is described, the end result of recovery is the reconstruction of meaning following its disruption
through trauma.[48]

Forming a narrative is critical to this work. Thus, Charles
Figley speaks of the development of a "healing theory" as a
means of modifying the assumptive world to incorporate loss.[49]
The main benefit of such cognitive efforts is that they help
modulate the intrusive images and feelings that accompany loss
and "complete" or resolve the discrepancy between the old and
new worldviews that plague mourners.[50]

Kenneth Sewell and Amy Williams have offered a particularly elegant analysis of the attempt to recover a sense of
personal integrity following traumatic loss.[51] They rely on the
notion of "implicit construction" in developing a treatment plan
for trauma survivors. They begin their analysis by noting that
trauma affects primarily two domains of thought in survivors:
the domain of events and the social domain. Event disruption occurs when the trauma experience violates one's sense
of "how the world works." Social disruption, in contrast, occurs when the sense of social relations is upset in trauma. The
latter is more common in situations of emotional or physical
abuse, but Sewell and Williams note that most traumatic experiences disrupt *both* domains to some extent. Thus, a person
who experiences sexual violation from a family member may experience disruption of the beliefs that the home is a safe place
and that elder family members are trustworthy. While Sewell
and Williams do not explicitly mention the spiritual domain, I

would include it in the category of cognitive domains disrupted in trauma.

In their work with trauma survivors, Sewell and Williams use the notion of implicit constructions to organize psychological experience. Thus, they claim that experiencing any one pole of psychic life relies on the other pole for its meaning. One cannot experience happiness, for example, without implicitly anchoring it in sadness. Nevertheless, they argue that this process of construing happiness by comparing it with sadness is implicit. Arguing from this premise, they claim that recovery from post-traumatic stress disorder occurs when the traumatized person develops constructs for the trauma that can be integrated into his or her existing system of meaning. To create this new system, the survivor must build a network of implicit constructions regarding the trauma that allow him or her to anticipate and understand novel yet *non-traumatic* experiences. Thus, for example, a woman whose fiancé was murdered, and who was anticipating become a parent and growing old together with him, must now work to consider explicitly alternatives to her implicit notions of happiness shattered through the trauma she sustained. Doing so will allow her to imagine a more vital and satisfying future than she might anticipate otherwise.

Sewell and Williams use a process they call metaconstruction to assist in the development of a new construct system following trauma. Metaconstruction involves integration of one's past and future self-conceptions. As we have already observed, in the experience of trauma the present appears discontinuous with the past in some critical ways, and this discontinuity impedes one's ability to imagine or predict the future. Sewell and Williams believe that through trauma the incongruity between past and present may be so extreme that it can be difficult to see one's present psychological state as being connected in a coherent way to the remembered past. The process of therapy thus involves elaborating the past and present metaconstructions so that they may be seen as continuously linked. This linking then allows the construction of a sense of future events, of relationships, and of a sense of self to emerge. For example, women who are raped may lose any sense of personal security they had constructed prior to their assault and view the world as a dangerous and uncertain place. In recovering a relative sense of safety, the women must build both on their past strategies for safety-making and the reality of their violations to create a more realistic and effective understanding of self-protection strategies in the future.

Sewell and Williams's metaconstruction process makes use of five strategies:

In the first phase, they emphasize the importance of *symptom management*. Cooperating with survivors to ease anxious symptoms allows the clinician to join with them and to begin to establish a sense of hope.

The second tool important in treatment is *life review.* The purpose of this review is to begin to evoke the survivor's understandings of his or her world and self in the past. This process is undertaken in a reflective way, so that the survivor has the opportunity to become reacquainted with aspects of his or her own history that provide a context within which the trauma took place and was interpreted.

The third tool Sewell and Williams draw on in treatment is *trauma reliving.* Here, they encourage the client to deeply remember the experience of trauma — to talk from within the experience as he or she reconnects with all of the pain, confusion, fear, and shame associated with it. In trauma reliving, the clinician asks the survivor to relive the experience slowly and at as many levels of awareness as possible. Through this process, the clinician has an opportunity to normalize the client's response to the trauma through drawing on his or her context and past experience. They then work with the client to identify ways in which the experience might be viewed differently.

Constructive bridging is the fourth tool Sewell and Williams draw on to promote healing. Through this tool, the clinician encourages the trauma survivor to provide narrative segues from past to present and present to past. Bridging in this way allows for a richer conceptualization of the connections between past and present, thus promoting healing of the split between them that plagues trauma survivors.

Finally, in *intentional future metaconstruction*, the clinician works with the survivor to assess what may lie ahead. Thus, for example, Sewell and Williams describe how a man who was raped faced the task of recovering a balanced sense of his own masculinity following the assault. Healing included recovering the memory that during the rape his assailant labeled him with a homosexual epithet. Reliving the experience and reviewing his experience of his own sexuality prior to the trauma helped him to move toward a future in which he would no longer be compelled compulsively to prove his masculinity. Through this process, the client was then freed to imagine future relationships in which his sense of sexuality might be more fluid, nuanced, and gentle. Sewell and Williams note that after experiencing trauma, some clients cannot see a future; whereas others, in looking ahead, see only continual trauma. However, through stimulation of fantasies and the use of metaphors, they encourage survivors to build bridges between the present and the future that are less constricted by the trauma they have sustained.

In its attempt to restore the disruption in continuity at the heart of trauma, this elegant model attends to the holistic experience of survivors in an imaginative, empathetic, and multivalent way. However, one shortfall of this particular approach is its failure to explicitly address the spiritual disruptions

trauma survivors experience. Typically, the concerns and ex-
pertise of psychotherapists lie in the cognitive, emotional, and
behavioral domains. Incorporating the spiritual concerns of survivors, as pastors and pastoral counselors are able to do, may
provide for greater healing and integration of loss. So we turn
to a consideration of the spiritual issues facing survivors of
traumatic loss.

The Quest for Wholeness in the Face of Traumatic Loss

Perhaps the greatest shock at the core of traumatic loss is the
confrontation survivors face with *the inevitability of their own
deaths.* In coming to terms with the reality of trauma, survivors
must find a way of accepting their human vulnerability and
mortality. As Lifton notes, survivors who have an encounter
with massive death take a psychic journey to the very edge of
the land of the living. In the healing journey, they must find a
way to return fully to it. However, the resolution they seek must
be large enough to encompass both the depth of the tragedy
they have encountered and their finitude. Lifton uses the term
"formulation" to describe the process through which survivors
heal from the insult they have experienced.[52] He notes, however, that not all formulations contribute to wholeness. For
example, some survivors develop an embittered worldview in
the wake of the destruction they have witnessed. He observed
this in certain Hiroshima survivors who developed a taste for
total retaliation. Other survivors may choose to scapegoat the
vulnerable as a way of coming to terms with loss. The flagellants' attacks on Jews during the Black Death pandemic of
the fourteenth century represented this destructive tendency
in formulation. Finally, Lifton notes that some survivors create "indelible images" of the destruction they have experienced,
images that fail to serve them in the quest for healing because of

their static quality. These indelible images, composed of memories frozen in time, do not lend themselves to integration or resolution. It is as if the survivor is paralyzed in his or her attempt to make meaning of the trauma and remains fixed upon images of destruction and annihilation.

Creation of a survivor mission is an important characteristic of survivors of massive loss who seek to bear witness to the suffering they have observed. However, the task survivors face is to bring to their survivor mission their best experiences of love, nurture, and harmony, so that they move toward wholeness in addition to healing.

My own work with survivors of AIDS loss suggests to me that survivors face three spiritual tasks in recovery. First, for healthy resolution from loss, they are aided when they recover a sense of purpose that moves them beyond themselves, provides integration, and is faithful to an ultimate value they hold dear. This ultimate value may be God, but it may also be nontheistic in nature, such as justice or the good of the community. This first task, which derives from Sandra Schneiders's definition of spirituality, is one way of rephrasing what Lifton has described as a "survivor mission." Second, survivors benefit greatly from learning to accept themselves — to forgive themselves for their failings and to treat themselves with mercy and loving kindness.[53] Finally, survivors also benefit from achieving an empathic connection with the human community. They grow as they move toward forgiveness of those who have caused them harm and learn to empathize with survivors of other forms of trauma and oppression.[54] As difficult as this may seem, developing empathy is crucial to the acceptance of one's own fragile humanity. Recognizing that one is not God, that one is human, and that each of us is inextricably connected to all of humanity are key aspects of recovery. We must learn to accept in others the same limitations of power and knowledge that we experience in ourselves.

The main purpose of this book is to explore these spiritual tasks of recovery from traumatic loss, particularly through considering their impact upon Julian's healing and the development of her distinctive theology and spirituality. In the next chapter, we explore the context in which she lived and developed her compassionate theology of human wholeness and divine mercy. Then we explore, in turn, her identity as a survivor and the theology and spirituality she developed in response to loss. Finally, we consider the implications of her mature reflection for survivors in our own day.

T W O

The Fourteenth Century
and Its Perils

And there was in those days death without sorrow, marriage without affection, self-imposed penance, want without poverty, and flight without escape. — The Plague according to John of Reading[1]

The 14th century suffered so many "strange and great perils and adversities" (in the words of a contemporary) that its disorders cannot be traced to any one cause.... The four horsemen of St. John's vision...had now become seven — plague, wars, taxes, brigandage, bad government, insurrection, and schism in the Church.... Simply summarized by the Swiss historian J. C. L. S. de Sisimondi, the 14th century was "a bad time for humanity." — Barbara W. Tuchman, *A Distant Mirror*[2]

Sin is necessary, but all shall be well.
All shall be well; and all manner of things shall be well.
— Julian of Norwich, *Revelation of Love*[3]

Julian of Norwich's experiences with the Black Death markedly influenced the development of her theology and spirituality — in fact to such an extent that I think she can be helpfully understood as a survivor of traumatic loss arising from the plague. Given her theology, I believe that Julian would characterize the attribution of loss and suffering to God's anger as a spiritual form of traumatic loss. In my view, Julian's experience of plague loss shaped the form of her religious experience — including her visions — influenced the effects they had upon

41

her, and motivated her to articulate and disseminate her theological reflections upon them, despite the personal risks this
venture posed. Clearly, understanding Julian's experience and
her theological reflection upon it will provide a helpful resource
for contemporary survivors.

In developing this argument, I first explore certain partic-
ulars about Julian's life and the wider historical and religious
context within which Julian was situated. Second, I examine
the Black Death, since it was a key influence upon the development of Julian's distinctive theological vision. Finally, I attend
to the phenomenological experience of plague loss, the extent
of plague loss, its social effects, the religious response to it,
pastoral concerns associated with it, and the dominant theological interpretations to it offered in Julian's day. Consideration of
these historical data will pave the way for the characterization
of Julian as survivor that I shall advance in the next chapter
and help contemporary survivors to consider parallels between
Julian's experience and their own.

Julian's Life and Times

To fully appreciate Julian's vibrant theology and distinctive spirituality, we must view them against the backdrop of fourteenth-
century British life, where death was both an omnipresent and
"grim business."[4] Julian's time was violent and brutal, marked
by cruel warfare, brigandage, the torture and persecution of
Jews, and extremes of destructive piety. The masochistic rites
of the flagellants and the fiery execution of convicted heretics,
including the Lollards of Julian's own Norwich, testify to the
spiritual disruption that accompanied the terrors of the age. The
ever-present reality of violence, along with the ecological insta-
bility manifested in recurring famines and plagues, undoubtedly
contributed to the grotesque fascination with death expressed

in fourteenth-century art. Ironically, the well-developed penitential system and eschatological teachings about the afterlife,
designed to comfort sinners, may also have heightened anxi-
eties about salvation. As we shall see, Julian placed primary
emphasis upon questions concerning salvation, and, in her
focus on these concerns, she was quite representative of her age.
In many ways, Julian lived in a transitional time. In her day, a
decided belief in the superiority of the spiritual world and the
afterlife was giving way to a more secular worldview. This outlook was focused upon the value of the individual and upon
an active, but not necessarily religiously oriented life in the
present.[5] As Barbara Tuchman reminds us, the seeds for this
change lay within the church and its associated institutions,
including the papacy and the university. Both the corruption
and lavish extravagance of the papacy, on the one hand, and
the development of new philosophies such as nominalism, on
the other hand, laid the groundwork for the development of a
more secular worldview. Each contributed in its own way to the
decline of the medieval world's grand synthesis.

We know few things for certain about Julian and her life. She
tells us in her text that she experienced her life-changing vision
on the eighth day of May in 1373 when she was thirty and a half
years old.[6] Thus, we can infer that Julian was born close to the
end of 1342. A bequest by Roger Reed, rector of St. Michael's
Church at Coslany, to "Julian anakorite" in 1393 suggests that
Julian had adopted the distinctive lifestyle of an anchoress by
that time. That she continued in this ministry into the next
century is supported by the prologue to the Short Text identifying her as "a recluse at Norwich living yet in 1413."[7] Evidence
from wills suggests that Julian lived to be at least seventy-four
years old.[8] Two bequests to support Julian, including one in November 1415 by John Plumpton for forty pence to "the ankeres
in ecclesia sancti Juliani de Conesford in Norwice" and another

in 1416 by Isabelle Ufford, countess of Suffolk, imply that Julian lived to a ripe old age.[9] The testimony of the colorful Margery Kempe, a contemporary of Julian's from nearby King's Lynn in southeast England, indicates that Julian's reputation as a spiritual counselor was well established, for Margery refers to her as "an expert in such things [who] could give good advice."[10] In fact, scholars have commented on the congruity between the advice Margery received and the theology of Julian's text, supporting the view that the anchoress Margery consulted was indeed the author of the *Revelations*.[11]

Aside from this "external" data about Julian's life, we can glean other critical information from Julian's texts. Julian's *Revelations* exists in two versions, normally described as the Short and Long Texts. These texts are found in several manuscripts. Four of them are held in the British library. These holdings include Additional 37790, a mid-fifteenth century version of the Short Text known as "Amherst," and three mid-seventeenth century versions of the Long Text: Sloane 2499, Sloane 3705, and Stowe 42. In addition, the earliest version of the Long Text, Anglais 40, dating from the sixteenth century, resides at the Bibliothèque Nationale in Paris. Finally, Westminster Cathedral owns the second oldest version of the Short Text, dating from around 1500.

Denise Baker rightly raises a question posed by other Julian scholars: "Is the short text in Amherst the earliest extant manuscript, an abridgement of, or an antecedent to the long text witnessed by the remaining five documents?"[12] In short, did Julian compose both documents, and if so, when did she write them?

Most scholars, following Edmund Colledge and James Walsh, editors of the critical edition in Middle English, believe that Julian composed both versions herself and that the Short Text preceded the Long Text by twenty or more years. If we assume that Julian wrote the Short Text soon after her vision in 1373, and further assume, based on her own words, that she reflected on the Vision of the Lord and Servant for twenty years before including it in the Long Text, then the earliest possible date for the Long Text is 1393.[13]

We can therefore conclude with some certainty that a devout anchoress known as Julian had a series of life-changing visions focused primarily, but not exclusively, on Christ's crucifixion. Further, she wrote two accounts of her visions: a short version assumed to be written soon after the event and a second, longer version written after nearly twenty years of sustained reflection on it. Aside from this, it is difficult to establish with certainty Julian's marital status, religious vocation, social class, or level of education, despite the fact that a plethora of theories have been advanced about these more personal details of her life.[14]

As intriguing as speculation about these matters may be, perhaps the most pertinent fact about Julian is that she survived a series of outbreaks of the plague. The first and most serious one occurred when she was just six years old. This epidemic constituted one of the greatest disasters the Western world has ever experienced. Besides this initial outbreak, Julian also survived additional plague epidemics, including those in 1361 and 1369. While we cannot be certain that Julian was living in Norwich at this time, we do know that wherever she was living in England she would have experienced the plague. We may also assume that the people in Norwich would not soon have forgotten the suffering they experienced as a result of it. This factor would surely have influenced the ministry of spiritual care that Julian exercised later in her life. So we turn to a brief exploration of the religious and political climate of fourteenth-century Norwich, especially as it shaped the turbulent context in which the fourteenth-century experience of the plague was mediated, noting important parallels between the experiences of plague-related pain and loss and contemporary experiences of trauma.

The Religious and Political Context of Fourteenth-Century Norwich

The best and worst of human achievement characterized the late fourteenth century, in which Julian experienced her life-transforming vision. On the one hand, religious and artistic writing flourished. Julian's literary contemporaries included such towering figures as Franceso Petrarch, Giovanni Boccaccio, Geoffrey Chaucer, and William Langland. Further, during her lifetime, both England and the continent experienced one of the greatest known flowerings of mystical piety. England alone witnessed the work of Walter Hilton, that of the anonymous author of *The Cloud of Unknowing*, and the writings of Richard Rolle and Margery Kempe. Continental mystics included many significant women: Birgitta of Sweden and Catherine of Siena are the best known, but other contemporary and near contemporary women religious writers included Mechtild of Magdeburg, Mechtilde of Hackeborn, Gertrude of Helfta, Angela of Foligno, and Margaret Ebner.[15] Male continental mystics active at this time included such giants as Jan van Ruysbroeck, Jean Gerson, Meister Eckhardt, John Tauler, and Henry Suso.

Despite the towering accomplishments of these figures and the energy and vibrancy associated with them, a great discrepancy also marked the fourteenth century. This was the split between the moral and philosophical ideals of the day and the behavior that these ideals were intended to guide. Barbara Tuchman expressed this lapse most clearly in her evaluation of the failure of the chivalric ideal: "if the [chivalric] code was but a veneer over violence, greed and sensuality, it was nevertheless an ideal, as Christianity was an ideal, toward which man's reach, as usual, exceeded his grasp."[16] This failure of ideals described the essence of the period, and the most destructive scourges of the century — war, brigandage, papal schism, and plague — exacerbated it. Each of these forces contributed to the dissolution of medieval ideals and the eventual re-creation of secular and religious society experienced in the Renaissance and Reformation.

The city of Norwich was not insulated from the best and worst influences of the time, for in Julian's day the city was far more prominent than it is today. In the late fourteenth century, Norwich was the second largest city in England, and it was a thriving center for shipping and for trading textiles. Its prominence was due to an accident of geography and politics. Norwich was an inland port situated on the river Wensum and was handily positioned for trade with England's economic partners in Flanders and the Rhineland. This protected location provided the city with an economic boost, as wartime raids on southern English ports caused the diversion of traffic to Norwich.

The city's economic and geographical prominence also led to intellectual trade.[17] The exchange of religious ideas between Norwich and the continent may have been responsible for such innovations as a house of beguines in Norwich, the only one in England, and the existence of a full array of religious communities in the city, including Benedictines, Dominicans, Franciscans, and Augustinians. While writers speculate about the influence of these communities upon Julian's life, little is actually known about Julian's intercourse with these religious orders and their distinctive theologies and pieties.

Modern studies highlight the existence of a thriving religious life in fourteenth-century Norwich. Even today, tangible evidence remains in the many medieval parish churches that dot the city. Norman Tanner notes that Norwich possessed

forty-six parish churches in the late medieval period, second
only to London. Of course, in Julian's day, the Norman cathedral and its Benedictine priory were at the geographical and
spiritual heart of the city. Herbert Losinga, the first bishop of
Norwich, began construction of this impressive and breath-
takingly beautiful structure in 1097. Besides providing a focus
for the city's spiritual life, the cathedral provided a "canvas" for
artistry and craftsmanship. Forty-six guilds and religious confraternities thrived in the city in Julian's day, and the cathedral's
beauty demonstrates the sheer skill and wealth of the many ar-
tisans and craftsmen who plied their trade in Norwich. Surely
Julian herself would have worshipped in and appreciated the
beauty of this structure.

Tanner, along with Roberta Gilchrist and Marilyn Oliva, provides evidence for a dynamic religious culture in Norwich in the
late medieval period.[18] In Tanner's view, the older and more
clerical aspects of the church in Norwich continued to thrive.
At the same time, the city was enriched by the presence of
new religious movements, largely directed toward laity, that
arose in the late medieval period.[19] These included the proliferation of religious lifestyles, including hermits, anchorites, and
groups resembling beguinages; craft guilds and their associated
guild-days, processions, and mystery plays; pious confraternities; pilgrimages and devotions to the saints; improvements
in the religious education of the laity; and the multiplication
of Masses and prayers for the dead.[20] In fact, the studies of
both Tanner and Gilchrist and Oliva provide helpful and concrete data to support the view that alternative religious lifestyles
thrived in Norwich.

First, Tanner notes that more hermits and anchorites lived
in Norwich in the fifteenth and early sixteenth centuries than
in any other town in England.[21] One wonders, what effect, if
any, Julian's renown had in influencing this trend.

Second, Gilchrist and Oliva's study of religious women in East Anglia clearly supports the view that women as well as men participated in these movements. In fact, they conclude that the preponderance of religious women of various sorts in Norfolk and Suffolk strongly supports the conclusion that members of the laity in this region were active participants and generous supporters of a lively religious life. They identify at least six categories of religious women in East Anglia in Julian's day: nuns, hospital sisters, women who lived in informal religious communities, anchoresses, vowesses, and other single religious women of uncertain status. They conclude that the female piety associated with these vocations greatly enriched the local community. They also suggest that communities of religious women, in contrast to communities of men, were never intended to be self-supporting; thus, they existed in a more interdependent relationship with the local community, benefiting from their gifts and favors as they shared prayers and charitable works of mercy with those in need. The evidence of support Julian received from wills testifies to these interconnections.

This evidence provides an optimistic picture of the health of religious institutions in Norwich, yet there are indications that dissent and disillusionment with the church were not by any means unknown. Dissatisfaction with the institutional church arose from the nature of the papacy in the fourteenth century, the leadership of Bishop Henry Despenser, and the influence of Wyclif sympathizers in Norwich.

Scandals surrounding the papacy undoubtedly provided a great source of discontent with the church in Julian's day. Relations between the papacy and state in the fourteenth century began badly with the assault on Pope Boniface VIII by agents of Philip IV, king of France, in 1303. The monarchs clashed over temporal versus papal authority: Philip wanted to tax clerical income without support from the pope. Boniface forbade the clergy from complying, fearful that clerics might develop greater allegiance to the king than the pope. In the Bull *Unam Sanctam* in 1302, Boniface boldly asserted, "It is necessary to salvation that every human creature be subject to the Roman pontiff."[22] Philip did not respond well to this pronouncement. He called for a council to judge the pope on charges of heresy, blasphemy, murder, sodomy, simony, sorcery, and failure to fast on feast days; Boniface, in return, excommunicated him. Philip's response was to seize the pope at his summer estate in Anagni in an attempt to delay the excommunication and bring the pope before a council. While local citizens quickly freed him, the pope soon died from the shock of these events.[23]

The papacy eventually moved from Rome to Avignon, in part because of this unfortunate situation. Under Philip's influence, Clement V, a French pope, was elected. Because he feared reprisal from the Romans and separation from his French mistress, Clement chose to reside in Avignon. The next six popes in succession, following in Clement's footsteps, also chose to reside in Avignon. As Barbara Tuchman sagely notes in her commentary on these events, the papacy sought to make up what it lacked in spiritual power through amassing temporal power. Thus, the papacy concentrated on finance and the organization and centralization of all revenue-bearing processes at its disposal. This development proceeded to such an extent that, in the end, "every pardon, indulgence and absolution, everything the Church had or was, from cardinal's hat to pilgrim's relic was for sale."[24] Other sources of papal income included benefices, payments to avoid excommunication and anathema, and dispensations of every sort. Petrarch aptly captured the irony of the situation when he noted that the popes, "successors of the poor fishermen of Galilee," were now "loaded with gold and clad in purple."[25]

Certainly, the political tensions between France and England in this period jaded and undermined English views on the papacy. Tuchman herself believes that fallout from the Avignon captivity of the papacy helped to move England toward the development of a national church.[26]

Unfortunately, corruption and greed were not limited to the papacy as "corruption spread through every level of the church hierarchy from canons and priors down to mendicant friars and pardoners."[27] Reviewing the list of papal and clerical abuses calls to mind Julian's observation that "God's servants, that is to say holy Church shall be shaken in sorrow and anguish and tribulation in this world, just as people shake a cloth in the wind."[28] As the century wore on, the problems of the papacy culminated in the Great Schism in 1378: the election of two competing popes, one based in Rome and the other in Avignon. The existence of the schism had less to do with questions of doctrine than with complex political alliances between church and state. The scandal of two competing popes was compounded in 1409 with the election of a third, and the papal schism was not resolved until the end of the eighteen-year-long Council of Basle in 1449. Thus, the power and prestige of the papacy were considerably diminished, and this development paved the way for the Protestant Reformation that soon followed.

While Norwich was at some remove from both Avignon and Rome, the rivalry between competing claimants for the papal throne came quite close to home for Julian and her fellow citizens. The deplorable military activities of Henry Despenser, who served as bishop of Norwich from 1370 until 1406, contributed to local disillusionment with the institutional church. Despenser, described by the chronicler Thomas Walsingham as youthful, arrogant, and insolent, became known for two ruthless acts.[29] The first was his cruel suppression in 1381

of the Peasants' Revolt, a violent uprising partially resulting from labor shortages following the 1349 pestilence. The
second was his organization, promotion, and oversight of a
"crusade" in 1383 against the French and Flemish supporters
of Pope Clement VII on behalf of Pope Urban VI. As Tuchman notes, this ill-conceived operation began in scandal and
ended in fiasco. Despenser's means of financing the campaign
did far more harm to the papacy than success in the cause
would have achieved. Agents of the church virtually extorted
financial support from the faithful in their attempts to finance
the disastrous campaign.[30] Even the sacrament was withheld
from parishioners who refused to contribute to the "crusade,"
demonstrating the unscrupulous lengths to which the clergy
and bishop were willing to go in support of this doomed cause.

The Lollards' protest against the war constituted one of the
first damaging consequences of this campaign. A second was
the disgraceful outcome of the "crusade" itself. Upon landing in
Calais, Despenser and his troops experienced some initial victo-
ries against the Flemish. When they were overcome in the fields
in northern France by a greatly superior French force, however,
the bishop's men deserted him in battle. Thereupon, he beat
a hasty retreat to Bourbourg, where he remained for several
months, until a negotiated settlement with the French resulted
in the war's end. The French simply had no desire to fight.
Thus, the bishop was left with neither gain nor glory. In fact,
as Tuchman notes, he was bought off and then returned home
to deficit and disgrace.[31] While it is certainly difficult to fathom
fully the sentiments about the bishop's behavior six hundred
years later, every indication suggests that his ruthless mili-
tarism received little support. The Great Schism scandalized
the faithful and vexed those most responsible for its occurrence.
Given these already complex dynamics, it seems unlikely that
many would have favored a military solution to the schism. It

is interesting to speculate about how the news of and effects of this ill-conceived campaign may have influenced Julian's reflection upon and ministry of soul care, particularly since she was directly under the authority of the bishop.

A third form of evidence for religious dissent in Julian's day arises from the presence of the Lollards. The Lollards were religious dissenters whose views accorded with those of John Wyclif, the Oxford preacher, scholar, and posthumously condemned heretic.[32] Like Wyclif, the Lollards attacked clericalism and religious abuses, denied transubstantiation, and promoted the translation and reading of the Bible in English. Further, they were devoted to the humanity of Jesus. While known primarily for their heterodox religious views, the Lollards also participated in the Peasants' Revolt of 1381 and the Oldcastle uprising in 1414. Thus, the movement posed both a religious and civil threat, and, as Tuchman notes, its primary sympathizers were drawn from the commoners and lower clergy. From 1385 onward, Lollards were persecuted in England, and in 1398 the bishops requested authorization for the death penalty against them. According to Tanner, Lollardy never gained the prominence in Norwich that it achieved in other centers, such as London; however, at least three Lollards were burned in Norwich in 1428. Numerous other Lollard sympathizers were sentenced to be flogged or to do "solemn penance" in the city.[33] Therefore, Julian would undoubtedly have heard of the current of dissent associated with Lollardy, and scholars have suggested that she may have consciously framed several of the disclaimers present in her text to distinguish herself from its adherents. For example, this situation may account for her remarks in the Short Text in which she discounts her authority as teacher: "But God forbid that ye should say or take it thus, that I am a teacher for I do not mean that, nor meant I ever so. For I am a woman, unlettered, feeble and frail."[34]

The care that Julian takes to indicate that nothing in her vision draws her away from the teaching of the church may represent a second influence of Lollardy on her writing.

> Although the revelation treated of goodness, with little mention of evil, yet I was not drawn away from it by any single detail of the faith that holy Church teaches me to hold. . . . And I was strengthened and taught in general to keep my faith in every detail and in all I had understood before, hoping in this way that I was held in the mercy and grace of God, only wishing and praying in my every intention that I might continue in such way to my life's end.[35]

Here Julian takes care to uphold her orthodoxy, perhaps because of the life-threatening danger that may have come to her through too close an association with Lollard views.

The Hundred Years' War between France and England, which raged off and on from 1337 to 1453, was a final factor significantly shaping life in medieval Norwich and throughout Western Europe. Its cause was twofold: first, England claimed territory in lower western France in Guienne and Gascony, remnants of the inheritance of Henry II through Eleanor of Acquitaine. Second, Edward III, king of England from 1327 to 1377, launched a claim to the throne of France through his mother's line. This war exerted its effects in several ways. First, it caused a severe drain of money and manpower in England and promulgated a climate of lawlessness. English troops learned to survive on the plunder of war in France, and once they returned home, they terrorized travelers, looted and destroyed homesteads, took captives, held villages for ransom, and spread both terror and violence[36] The war contributed to the death of ideals; it severed the bonds of chivalry that had united the nobility and created a climate of mutual antagonism between England and

France that was to last for centuries. In combination with the Great Schism, the war also stimulated a growing climate of nationalism and the rise of the nation-states. Throughout Julian's lifetime, under a variety of monarchs, England was at war with France, Scotland, and Wales. The pain of wartime losses and their wide-ranging effects may have touched many of those who sought counseling from Julian.

As this survey of the century's climate demonstrates, Julian lived in an age of intellectual, moral, political, and religious ferment. While the political and religious structures of medieval life continued to flourish, the social and theological underpinnings supporting them were corroding through violence, greed, excess and the disillusionment associated with suffering. This disillusionment was fostering the development of dissenting voices, such as those of the Lollards in England. As a result of the papal schism and growing nationalism, medieval unity increasingly disintegrated and political, religious, and interpersonal autonomy were increasingly prized. Ecological conditions played an equally important role in social change because of their effects on the availability and price of labor. In the face of these varying pressures, a profound cynicism emerged and it was writ large. Human pessimism in the late Middle Ages fastened on God's disapproval as a cause of suffering. Julian lived, prayed, and wrote in this gloomy climate, and her distinctive voice offered a creative alternative to the prevailing theology of her day.

The Black Death in Fourteenth-Century Europe

The arrival of the "pestilence" or "Great Mortality," which appears to have originated in fourteenth-century Asia, heralded one of the greatest disasters ever known. According to the traditional account, the plague was spread to Western Europe primarily through well-established trade routes from parts of Eurasia where it was endemic. An Irish chronicler recorded one of the most chilling descriptions of its anticipated arrival.

> And I, Brother John Clynn, of the Friars Minor of Kilkenny, have written in this book the notable events which befell in my time, which I saw for myself or have learnt from men worthy of belief. So that notable deeds should not perish with time, and be lost from the memory of future generations, I, seeing these many ills, and that the whole world is encompassed by evil, waiting among the dead for death to come, have committed to writing what I have truly heard and examined, and so that the writing does not perish with the writer, or the work fail with the workman, I leave parchment for continuing the work, in case anyone should still be alive in the future and any son of Adam can escape this pestilence and continue the work thus begun.[37]

Two features of this account are noteworthy: first, Clynn's impression that death from the plague might be total and, second, the frightening sense he had of "waiting among the dead for death to come." To contemporary chroniclers, the first plague epidemic seemed to be a harbinger of the world's end. Waiting for what appeared to many to be certain death must have created an ominous sense of doom, indeed. Certainly, those living with AIDS before the advent of retroviral treatment experienced similar fears and forebodings.

   This sense of impending disaster was clearly grounded in real and massive mortality. As Horrox notes, historians have tended to be of two minds about the plague and its effects. Late nineteenth-century historians, such as Cardinal Francis Gasquet, believed that the plague "wrought cataclysmic change, not only in society but within the individual."[38] These historians postulated grand and sweeping effects of the plague and attributed the decline of medieval certainty to the plague's devastation. Yet succeeding generations of historians tended to downplay the effect of the Black Death. However, Horrox notes that recent trends in scholarship are tending toward increased acceptance of the notion that plague mortality was much higher than historians believed in the 1970s.[39] At that time, the figure of a third was normative; historians now believe that mortality, particularly in some areas, may have been considerably greater. As Horrox indicates:

> Many medieval estimates of mortality are indeed suspect, but they are testimony to a sense of dislocation and shock which it is unduly (and offensively) arrogant to ignore, whatever the actual mortality levels may have been. In recent years English assessments of the mortality in 1348–49 have also been rising steadily back towards a death rate of almost one in two, providing a context in which any contemporary exaggeration seems entirely understandable.[40]

Thus, estimates of plague mortality have risen from 30 percent in the 1970s to 40 percent in the early 1980s to an average mortality of 47 to 48 percent today. These estimates are based on an increasing number of local studies that allow for more precise estimates of plague death in a given region.

Scholars have established with certainty that one cause of the spread of the Black Death was the bacterium *Yesina pestis* or *Pasteurella pestis,* carried in the stomach of a flea such as *Xenopsylla cheopsis.* This flea is normally carried by black rats, and historians have long believed that these rats and the parasites they carried were disseminated by shipping and carried along principal trade routes, thus accounting for the patterns of infectious spread historians have documented. However, Norman Cantor cites recent biomedical research that suggests that peculiarities about the spread of the Black Death, particularly in England, have led scientists to conclude that other diseases in addition to bubonic plague may have contributed to the patterns of mortality observed.[41]

Drawing on the research of Graham Twigg, Cantor proposes that the Black Death either involved or was even exclusively the cattle disease anthrax.[42] Several factors lend credence to this theory: first, both anthrax and bubonic plague begin with similar flu-like symptoms and may easily have been confused by medieval physicians. Second, the very rapid spread of the diseases seems more typical of cattle diseases such as anthrax, hoof and mouth disease, or mad cow disease. Until this point, as Cantor notes, research has not clearly suggested whether an anthrax mutant could be spread to humans. However, it now appears that the mad cow disease that killed nearly seventy people in Great Britain in the 1990s was spread to humans who ate tainted meat.

These results have taken on increased significance since 1998 when the scientist Edward I. Thompson, cited in Cantor, described evidence arising from an archeological excavation at Soutra, Scotland, near Edinburgh. Scientists found evidence of anthrax spores in a cesspool where human waste was discharged on the site of a medieval hospital located near a mass grave for Black Death victims. Thompson also provided evidence of ten medieval abbeys or priories whose cattle herds were diseased. Finally, he documented that meat from cattle that had died of cattle disease was sold on the open market prior to the Black Death. In the light of this data, Thompson concludes that "bubonic plague and anthrax probably co-existed during the fourteenth century," and Cantor affirms that this conclusion is the best that science can provide at present to account for the 1349 mortality.[43]

As Tuchman notes, Western Europe had heard rumors of a terrible plague arising in China and spreading to India, Persia, Mesopotamia, Syria, Egypt, and Asia Minor as early as 1346.[44] However, the threat of death did not clearly emerge until the plague made its entry into the Sicilian port of Messina in October 1347. It arrived through Genoese trading ships returning from the Black Sea port of Caffa in the Crimea, according to the traditional account of the Piacenzan chronicler Gabriele de Mussis.[45] From Sicily it progressed to North Africa by way of Tunis, to Corsica and Sardinia, to the Balearics, Almeria, Valencia, and Barcelona, and then to Southern Italy.

Once it entered the European mainland, the spread of the plague was rapid and relentless. It spread from Italy north to the heart of the Holy Roman Empire within a year. It reached Bavaria by June 1348 and Austria by November of that year. It reached Vienna and northern Germany in 1349. The plague apparently spread to the western Mediterranean coast through Italian sailing ships. It entered France through coastal towns and then infected Avignon in the south in the spring of 1348 and Paris in the north in June of 1348. Death rates were stunning: between February and May, up to four hundred people a day died in Avignon. As Gottfried notes, in Avignon in one six-week period, eleven thousand people were buried in a single graveyard, one out of three cardinals died, and the total mortality likely exceeded 50 percent.[46] Paris, the largest city of Northern Europe with a population of between eighty thousand and two hundred thousand, experienced eight hundred deaths a day in November and December.[47]

At the same time as it was moving northward, the plague also moved to the west. It passed through Toulouse to Bordeaux and probably traveled from Gascony in western France to England in the summer of 1348. Accounts of the port of entry differ, with Bristol, Melcombe, and Southampton in the south of England as likely candidates. However it arrived, the plague reached London by the fall of 1348. England was extremely hard hit by the plague, for, as Horrox notes, nearly half the population of England died from it within eighteen months.

While the rate of infection and death varied from region to region, nearly all agree that East Anglia, the region of England surrounding Norwich, was the most severely afflicted. It is possible that Norwich was infected with several strains of the plague: one arriving by means of sailing ships from the Netherlands and others arriving overland from London and the Essex area.[48] At the time of the first outbreak, Norwich's population was between ten thousand and twelve thousand. The plague arrived in Norwich in January of 1349, eventually took the pneumonic form, and remained until the spring of 1350. It is estimated that half the beneficed clergy and 40 to 45 percent of the general population died in the first epidemic. Equally hard hit was the nearby town of Bury St. Edmonds, and in its surrounding villages mortality is estimated at 60 percent. As Gottfried notes, "It is likely that for all of East Anglia, plague mortality approached 50 percent, ranking it with Tuscany and parts of Scandinavia as the European areas most devastated by the Black Death."[49]

From England, the plague spread to Scotland, Ireland, and Wales in 1349. It continued its march across the European mainland, finally reaching Russia in 1350 or 1351. By the end of 1351, it had run its course. In 1351, agents for Pope Clement VI calculated the total number of dead at 23,840,000. This figure assumes a mortality rate of 30 percent. As Gottfried notes, "It is unerringly close to Froissart's claim that 'a third of the world died,' a measurement probably drawn from St. John's figure of mortality from the plague in the Book of Revelation, a favorite medieval source of information."[50]

As a result of this great mortality, the European population experienced an initial decline. Many experts believe that it eventually began to recover. However, because the plague was to recur repeatedly for the next century, population growth eventually became flat and showed few signs of recovery until at least 1460. Plague recurrences at the national and regional levels were observed in England in 1361, 1369, 1379–83, 1389–93, 1400, 1405–7, 1413, 1420, 1427, 1433–34, 1438–39, 1457–58, 1463–64, 1467, 1471, 1479–80, and 1485.[51] While subsequent outbreaks do not appear to have been interpreted with the apocalyptic note that accompanied the first epidemic, the resulting climate of death in the wake of these repeated outbreaks is poignantly expressed in the macabre art and literature of the dying in the fifteenth century, and the striking transitombs favored by the nobility. These tombs show with gruesome accuracy the decay of the body, including the depiction of skeletal remains and mice, snakes, and snails preying upon the corpse or the stitches of the embalmers.[52] Reflection on mortality and human frailty characterized the aftermath of the plague in Julian's day in the same way as exposure to massive death has led to contemplation of these same concerns in our time. A consideration of the short- and long-term effects of the plague helps us to understand the social, religious, and psychological implications of this "Great Mortality."[53]

Social, Psychological, and Religious Effects of the Plague

In assessing the effects of the Black Death as revealed through a great variety of primary texts, Horrox observed what she describes as the frequent repetition of various details in the account of the plague's devastation. She describes these repeated details as clichés. The chroniclers repeatedly note that there were not enough living survivors to bury the dead, that whole families died together, and that priests were buried alongside penitents who had confessed to them a few hours earlier. In Horrox's opinion, this repetition robs the accounts of vitality, with only a few concrete details helping contemporary readers to assimilate the horrors wrought by the relentless spread of the disease.[54] I also observed the repetition of such descriptions in the chroniclers' accounts of the plague, but rather than clichés, the descriptions struck me as a repetition of the unthinkable, testifying to the attempts of survivors to assimilate fully the trauma they had experienced. We have seen similar trends in recent traumatic events — for example, the continuous repetition in the media of images of airplanes striking the Twin Towers and of beaches, streets, and hotels being overrun by the tsunami in Southeast Asia.

It is indeed clear from reading the chroniclers' accounts of the plague's devastation that those remaining alive survived a situation of unspeakable horror. In our survey of the plague's effects, we consider dimensions of the experience that were particularly difficult for survivors, explore the religious response to the plague, and then assess the long-term consequences of the fourteenth-century pandemic.

Social and Psychological Effects of the Plague

Undoubtedly, the massive amount of death caused by the plague was its most horrifying aspect and had two consequences. First, *observers were overcome with the sheer number of dead and decaying bodies they encountered.* Giovanni Boccaccio describes the situation in Florence.

> As for the common people and the bourgeoisie . . . many dropped dead in the open streets, both by day and by night, whilst a great many others, though dying in their own

houses, drew their neighbors' attention to the fact more by the mere smell of their rotting corpses than by any other means. And what with these, and the others who were dying all over the city, bodies were here, there and everywhere.[55]

Here is a comparable description from Vienna taken from the chronicle of the monastery of Neuberg in southern Austria.

The contagious plague came in due course to Vienna and all its territories, and, as a result, countless people died and scarcely a third of the population remained alive. Because of the stench and horror of the corpses they were not allowed to be buried in churchyards, but as soon as life was extinct they had to be taken to a communal burial ground in God's Field outside the city, where in a short time five big deep pits were filled to the brim with bodies.[56]

Or again, from England from the chronicle of the cathedral priory of Rochester:

Alas, this mortality devoured such a multitude of both sexes that no one could be found to carry the bodies of the dead to burial, but men and women carried the bodies of their own little ones to church on their shoulders and threw them into mass graves, from which arose such a stink that it was barely possible for anyone to go past a churchyard.[57]

Contemporary accounts of the Southeast Asian tsunami and Hurricane Katrina also emphasize the volume of corpses and the inability of medical examiners and morgues to process and identify the dead. The extent of death in northern Indonesia following the tsunami also necessitated burial of the dead in mass graves.

These accounts create the impression of a population overwhelmed with and revolted by the sight and stench of death.
It is difficult to imagine what it would have been like for
plague survivors to face such sights on a daily basis through
the plague's extended course in a given region, and it is clear
that over time survivors simply became insensitive to the horror
in order to survive. Boccaccio captures the second consequence
of this confrontation with massive death, that is, the growth of
apathy:

> In fact, no more respect was accorded to dead people
> than would nowdays be shown towards dead goats. For
> it was quite apparent that the one thing which, in normal
> times, no wise man had ever learned to accept with patient
> resignation . . . had now been brought home to the feeble-
> minded as well, but the scale of the calamity caused them
> to regard it with indifference.[58]

The tremendous delay experienced in the recovery of the
dead following Hurricane Katrina's devastation provides an
important contemporary parallel to this medieval phenomenon.
    The third consequence of the overwhelming death toll was
the collapse of normal customs for death and burial. The account of Gilles li Muisis, abbot of St. Giles at Tournai in
Flanders, describes this effect:

> Later, when the calamitous mortality was growing much
> worse, a proclamation was made on St. Matthew's Day
> [September 21] that nobody at all should wear black, or
> toll bells for the dead, that palls should not be placed over
> the bier, and that crowds should not be invited, as usual,
> to attend the funeral, but only two to pray for the dead and
> to attend the vigils and masses. The authorities had these
> things proclaimed, together with numerous other matters

for the good of the city, under pain of certain penalties at the discretion of the *jures* and council.[59]

One reason this custom arose was because the repeated tolling of the "passing bells" was filling the populace, men and women alike, with fear. However, it is also true that the magnitude of death simply made it impossible for clergy, physicians, and society in general to respond in the customary ways to individual cases. This same phenomenon was also observed in the aftermath of the tsunami as imams protested the indignity with which the dead were being treated in heavily damaged areas of Indonesia. During the plague years, the difficulty in obtaining clergy, in particular, led to a great deal of anxiety. This caused at least one bishop, the bishop of Bath and Wells, Ralph of Shrewsbury, to counsel priests to advise their parishioners that "if they are not able to obtain any priest [in time of illness] they should make confession of their sins (according to the teaching of an apostle) even to a layman, and if a man is not at hand, then to a woman."[60] However, to avoid such extreme measures, the bishop did provide a forty-day indulgence to those who confessed to a priest before becoming ill. Further, penitents who confessed to lay ministers were exhorted, in the event of their recovery, to confess to a priest. Thus, tolerance for lay confessional ministry seemed clearly reserved for extremity.

The chroniclers' accounts also describe a fourth painful effect of the plague deaths. Fear of contagion resulted in *abandonment of the dying and dead.* This effect manifested the dehumanization wrought by the plague. The dying were not cherished but were treated instead as objects to be avoided. This is most poignantly captured in Boccaccio's description of the plague in Florence:

[In the wake of the plague] it was not merely a question of one citizen avoiding another, and of people almost

invariably neglecting their neighbors and rarely or never
visiting their relatives, addressing them only from a distance; this scourge had implanted so great a terror in
the hearts of men and women that brothers abandoned
brothers, uncles their nephews, sisters their brothers, and
in many cases, wives deserted their husbands. But even
worse, and almost incredible, was the fact that fathers and
mothers refused to nurse and assist their own children as
though they did not belong to them.[61]

We read in de Mussis's account of the plague in Piacenza that

... when the sick were in the throes of death, they still
called out piteously to their family and neighbors, "Come
here. I'm thirsty, bring me a drink of water. I'm still alive.
Don't be frightened. Perhaps I won't die. Please hold me
tight, hug my wasted body. You ought to be holding me in
your arms."[62]

De Mussis goes on to ask, "What a tragic and wretched sight!
Who would not shed sympathetic tears? ... But our hearts have
grown hard now that we have no future to look forward to."[63]

Fear of contagion led, in some places, to isolation of the sick,
who were ejected from towns. In Milan, in draconian style,
the citizens walled up the windows and doors of the first three
homes containing the plague, where all the inhabitants were
left to perish.[64] But, as Horrox notes, the best safeguard was
flight—as advocated in a German manuscript, "Clever doctors
have three golden rules to keep us safe from pestilence: get out
quickly, go a long way and don't be in a hurry to come back."[65]
The rich, in particular, preferred flight, but those who fled were
not always at ease with the solution, since they understood that
God's anger, in the form of the plague, could follow them anywhere. Clearly, those who were well harbored ambivalence and

guilt about abandoning the sick, factors that may only have contributed to their burden of grief. The frequency with which flight was adopted, even by the clergy, underscores the human instinct for survival at the same time as it highlights the disruption of the fabric of community that invariably accompanies disaster.[66]

A fourth effect of the plague was *ambivalence among the worried well*. How were they to live while the plague raged? As we have already noted, some chose to flee and, in their flight, to create a peaceable existence with good food, fine wine, and pleasant conversation. Others, perhaps more surely anticipating death, chose to "drink heavily, enjoy life to the full, go round singing and merrymaking, gratify all of one's cravings whenever the opportunity offered and shrug the whole thing off as one enormous joke."[67] Others, of course, steered a middle course between complete denial and total abandon. According to Boccaccio, these did not restrict their diet as much as the cautious, nor indulge as freely as the reckless. Instead, they moved about freely with flowers or other aromatic substances in their hand to protect themselves from the stench of the sick and dead. Since there was no clear consensus either about the cause of the plague or its treatment, it was anyone's guess as to which strategy would ultimately prove most effective.

One final, troubling effect of the plague was to prove particularly damaging to society, namely, *suspicion of outsiders*. This effect was to lead ultimately to the death of thousands through persecution. Evidence for this fear occurs in several accounts, such as one from Padua, where it was believed that a single outsider brought the plague. As a result, cities banned the entry of all outsiders, and merchants were unable to travel easily from city to city.[68]

A comparable account may be found in the autobiography of the fourteenth-century German mystic Henry Suso. Suso describes how his traveling companion was accused of poisoning wells when he traveled to a strange village. The unfortunate man was seized and imprisoned, and he was released only when Suso paid a stiff fine on his behalf. In the end, Suso himself was accused of being a poisoner, and he was able to escape this danger only with the help of a priest who overheard his desperate prayers for deliverance. The priest took him in, kept him overnight, and helped him make his way safely out of the town in the morning.[69] This tendency to blame strangers and foreigners for inexplicable misfortune points to a nearly universal psychological phenomenon, the punishing of scapegoats, which continues to persist in times of tragedy.

Clearly, the advent of the plague brought many difficult emotions to those unfortunate enough to experience the suffering and death it wrought. Contemporary accounts attest to the following range of feelings: helplessness, numbness, shock, apathy, denial, guilt, relief for survival, gratitude for life, a loss of certainty, a sense of hopelessness, vulnerability, pessimism, an inability to assimilate the extent of disaster, an awareness of the irony of life, a sense of life as precarious, a loss of direction, and an awareness of paradox. Many of these same emotions were present in the survivor vignettes in chapter 1. Living with this full panoply of emotions was certainly unsettling. Perhaps the most unsettling experience of all, however, *was attempting to understand why: why had this suffering come to afflict the population?* While several scientific explanations were advanced, the most common and compelling belief was that the plague resulted from the action of the Divine.[70]

Religious Explanations for the Plague and Their Effect on the Faithful

Perhaps the most common and most troubling explanation for the plague was theological: specifically, the plague was understood as a form of divine vengeance for human sinfulness.

One of the most sustained theological accounts of the plague is found in Gabriele de Mussis's *Historia de Morbo.*[71] His description of the plague's arrival in Italy is the most frequently cited; as Horrox notes, what is less well known is that it occurs in the context of an extended meditation on the plague as an expression of divine anger. De Mussis's account begins as follows.

> May this stand as a perpetual reminder to everyone, now living and yet to be born, how almighty God, king of heaven, lord of the living and of the dead, who holds all things in his hand, looked down from heaven and saw the entire human race wallowing in the mire of manifold wickedness, enmeshed in wrongdoing, pursuing numberless vices, drowning in a sea of depravity because of a limitless capacity for evil, bereft of all goodness, not fearing the judgments of God, and chasing after everything evil, regardless of how hateful and loathsome it was. Seeing such things he called out to the earth: "What are you doing, held captive by gangs of worthless men, soiled with the filth of sinners? Are you totally helpless? What are you doing? Why do you not demand human blood in vengeance for this wrongdoing? Why do you tolerate my enemies and adversaries? When confronted by such wantonness, you should have swallowed my opponents. Make yourself ready to exercise the vengeance which lies within your power."[72]

De Mussis describes an extended dialogue between God and creation in which God pronounces the following judgment on humankind.

> I pronounce these judgments: may your joys be turned to mourning, your prosperity be shaken by adversity, the

course of your life be passed in never-ending terror. Behold the image of death. Behold, I open the infernal floodgates. Let hunger strike down those it seizes, let peace be driven from the ends of the earth; let dissensions arise; let kingdoms be consumed in detestable war; let mercy perish throughout the world; let disasters, plagues, violence, robberies, strife and all kinds of wickedness arise. Next, at my command, let the planets poison the air and corrupt the whole earth; let there be universal grief and lamentation. Let the sharp arrows of sudden death have dominion throughout the world. Let not one be spared, either for their sex or their age; let the innocent perish with the guilty and no one escape.[73]

This diatribe continues with a condemnation of the clergy and ends with a description of God's vengeance unleashed on the earth, in which de Mussis describes God as shooting arrows bearing disease toward humankind, thus infecting the entire human race. Clearly, in de Mussis's view, the plague is a form of divine punishment sent directly from God's hands to afflict the populace. Similar theories were advanced in the early days of the AIDS epidemic, which was viewed by some religious commentators as God's punishment of gays.

De Mussis's account conceives of the plague as a reversal of creation and may explain the common scriptural allusions to Noah that occurred at the time of the Black Death. The plague was understood as an "undoing" of the goodness of the world, because of human sin, in the same manner as the flood described in Genesis.

Undoubtedly de Mussis, an attorney, was trained as a rhetorician rather than as a theologian. This background may account, in part, for his stark portrayal of God's anger. Nevertheless, even the theologians of the day turned to divine anger as an explanation for the plague, although their rhetoric was softened a bit and tends to portray a more kind and merciful God who may be moved through the repentance of the faithful.[74]

What sins were understood to be the occasion for the unleashing of such terrible wrath? Several catalogues of sin are cited, but the sins most commonly mentioned included the seven deadly sins: pride, avarice, envy, lust, anger, sloth, and gluttony. Other sins invoked as explanations included the lack of good faith and equity among judges, lawyers' use of unethical or petty methods in bringing forth trumped-up charges, the hypocrisy of religious, and the vanity of ladies. Critics also condemned the failure of those in leadership, including the unjust favoritism of kings and the greed of clergy and prelates. But perhaps the most commonly cited causes for God's disfavor included the divine disapproval of tournaments and the scandalous styles of the times. The moralists criticized the tournaments for their frivolity and excess and the fashions for their indecency and for inciting the faithful to vanity and immorality.[75] Finally, in the fourteenth century as in the twenty-first, the failure of youth and adolescents to obey their elders is noted as one cause of misfortune, in the face of which parents are exhorted to discipline, in this case by Reason in *Piers the Plowman.*

And then he charged chapmen to chastise their children
"Don't let wealth spoil them while they are young
Nor for fear of the pestilence indulge them beyond reason.
My mother and father both told me
That the dearer the child the more teaching it needs.
And Solomon said the same, in his book of Wisdom:
Qui parcit virge odit filium,
Which is in English, if you want to know:
Who spares the rod spoils the child."[76]

Clearly, the dominant religious explanation was not flawless. Astute observers in every age have noted that the innocent as well as the wicked suffer. When faced with objections on these grounds, theologians resorted to a second explanation, namely, the view that "plague is a spiritual blessing and a sign of God's mercy, since it prompts men to repent in this life and be spared the pain of hell in the next."[77] Thomas Brinton, one of the most famous preachers in England in the fourteenth century, articulated this view. Of course, this understanding might explain the dynamics that led some to survive, but it did not explain the deaths of innocents. These Brinton attributed to the sins of others; he believed, for example, that the deaths of innocent children were due to the sins of their parents. He viewed these deaths as "a release from prison, an end of exile and toil, an escape from all danger, breaking of chains, a return to the homeland, a going forth to glory."[78] The death of innocent children, therefore, provided just one example of the way in which God sometimes punished the innocent to chastise sinners.

A final theological explanation advanced for the 1348–49 outbreak of the plague was the view that it heralded the end of the world. Of course, this explanation lost force in repeated epidemics; nevertheless, in the first and most damaging outbreak, the invocation of apocalyptic imagery and explanation seemed both appropriate and compelling.

Pastoral Responses to the Plague

Clearly, people faced with the plague turned to religious explanations. Whether the plague was viewed as a punishment for sin, a wake-up call, or a harbinger of the end times, the same remedy was invoked: the faithful must repent and be saved. Therefore, the church developed a variety of vehicles toward this end.

Processions were one of the most common religious resources mustered against the plague, and indeed had a venerable
history: Gregory the Great led a procession through Rome in
590 during Justinian's Plague, chanting the great litany composed for the occasion. As the procession made its way through
the streets of the city, Michael the Archangel appeared on top
of the mausoleum of Hadrian sheathing his sword. Believers
interpreted this as a sign that God had been appeased, and it
led to the christening of the mausoleum as Castel Sant'Angelo.
To commemorate the occasion, a great statue of the archangel
was placed atop the building.[79] When the plague returned in the
Middle Ages, the pope and bishops again organized processions
as a first line of resistance. As Tuchman notes, some of these
penitential processions lasted three days and were attended by
as many as two thousand people. Unfortunately, they also encouraged the spread of the infection, and when this became
clear, Pope Clement VI finally prohibited them.[80]

Other pious activities encouraged in the face of the plague
included reciting psalms, making a pilgrimage, embracing acts
of penance, and attending Mass. Brinton's program for repentance included confessing one's sins, praying for other believers,
serving God, adopting a habit of watchfulness, and meditating
on the Passion of Christ.[81]

Medieval art and documents testify to the importance of
intercession as an aid in the plague. Three saints, in particular, were considered as powerful protectors. The first was the
Blessed Virgin Mary. In his survey of late medieval iconography
developed in response to the plague, John B. Friedman provides
an image of the Virgin and plague victims taken from a German altarpiece. In this image, the Virgin extends her mantle
over plague victims to ward off the arrows of God's wrath.[82]
This realistic depiction places arrows in the spots where plague
victims normally experienced buboes, inflammatory swelling

of the lymph glands from which the bubonic plague takes its name.

Friedman also cites two popular prayers to the Virgin for protection against the plague, both works of John Lydgate. In one poem, he asks the Virgin to "Pray / Thy swete son ... / That no perylous plage of pestilence ... / Entyr in England." In the second, he begs her:

> do not now disdeyne
> Contraryous planetis to Appeese & Represse,
> Whos dredefull werrys do men full Mortall peyne,
> Be vnwholesome Eyres Cawsyng greete syknesse.[83]

Devotion to two other patrons grew at this same time. St. Sebastian became particularly popular because he was associated with arrows, being the patron of archers and crossbowmen. According to legend, he was a member of the imperial guard martyred by the emperor Diocletian in the third century. He was shot with arrows and presumed dead, but he recovered through the ministrations of Irene, the widow of another Christian martyr. When the emperor discovered this, he had Sebastian bludgeoned to death. The image of being shot with arrows was a popular religious device for describing the onslaught of the plague, and the saint's body, pierced by arrows, yet alive, became a potent symbol for plague victims.[84] As a result, Sebastian's relics in Flanders and Italy drew many pilgrims, and medieval representations portray him interceding on behalf of plague victims.

A third popular patron was St. Roche. Unlike Sebastian, Roche actually contracted the plague, yet survived. In 1379, while on a pilgrimage during which he cured plague victims, he was falsely imprisoned as a spy near Montpelier, where he eventually died. Friedman notes that both Sebastian and Roche appeared on plague coins and tokens designed to avert the disease. Further, many pious confraternities took the names of these saints and developed images of them in wood sculpture, wall painting, and stained glass. Confraternities were composed of pious lay persons who banded together to arrange for masses for their souls after death and for prayer protection from the plague. The formation of confraternities was another common religious reaction to the dangers of the plague.[85]

Besides these pious practices designed to avert the plague, Europeans also resorted to extreme measures against fellow sufferers in the name of God. Two of the most disturbing and related chapters in the fourteenth-century history of the Black Death describe the penitential practices of the flagellants and the associated persecution of the Jews. These phenomena also shed light on the religious response to the plague.

Extreme Religious Reactions: Persecution and Flagellation

In the introduction to his discussion of the Jewish persecutions accompanying outbreaks of the plague, Philip Ziegler attempts to explain the rationale and tactics accompanying this horrible practice. Persecution in the Middle Ages was rooted in the sense of helplessness people felt when facing suffering. Seeking explanation and relief, they attempted to find solace in action rather than to endure the paralysis that accompanies helplessness. In the absence of satisfying medical explanations, the population sought a scapegoat: someone near at hand who could be blamed for the present suffering. As Ziegler notes:

> Few doubted that the Black Death was God's will but, by a curious quirk of reasoning, medieval man also concluded that His instruments were to be found on earth and that, if only they could be identified, it was legitimate to destroy them. What was needed, therefore, was a suitable target for

the indignation of the people, preferably a minority group, easily identifiable, already unpopular, widely scattered and lacking any powerful protector.[86]

Strangers and outsiders were among those targeted for persecution and violence as the plague advanced. Ziegler describes the ways in which the category, "stranger," was nuanced depending on circumstances. In Spain, Arabs were suspect, while throughout Europe, pilgrims were viewed with suspicion. In Narbonne, a city in southern France, the English were targeted. The lepers were the second most widely feared group. In the southern French region of Languedoc, in 1321, lepers were burnt on the suspicion of poisoning wells, yet even in this situation, it was assumed that they were complicit with Jews.[87] Drawing on these findings, it is interesting to speculate about the extent to which suspicion of religious difference also fueled the militant response to 9/11 in the United States.

A number of factors combined to highlight the Jews as the preferred target of persecution. As Cantor notes, Jews lived in tension with their neighbors for both religious and economic reasons.[88] The emergence of Kabbalah — an esoteric form of religious thought among the Jewish elite, concerned with God, creation, and nature — may have led to suspicion against them, particularly since, in some places, there was an overlap between Kabbalah and Christian Catharism. The beliefs of the latter, a movement with a dualistic and Gnostic theology, were officially denounced as heresy.[89] In addition to their differing religious beliefs, the profession of many Jews provided a further inducement for violence against them. In the Middle Ages, the Jews served as moneylenders, because Christians were forbidden from using money to make money. Over time, as the banking industry developed, the Jews experienced increasing marginalization as bankers, until in many places they functioned more as petty lenders and pawnbrokers. Nevertheless, as Cantor notes, "there were large amounts of money to be made from the destruction of the Jews."[90] In some cases, archbishops themselves directly profited from persecution. Finally, a visibly lower incidence of the plague among Jews may also have ignited violence against them. Cantor attributes this decreased rate of disease to legislated impediments against Jewish farming, their segregated living quarters where they were cut off from wharves and cattle and thus from the main carriers of disease, and rabbinic laws that prescribed personal cleanliness, good housekeeping, and selective diets.[91] As Cantor notes, "their practical quarantine aroused suspicion that they were responsible for the disease to which they themselves seemed immune."[92]

A tradition of anti-Semitism in Christian theology also contributed to the violence against the Jews. Anti-Semitism was reflected in canon law and in the writings and preaching of such respected theologians as John Chrysostom, Augustine, and Thomas Aquinas. The latter, in fact, concluded that "since Jews are the slave of the Church, she can dispose of their possessions."[93] This intellectual climate of intolerance led inevitably to persecution and violence. During the Crusades, massacres of Jewish communities accompanied the Crusaders' march to Palestine as the cry, "HEP, HEP" for *Hierosolyma est Perdita* (Jerusalem is lost) became the battle cry against them. The violence seemed justified, since Christians blamed Jews for the capture of the Holy Sepulcher by the Moslems. With the arrival of the Inquisition in the thirteenth century, the Jews were faced both with charges of ritual murder and the wearing of badges.[94] The existence of the Jews in Medieval Europe was precarious, indeed, and Jews were dependent on the favor of kings and rulers to maintain their tenuous toehold on property and possessions.

In the advent of the plague, the charge leveled against Jews was the poisoning of wells "with intent to kill and destroy the whole of Christendom and have lordship over all the world."[95] The first persecutions occurred in Spain and in southern France in the spring of 1348. In May of 1348, there was a massacre in Provence and widespread extermination of the Jews in Narbonne and Carcassone. The movement against the Jews gained particular momentum, however, following the extraction under torture of a confession of guilt at Chillon, in Savoy, in September 1348. Following the circulation of this confession, violence erupted with unspeakable brutality throughout central Europe. In some places, Cantor notes that persecutions even began to precede the arrival of the plague. This was the case in Chillon, were Jews were attacked four months before the plague arrived. Jews were also banned from the city of Zurich in Switzerland for all time on September 21, 1348. This persecution in Zurich preceded the arrival of the plague in the city by a whole year. In November of 1348, Jews were burned at Solothurn, Zofigen, and Stuttgart in Germany; in December at Landsberg, Burren, Memmingen, and Lindau; and in January at Freiburg, Ulm, and Speyer, all also in Germany. In January, Jews in Basel, Switzerland, were burned after being imprisoned in a house on an island in the Rhine built expressly for their destruction. In February, Jews were massacred at Gotha, Eisenach, and Dresden in what is now the eastern part of Germany, and two thousand Jews were murdered in Strasbourg at the German border with France. In March, Jews were killed at Worms, Baden, and Erfurt in Germany. For a time, the violence ceased, but its return in the summer of 1349 resulted from the influence of the flagellants.

The flagellants were extreme penitential groups in Europe that arose in conjunction with the plague and were particularly evident in Germany, France, and the Low Countries. These groups practiced public self-scourging, the aim of which was to avert God's anger against sinners. The movement had its roots in Italian monastic communities in the eleventh century, but the practice of group flagellation underwent a metamorphosis, reemerging at the height of the plague with a strong public focus. The flagellants would march into a town in a long procession, two by two. Sometimes they came by the thousands and, at other times, hundreds. They wore distinctive clothing marked with red crosses and segregated themselves by sex. Upon entering the town, they would process to the church, accompanied by the ringing of church bells. The flagellants chanted special litanies and sang the "Stabat Mater" and other hymns devised to accompany their rites. The central focus of their activity, usually conducted in the public square, was thrashing by the group's master for particular sins. This was followed by self-flagellation with scourges fashioned from sticks with knotted tails from which protruded needle-like spikes. The flagellants proceeded to whip themselves with these instruments until they drew blood. These rituals were accompanied by public hysteria, with spectators crying, sobbing, howling, and tearing at their hair and body in reaction to the excesses they witnessed.

At first, Ziegler notes, the movement was well-regulated and disciplined. New entrants had to obtain permission of their spouse, confess their sins, show that they were able to support themselves, and vow obedience to their master. Over time, however, the group's arrogance grew, and this led to conflict with the church. Conflict was rooted in the group's repudiation of church authority, their ridicule of the Eucharist, and their refusal to reverence the host. Eventually, their actions became more extreme, and they were known to interrupt church services, drive clergy from their churches, and loot church property. As the group became more and more revolutionary, it also became more violent, and unfortunately, the flagellants directed their violence against the Jews. As Tuchman notes, "In every town they entered, the flagellants rushed for the Jewish quarters, trailed by citizens howling for revenge upon the 'poisoners of the wells.'"[96] Their actions led to the massacre of Jews in Freiburg, Augsburg, Nürnberg, Munich, Königsberg, Regensburg, Worms, Frankfurt, Cologne, and Mainz. Horrified by these massacres, church and civil authorities took action to suppress the movement. On October 20, 1348, Clement VI issued a papal bull denouncing the flagellants for contempt of church discipline and ordering prelates to suppress their pilgrimages. Further, the University of Paris denied their claim of divine inspiration. Then, in the words of the chronicler Henry of Herford, the flagellants vanished "as suddenly as they had come, like night phantoms or mocking ghosts."[97]

Yet in their heyday the flagellants did irreversible damage to the Jewish population and their sympathizers.[98] So although the persecution of the Jews was over by 1351, the loss of 60 large and 150 smaller Jewish communities considerably weakened the Jewish presence in Europe. And no wonder, for in all, Jews had experienced some 350 massacres during the plague years.[99] This legacy of suffering remains as a painful reminder of the human thirst for vengeance in the face of massive and inexplicable pain and suffering. That such vengeance is wrought in the name of God makes it especially disturbing. These events also point to ways in which religious differences may magnify and intensify conflicts and retaliation, both phenomena we have observed in the wake of 9/11.

The Longer-Term Effects of the Plague

In attempting to assess the repercussions of the plague, Rosemary Horrox notes that late nineteenth-century historians had given the plague a "starring role" in the drama of change. The plague was viewed, for a time, as an agent of cataclysmic change in a number of domains, including art, religion, social arrangements, and the economy. Over time, however, historians have moderated this view somewhat. As Horrox notes, historians are less likely to attribute change to a single cause. Instead, they are more apt to see change as arising from a complex intersection of forces. However, the emphasis on the plague as a catalyst for change is again on the rise.[100]

Clearly, the plague significantly affected several aspects of religious life, such as the composition of the clergy, their status and educational level, and a growing restiveness in the face of traditional theologies. However, in assessing the effects of the plague on the religious life of the late fourteenth century, we must not overlook the importance of equally significant factors, such as the papal schism, which had far-reaching implications for the institution of the church and the piety of the faithful. As Harper-Bill notes in accounting for the rise of Wyclif and his followers, we must remember that this first notable outbreak of heresy in England coincided with the Great Schism and that religious dissent in England quickly dissipated once church unity was restored.[101]

We shall examine three areas in assessing the long-term effects of the plague: mind-set, morality, and mood.

Ziegler offers a very cogent analysis of the mind-set of the faithful. He believes that medieval people undoubtedly felt let down by the church. While the faithful were willing to accept that the plague was the work of God and a response to sin, they found it difficult to understand why the church had not been able to warn them earlier that the patience of God was being tried to such an extreme degree. When suffering came, people were disillusioned with the church for failing to issue more timely and effective warnings.[102]

Clearly, there must have been a gap between people's expectations of the church and the church's ability to respond to them. The reality of the schism and the rhetoric of sin in the time of the plague undermined the authority of the institution, for each of these factors highlighted discrepancies between ideals and reality. The rhetoric of sin seemed inadequate when the innocent appeared to die at as great a rate as sinners in the plague. Further, the schism highlighted the church's seemingly greater concern with temporal than spiritual matters. These developments strained credulity. The disappointment they wrought was at least partly responsible for the pessimism of the late fourteenth and early fifteenth centuries that is everywhere expressed in its art and literature. Further, contemporary observers could not have failed to note that "God's wrath seemed just as hot against the Church as against people," for clergy died in even greater numbers than laity.[103] In Ziegler's opinion, this fact along with clerical abuses, such as abandonment of the sick and dying during the plague and clerical greed and laziness after the plague, must surely have exposed the vulnerability of the clergy and been a factor in their decreased popularity.[104] The fact that they represented a God increasingly portrayed as wrathful and retributive could not have helped their popularity either. Finally, clergy fitness and education were depressed after the plague in comparison to pre-plague standards. At a time when the church faced terribly perplexing pastoral problems, the average priest was increasingly ill-equipped to respond.

A second significant effect was the growing moral laxness of the populace. According to the chronicler Jean de Venette, in the aftermath of the plague, "men were more greedy and quarrelsome; women became sexually degenerate; clergy haunted taverns and gambling dens; [and] little men bustled about to make themselves the equals of their betters."[105] So on the one hand, we have accounts of post-plague life which describe decreased morality. Ziegler attributes this trend to relief from tension and the enjoyment of more money, since one notable effect of the plague was a marked increase in wages.[106] On the other hand, when the fabric of community unravels, as it surely did in the aftermath of the Black Death, both loss of morale and of community consensus may explain the decline of morality.

Finally, the plague affected the mood of the populace. In the wake of the Black Death, all commentators agree that the psychological climate was marked by a pervasive pessimism, a "neurotic and all-pervading gloom."[107] This gloom was evident in the moralistic tone of certain literature, such as Langland's *Piers Plowman*, and in the obsessive fascination with death that characterized the art and literature of the fifteenth century, with its "Dance of Death" theme. As Horrox rightly notes, most survivors lived with an increased sense of guilt and vulnerability that came with the knowledge that "the increased expectations of survivors derived ultimately from the deaths of family and friends."[108]

This sense of vulnerability was reflected in increased emphases on the unpredictability of death and on the corruptibility of the body. People also seemed more aware after the plague that even seemingly healthy people might be struck down without warning. As Horrox notes, "the association of plague with unprepared death was one of its particular terrors."[109] As twentieth-century research with survivors makes clear, exposure to death on both the grand and disturbing scale associated with the plague leaves an indelible imprint on the memory and psyche of survivors, one that continues to exert powerful effects for years after the initial trauma.

As a plague survivor herself, Julian was not exempt from these dynamics. So we turn now to examine her revelations and her theological reflection upon them to explore in what ways they may have exerted their effects.

Julian as Survivor:
"You Are My Heaven"

For individual hibakusha [Hiroshima survivors] the experience of being loved and cared for could, gradually and against obstacles, re-create life-affirming imagery and reestablish the capacity to live.   — Robert Lifton, *Death in Life*[1]

The reason we are greatly troubled by [our pains] is our ignorance of love. . . . For some of us believe that God is all-mighty and may do everything, again that he is all-wisdom and can do everything, but that he is all-love and will do everything, there we hold back. And this ignorance, that is what most hampers God's lovers in my eyes. . . . Of all the properties of the blissful Trinity, it is God's will that we be most sure of and take most delight in his love; for love makes us strong.   — Julian of Norwich, *Revelation of Love*[2]

Julian as Survivor: Setting the Stage

The twentieth and twenty-first centuries have certainly witnessed dramatic and overwhelming death tolls from war, genocide, terrorism, and disease. Nevertheless, casualties exacted by the Black Death of 1348–49 rival those attributed to World War I and World War II. Those who study disasters professionally have ranked this pandemic as one of the most devastating crises of all time.[3] Julian, born almost midway through the fourteenth century and living in what was then one of England's greatest cities, knew this suffering personally. She survived several outbreaks of the second plague pandemic. Further, she was

84

not immune to the effects of war or to the disillusionment and dissent that marked the religious culture of her day. Her ministry of counseling would surely have exposed her to the former, while her text itself testifies to the latter. In this way, she has much in common with contemporary survivors, many of whom have been exposed through the media to a variety of forms of suffering beyond those they may have personally experienced.

While Julian's many interpreters have named the Black Death as an influence upon her theology, none has attempted to explore specifically how Julian may have suffered from the plague and how the experience of grief may have influenced her desire for spiritual transformation, the form in which it appeared, and its effects. So I suggest in this chapter that Julian may be more deeply understood as a survivor of traumatic loss from the plague. To this end, I first lay out several assumptions about the effect of the plague on Julian that help to situate her clearly as a survivor. Then I use Lifton's psychology of the survivor as an interpretive lens. I am particularly interested in demonstrating how that psychology helps to interpret the effects of loss on Julian's religious development, on her visions, and on the theology she fashioned in response to them. This analysis will put us in a better position to explore the positive resources available in Julian's work for survivors of traumatic loss today.

Julian's Experience of Traumatic Loss

Certain crucial assumptions about the effects of the plague on Julian provide grounds for my belief that Julian may be more deeply understood as a survivor of the plague. These assumptions flow from what is known about the magnitude and effect of plague loss on Julian's contemporaries. The experience of twentieth- and twenty-first-century survivors of traumatic loss also informs these assumptions. While the circumstances of loss certainly differ across time, research on traumatic loss suggests important similarities between the experiences of survivors of all forms of overwhelming loss, regardless of the particular cause of their loss. Thus it is not unreasonable to compare contemporary and historical experiences of loss in creatively reconstructing Julian's experience.[4]

The first and most significant assumption about the effects of the plague is that *Julian would have been exposed to the physical horror of death on a large scale at a young age.* This assumption flows directly from two facts: that Julian, who was born in 1342, would have been six or seven when the first plague epidemic arrived in England; and that according to the best estimates available Julian would have experienced the death of roughly half the people she knew. Thus, the extent of her loss is comparable, for example, to that sustained by citizens of northern Indonesia in the 2005 tsunami.

Second, *Julian would have experienced a diminished psychic capacity to absorb these deaths and to feel their effects. In addition, disruption of the normal customs for death and burial that accompanied the plague would have impaired her mourning.* Two facts undergird this assumption: they include, first, the testimony to apathy and psychic numbing widely described in the chroniclers' accounts of the plague and, second, the disruption in normal death rituals that accompanied the 1348–49 epidemic, due to the sheer magnitude of loss. Once again, the recent tsunami in Southeast Asia, in the extent of death it created, provides an important parallel to this aspect of Julian's experience.

Third, *Julian would have experienced cumulative effects of loss,* since she lived through several outbreaks of the plague.

Fourth, there is also every reason to expect that *Julian's memories of these events would have been vivid and lasting.*

As we have seen, vivid sensory memories trouble contemporary survivors of post-traumatic stress; as a plague survivor, Julian would undoubtedly have experienced a marked death imprint through her exposure to the plague. If anything, she may have been more susceptible to this phenomenon because of her youth.

Fifth, as all survivors do, *Julian would have encountered the question, "Why did I survive when so many others have died?"* This question, voiced in the sermons of Thomas Brinton, her contemporary, must also have disturbed Julian. As we shall see, it has also been voiced by survivors of contemporary disasters in their attempts to find meaning in loss. Indeed, as a plague survivor, Julian would have struggled with guilt about her survival. Surviving several outbreaks of the plague may have made this question even more urgent for Julian.

Sixth, *Julian and her contemporaries would have lived with dread about potential recurrences of the plague* and have asked, in living through repeated outbreaks, whether God and the world were reliable. Experiencing repeated outbreaks may have led to a diminished capacity for hope and increased Julian's death immersion. In this way she may be similar to contemporary survivors who articulate through their suffering an increased sense of their vulnerability to death.

Seventh, from what we know about the social disruption caused by the plague, we may assume that *Julian would have experienced ruptures in the fabric of her community.* Undoubtedly, she would have experienced a loss of social support because of deaths in her social network. Further, relationships are commonly strained in situations of overwhelming loss, as survivors attempt to cope with the magnitude of death they have experienced. The abandonment of the sick and dying, described frequently in the chroniclers' accounts, may have affected Julian deeply. Because Julian was a young girl in 1348–49, she may have been particularly vulnerable to familial loss. This sense of rupture within communities is perhaps most vividly present in natural disasters where citizens of entire regions experience the simultaneous destruction of the physical, social, and political structures that sustain life.

Eighth, *Julian may have experienced several psychological effects common to survivors of massive death: a sense of foreshortened future, a death-dominated life, unresolved or incomplete mourning, a restricted emotional range, and temptations to despair.* Later we shall consider evidence in Julian's text that suggests the presence of these effects prior to her visions.

Ninth, *plague experiences may have heightened Julian's concerns with sin and salvation, as she would have been exposed to the dominant theological explanation for the plague in her day, namely, human sinfulness.* The feelings of shame and guilt that often accompany traumatic loss may account for the heightened interest in salvation and redemption in the Long Text, in particular. Like Julian, many contemporary survivors of traumatic loss also suffer from shame and guilt, and many express anger at God because of their pain and grief. Some completely abandon their quest for religious explanations because they cannot reconcile the existence of their loss with a loving God.

Finally, in several striking ways, *Julian found herself living at the boundary of life and death.* She lived as an anchoress, she was a near death survivor, and she was a woman who survived multiple outbreaks of the plague. In addition, she may also have survived childbirth — not something to be taken for granted in those days.[5] The liminal quality of each of these experiences may have heightened her experience of survival and stimulated the penetrating quality of the reflections on suffering, death, and resurrection found in her texts.

A closer analysis of Julian's text helps us to understand how acknowledging her status as a survivor of traumatic loss provides deeper insight into the character of her visions and the healing they made possible.

Julian's Visions and Their Effects: Lifton's Psychology as a Hermeneutical Lens

Lifton's psychology, developed through analyses of interviews with contemporary survivors, offers a unique perspective on the healing character of Julian's visions. In the following analysis, I draw on his theory to explain how Julian's visions enabled her to move from grief to hope as the pain of suffering and loss became transfigured through the presence of love.

The Death Imprint and Death Anxiety

In our attempt to understand the transforming power of Julian's visions, we first explore how Julian's experience of death anxiety and the death imprint may have shaped their form and effects. Following Lifton, we may assume that Julian would have experienced both death anxiety and the death imprint as a result of her exposure to massive death in the plague. The chroniclers' accounts describe conditions that would have led to such phenomena, and Lifton himself describes the features that may have constituted the typical aspects of a death imprint caused by the plague.[6]

Julian experienced sixteen visions. The first fifteen occurred on May 8, while the sixteenth took place on the following evening. In the first chapter of the Long Text, Julian described in summary form the nature of the visions and the meaning of each. The primary focus of the visions is the crucified Christ. Through her vision of the crucifixion and her interaction with it, Julian developed her theology of redemption and salvation.

Other visions on the first day are concerned with the rightfulness and excellence of creation, the rewards of heaven, the
preservation of the soul in love, Christ's delight in the passion,
Christ's love for humankind, the nature of prayer, and the honor
due to the saints, especially the Virgin Mary. The sixteenth vision is of the Trinity dwelling in Christ within the human soul,
preserving it in love and protecting it from harm.

Julian's prayers prior to her vision suggested that she shared
two key traits with other survivors: first, she identified with
the dying, and, second, she had a heightened awareness of her
own death. The former is reflected in her prayer to be one with
those at the foot of the cross and to have knowledge of the
bodily pains of Christ's passion.[7] The latter is reflected in her
prayer for "a grave sickness even to the point of death ... in
this sickness [she] desired to have all manner of pains both in
body and spirit that [she] should have if [she] should die."[8] It
seems quite likely that Julian had anxiety about her eventual
death. Perhaps one reason why she prayed for a sickness unto
death was that she wanted the sickness to prosper her in her
own death, to enable her to withstand the temptations that she
anticipated in her final hour. Undoubtedly, Julian witnessed the
deaths of many in the plague who were spiritually unprepared
for death. Fearing for her salvation, she wanted a "dry run,"
an opportunity to encounter death so that she might prepare
herself in advance for its rigors.[9] Because Julian recognized the
unusual nature of this prayer, she asked for it on the condition
that it accord with God's will.

In addition, the text supports the notion that Julian suffered
from anxiety about her potential for premature death and an un-
fulfilled life. This, also, is a characteristic of survivors marked
by a death imprint. During her illness, she stated, "I was certain that I would die, which was both a wonder and a partial
sadness."[10] She also noted that "being still young, I thought it a

great sadness to die."[11] Clearly, Julian had ambivalent feelings about her own death, and her reluctance to face it is evident in the text.

Julian's experience of her vision provided her with an opportunity for healing from the impaired psychological dynamics characteristic of survivors of massive death. I hypothesize that healing occurred in the following way: Julian's vision of the crucified Christ may be understood as a type of death imprint, or indelible image of death, different from that arising from her plague experience. Her strenuous, and, at times, painful interaction with her vision of the crucifixion allowed her to heal from the destructive impact of her encounter with death in the plague. Julian's account of her visionary experience describes clearly how she was able to participate effectively in Christ's death. Her active engagement with the death imprint of the crucifixion may have relieved her of guilt associated with the "failed enactment" captured in the original, plague-related death imprint. That is, her ability to stay with the crucified Christ despite her pain in witnessing his sufferings perhaps compensated for ways in which she may have abandoned those suffering from the plague when she was younger. Her efficacious interaction with the vision, therefore, provided her with a chance to overcome both the damaging effects of the earlier death imprint and the death anxiety associated with it.

Central to this thesis is the argument that Julian's vision of the crucified Christ may be thought of as a death imprint. To use Lifton's language, this vision represents an "image of death" that is both "grotesque" and "absurd."[12] The grotesque quality of the imagery resides in the painful effects of the inhumane suffering that Christ experienced and that Julian described in excruciating detail. These effects include the copious bleeding of Christ's head and body;[13] the contemptuous treatment of the dying Christ, including the spitting, soiling, and buffeting of his body;[14] the discoloration and spoiling of his fair appearance;[15] the drying of Christ's body;[16] and the separation of Christ's skin from his skull.[17] Further, one may understand this death as "bizarre, unnatural, indecent and absurd."[18] These qualities, in Julian's view, derived from the fact that Christ experienced no human comfort in the midst of this painful death,[19] that he who was reduced to nothing was God,[20] and therefore, that he who was highest and most worthy was completely humiliated and utterly despised in this shameful death.[21] It is clear, therefore, that there was a degree of unacceptability and injustice in this death as Julian experienced it.

Clearly, also, Julian experienced death anxiety as she witnessed this vision, for she stated that she regretted praying the prayer that resulted in it. As she noted, "Little did I realize what pain I asked for and like a wretch I regretted it, thinking to myself, if only I had known what it were like, I would never have prayed for it. For I thought these pains of mine surpassed even those of bodily death."[22] Therefore, in witnessing this suffering, Julian had doubts about her ability to survive the pain associated with it. Nevertheless, she remained with the vision and expressed pleasure that she chose Christ as her heaven.[23]

Besides her ability to interact with the vision efficaciously, another important factor contributed to Julian's efforts to heal from the damaging effects of her earlier death imprint. In staying with the crucified Christ in her vision, despite the anxiety and pain that it caused her, Julian was able to move consciously through death to new life. This movement occurred in both the form and content of her experience. With regard to the content, Julian described in the eighth "showing" of the vision how Christ's painful death was changed into an image of life and glorification.

For at the very moment when it appeared to me that life could not be sustained and that the vision must of necessity come to an end, suddenly, as I still looked at the cross, I saw that his blessed face had changed. It was this change that at once affected me: for I was now as glad and happy as could be. Our Lord brought to mind the words: "Where now is there any point in the pain or in your grief?" In my new-found joy, I saw that in this life, in our Lord's plan, we are with him on his cross, dying with him in our pains and passion; when of a sudden his face will change in our sight, and then we will be with him in heaven. There will be no time between one state and the other: suddenly, we will be brought to his joy.[24]

Here Julian describes how Christ's passage from death to new life was instantaneous. In persisting with Christ in his pain, Julian's own experience of grief was transfigured as she witnessed the transformation of Christ's death to resurrection and the transformation of her own sorrow to joy.

The forcefulness of this passage from death to new life took on even greater meaning for Julian because her vision occurred when she herself was poised between death and life. Julian was at the point of actual death when she received her vision, yet she did not die. Her return to life following her encounter with death in her experience *and* vision undoubtedly provided her with healing from death anxiety. However, even after the first part of her vision, Julian's sense of her vulnerability to death remained strong. Her belief in her power to withstand the forces of death was not established on firm footing until her final vision on the next day in which Christ assured her that she would not be overcome.[25] It was the confidence that she gained from this final showing that truly empowered her in her "survivor mission" of reflecting and writing on her vision for the sake of her "even Christians."[26]

The argument, therefore, is that Julian's visionary experience of the crucified Christ provided her with a vehicle for effectively participating in a grotesque and absurd death. The effectiveness of her participation provided her with a measure of healing from the painful encounter with death that she had experienced in the plague, including the failed enactment associated with it. Further, her ability to understand Christ's death as painful, and yet as purposeful and yielding of new life, may also have provided a measure of healing.

Death Guilt and Identification with the Dead

Julian's ability to remain with the dying Christ, despite the pain this caused her, provided her with a sense of efficacy that may have counteracted the death guilt associated with her experience of the plague. This achievement was an important aspect of the healing arising from her vision.

In his discussion of death guilt, Lifton states that "death guilt begins . . . in the gap between that physical and psychic inactivation [survivors' experience] and what [they] feel called upon to do and feel. That is one reason the [death] imagery keeps recurring, in dreams and in waking life."[27] A key element in the healing that Julian experienced through her vision was her ability to remain compassionately with the dying Christ, despite the emotional pain she experienced in observing Christ's sufferings. Julian's ability to remain with Christ despite his and her pain was likely a departure from her earlier death encounter in the plague. She, like many, may have been immobilized or even have fled in the face of massive death accompanying the plague. Julian's ability to remain with the vision of the dying Christ becomes central to the development of her theology, for she derives her twofold anthropology directly from this experience. Julian describes her conscious decision to remain with the dying Christ in chapter 19 in the Long Text. After telling of the tremendous pain she experienced in seeing Christ suffer, she confides in the reader how she wanted to look away from the cross. In fact, as she contemplated this action, a "suggestion came to mind, just like a friend inviting me: 'Look up to heaven, to his Father.'"[28] While Julian does not say it explicitly, she implies that this suggestion to look away from the cross represented a temptation by "the fiend." Had she succumbed to it, Julian may have escaped the healing potential present in remaining with the vision. However, after considering the suggestion, she "was sure in her faith that there was nothing between the cross and heaven that could draw her aside."[29] She continued, "Either I must look up or else answer for myself. I did so inwardly with every power in my soul, saying [to the suffering Christ], 'No I may not, for you are my heaven.' I said this because I would not look up; for I had rather borne that pain until Doomsday than come to heaven other than by him."[30] Thus, Julian clearly resisted the temptation to abandon the suffering Christ.

She then goes on to elaborate the effect of this choice upon her spirit. "Thus I was taught to choose Jesus to be my heaven, whom at that time I could only see in pain. . . . And ever since then, this has always been my comfort, that, by his grace, I chose Jesus to be my heaven throughout this time of passion and sorrow. And that lesson has served me that I should do so evermore, choosing only Jesus for my heaven in weal and woe."[31] Julian's decision to remain compassionately with the dying Christ constitutes a significant turning point, and it reflects Julian's triumph over death guilt, for it demonstrated her successful enactment in the face of the death imprint represented in her vision. The sense of efficacy that she achieved through this choice is central to her healing from the sense of inactivation that she may have experienced in her earlier encounters with death.

A second aspect of her visionary experience may also have provided her with relief from the burden of guilt and self-blame characteristic of survivors and renewed her "right to live." Julian's encounter with Christ, who freely chose to die in order that she could live, may have provided her with relief from the survivors' question, "Why did I survive when others died?" Christ's willingness to suffer on her behalf is expressed in the ninth showing. Christ asks Julian if she is satisfied that he suffered for her. When she responded affirmatively, Jesus said, "If you are pleased, then I too am pleased. This is my joy, my bliss, my endless liking that I was ever able to suffer for you. For truly, if I could have suffered more, I would have suffered more."[32] And again in the Tenth Showing, she wrote:

> Our good Lord gently spoke, "Lo, how I loved you. . . . " To understand to the full these words of his, "See how I love you," it was as if he were to say: "Lo how I loved you. Behold and see that I loved you so much that before ever I died for you, I would die for you; and now I have died for you and willingly suffered all that I may. And now is all my bitter pain and all my hard travail turned into endless joy and bliss to me and to you."[33]

Thus, as a result of her vision Julian believed that Christ chose freely to suffer on her behalf and that his suffering and death were a source of life and joy for her. This is because the depth of Christ's suffering, freely chosen in love, revealed the depth of Christ's compassion for Julian and all of humanity. Christ's death, transformed through the power of love to new life, enabled Julian both to *live* and to live with a sense of freedom and joy. Because of Christ's willingness to die for her, she was relieved from the burden many survivors bear of living halfheartedly because of the guilt they feel for their survival.

Julian's encounter with the Christ, who chose to suffer on her behalf, provided her with an experience of meaningful death. This experience surely must have provided a sharp contrast psychologically to the arbitrariness of the many plague deaths Julian witnessed. At the same time, the psychological effect of Christ's willingness to suffer and die for Julian's sins was strengthened through Julian's awareness, derived from her vision, that Christ did not blame her for her sins. For, while Christ brought to Julian's mind the fact that she was not exempt from sin,[34] Julian also realized in the course of her vision that God does not respond to our sins with anger or blame.

> God also showed that sin shall cause us no shame, but will even be accounted to our honour. For just as every sin is answered in reality by a particular pain, so for every sin that same soul is given joy by love. And as different sins are punished by various pains in accordance with their gravity, so will they be rewarded in heaven by joys that differ according to the pain and sorrow they caused that soul on earth.[35]

Knowing that Christ did not blame her for the sin that resulted in his death must have relieved Julian from the considerable weight of self-reproach and shame that she undoubtedly felt as a survivor of the plague. Julian's vision helped her to understand that Christ did not blame her either for surviving or for her inability to help prevent the deaths of others she witnessed.

So Julian's vision freed her from death guilt in two ways: first, through the opportunity it provided her to participate efficaciously in death, and second, through the assurance she received from Christ that God did not blame her for causing Christ's death. Julian learned that Christ's atonement for sin freed her from the need to atone.

Psychic Numbing

Psychic numbing is the third trait Lifton describes as characterizing the psychology of survivors. Psychic numbing represents
the survivor's diminished capacity to feel. It arises in situations of trauma, where it appears that the survivor's capacity
to form mental symbols of the death experience is impaired. It
is as if survivors retain the capacity to form cognitive images of
the horror they are experiencing, yet disconnect these images
from the feelings that would normally accompany them. While
viewing the dying, survivors seemingly tell themselves: "If I feel
nothing, death is not taking place" and/or "I see you, but I am
not related to you or your dying." Lifton believes that in severe
psychic numbing the self becomes severed from such psychic
forms as compassion for others, communal involvement, and
other ultimate values. The end result of psychic numbing is a
sluggish despair characterized by chronic depression and a constricted life space that is often covered over by rage and mistrust.
The survivor takes on the identity of the dead as a result of the
experience of psychic numbing, for he or she lives a sort of "half
life" rather than a vital and fulfilling life.

   It is possible that Julian may have experienced the deleterious
effects of psychic numbing prior to her vision. Of course, evidence for this is limited. However, the fact of her illness prior to
her vision suggests that she may have been physically affected
by grief. Second, her prayer for a sickness unto death suggests
that she may have identified with the dying to the point of wishing to die herself. These are speculations, but it does seem clear
that Julian felt a vitality and joy for living after her vision that
seems discontinuous with the brief glimpses we obtain of her
life before the vision.

   I believe that Julian's vision provided her with an opportunity to heal from psychic numbing. She experienced healing

because she allowed herself to feel fully the compassion and empathy she held for the dying Christ. Yet Julian experienced these feelings at some personal cost, because they were much more intense than she anticipated.[36] Their intensity flowed from the unity of Christ's divinity with his humanity which increased the degree of suffering that Christ could sustain. That Julian remained with the vision despite her pain is evidence that she did not dissociate from her feelings of compassion for the suffering Christ. Julian's ability to remain with these feelings allowed her an opportunity to move through grief to a more fulfilling life, the movement at the heart of the paschal mystery. Two outcomes of Julian's vision, therefore, were an increased willingness to live and an increased capacity to experience joy in God's love for her.[37] The existence of these traits in the wake of her vision provides evidence for Julian's healing from the dampening effects of psychic numbing.

Counterfeit Nurturance

"Counterfeit nurturance" is the term Lifton has coined to describe the effects on interpersonal relationships of surviving trauma. These effects may range from struggles with autonomy, to concerns with contagion and consequent mistrust, to increased sensitivity to authenticity and inauthenticity in relationships, to rage in the face of scapegoating.

There is little evidence in the text to support the notion that Julian suffered from the degree of anger and mistrust in interpersonal relationships that sometimes characterizes survivors of traumatic loss, for the text reveals little about Julian's relationships. Existing evidence derived from the account of Julian's meeting with Margery Kempe and of Julian's description of her attitude toward her "even Christians" does suggest that Julian was a woman of deep compassion who felt great empathy for others. However, it is interesting to speculate about

Julian's choice to live as an anchoress. In making this choice, she effectively removed herself from the social sphere. Was she at all motivated by a fear of contagion, or did this lifestyle provide her with the time and means to engage in her "survivor mission" of sharing the fruits of her vision with others? Unfortunately, the text does not allow us to decide between these alternatives.

There is some evidence in the text, however, to suggest that Julian may have experienced life prior to her vision as counterfeit, that is, as lacking in authenticity. Julian did tell us, for example, that before her vision, she "had a great longing and desire, by God's gift, to be delivered from this world and this life. Frequently, [she said] I witnessed the woe that is here and knew the well-being and bliss that is there. And even if there were no other pain in this life apart from the absence of the Lord, sometimes this alone seemed to me more than I could bear. And this made me mourn and long more eagerly, and also my own wretchedness, sloth and very weakness made me reluctant to live and labor on as I knew I should."[38] Julian, therefore, appeared to experience life before her vision as tiresome and drab. Perhaps Julian's lack of enthusiasm for life may have motivated her to pray for a sickness unto death. One wonders, also, if the pre-plague spirituality expressed in her prayers was an attempt on her part to seek an enhanced appreciation of what was truly authentic in living and dying.

As a result of her vision, Julian was somewhat relieved of her sense of this present life as counterfeit, for Julian saw more possibility for joy in daily life through God's sustaining love. However, Julian seems very much a child of her age in one respect: it does appear that she awaits the hope of final bliss in the life to come. That is, her otherworldly eschatology causes her to relativize the joys and opportunities of the present life. The overwhelming impression one receives from the text, therefore, is that Julian believed that this present life pales in comparison with the life of the world to come.

Formulation

The final psychological characteristic Lifton has identified in survivors is formulation. Lifton uses the term to describe the way in which recovery from the trauma of multiple loss occurs as survivors are able to find meaning in their experience of death and dying and to make sense of trauma. He notes that survivors frequently undertake a mission, and Julian's efforts to write down and disseminate the contents of her vision may be understood in this way. Her efforts take on particular significance because, first, Julian's text was the first written in English by a woman and, second, she was at some risk of being condemned as a heretic for writing it. Her courage in producing this work is thus quite evident.

Julian's vision represented a creative attempt to give form and meaning to the experience of painful and absurd death. As a result of it, Julian achieved the symbolic immortality which Lifton states that survivors seek, for Julian emerged from her vision with Christ's assurance that she would not be overcome by sin and death. Freed from anxiety about her death and salvation, Julian was able to devote herself as an evangelist to sharing the good news of God's love. Her vision, therefore, represented a confrontation with death, a reordering of her emotions and imagery, and a renewal of a sense of life's meaning and vitality. Further, Julian's attempts to find meaning through her vision provide evidence for the three traits Lifton notes as crucial in survivors' attempts to make meaning. First, Julian experienced a heightened sense of connection both to God and to her fellow Christians as a result of her vision. Second, Julian emerged with a greater sense of symbolic integrity. She no longer seemed to dwell on Christ's suffering and her own fear of death, but, rather, emphasized the joy of Christ's life and love, and she continued to develop this emphasis through her long-term reflection and writing on her vision. Finally, she was enabled to "move forward" through life. No longer paralyzed or robbed of vitality through mourning, she was able to embrace the life of a theologian and counselor.[39] Julian's vision, therefore, was a potent source of transformation, one that provided her with integrity, purpose, and a new sense of her vocation.

Lifton's psychology of the survivor therefore provides us with a useful schema for understanding Julian's life and experience prior to, during, and after her vision. A closer examination of the character of Julian's theology offers much to other survivors of traumatic loss.

F O U R

Julian's Theology of Wholeness

And thus I saw our Lord Jesus lingering a long while; for the unity with the Godhead gave strength to the manhood to suffer in love more than anyone else might suffer. . . . Indeed the highest point in the passion is to think and know *who it is that suffered.*

— Julian of Norwich, *Revelation of Love*[1]

Julian offers the despondent a theological context in which they can ponder the significance of their particular sufferings. The visions of Christ in the *Revelations* form the substance of this theological discernment. The figure of Christ crucified focuses into one the human image of God and the divine image of humanity. Accordingly, we see the crucifixion not as an isolated episode in history, but as an epiphany of God's generative compassion. At the same time, we also see there the human race bound up in Christ's affliction. In this light, the experience of spiritual despondency, of desolation in prayer — even of God's absence — testifies to our union with the Crucified. Where once we had thought that sin and desolation indicated the absence of divine power, if not divine love, the visions now confront us with a God whose shocking debasement overturns our very questions.

— Julia Gatta, *The Pastoral Art of the English Mystics*[2]

To this point in our analysis of Julian's text, our primary concerns have been historical and psychological in that we have attempted to understand how Julian's work emerged in a particular context and how characteristics of that context may have influenced her development and vision in particular ways. In short, we have been concerned to a great degree with meanings lying "behind" the text.

As David Tracy points out, however, there is another aspect to the work of textual interpretation that demands our attention. This is the work of determining "the meaning 'in front of the text,' that is, that way of perceiving reality, that mode of being-in-the-world which opens the text up for the intelligent reader."[3] For religious texts, this work of interpretation requires us to specify the particularly religious manner of being in the world that is proposed in the text.[4]

In Tracy's view, authentic religious language "re-presents that basic confidence and trust in existence which *is* our fundamental faith, our basic authentic mode of being in the world."[5] Religious texts do not merely re-present that faith, however. They provide a vision that allows us to see the implications of this faith for our ordinary lives. They encourage us to live "with explicit faith, with complete trust and with unrestricted love."[6] In short, they "ask us to allow the limit experiences of trust and confidence in the final graciousness of reality itself to provide the basic orientation to our lives."[7]

In the course of Julian's vision, Christ provided her with a now famous reassurance:

Sin is necessary, but all shall be well.
All shall be well; and all manner of things shall be well.[8]

This statement certainly exemplifies Tracy's notion of a fundamental religious vision, and acceptance of it is central to Julian's theology. A primary question of textual interpretation, therefore, is articulating the grounds for Julian's confidence that all shall be well. What in Julian's vision provided her with the encouragement to adopt this degree of trust?

Understanding the grounds for Julian's faith is critically important for contemporary survivors who seek from Julian's experience a basis for faith and hope in their own suffering.

Thus, at the same time as we examine the foundation for Julian's trust that all shall be well, we shall test her analysis against contemporary experiences and insights related to the themes she explores. Can survivors living some six hundred years hence find reassurance and comfort in Julian's affirmation of faith?

In responding to this question, we shall explore two aspects of Julian's thought. First, in the present chapter, we examine her theology. What symbols, metaphors, and images underlie her understanding that all shall be well? How does she articulate the basis for her trust? Second, in the next chapter, we explore Julian's spirituality. What, in Julian's view, allows believers to live into these understandings? How may we transcend our finitude and be drawn toward an unshakable confidence in life's trustworthiness, even in the face of pain and disappointment? Attending to each of these aspects of religious life — the theological and the spiritual — may provide us with a more integrated understanding of Julian's religious synthesis.

Julian's Audience

Our understanding of Julian's theological enterprise is enhanced when we view the composition of her text as a "survivor mission," through which she shares both the contents of her extraordinary visions and her reflections on them for the sake of others who have experienced overwhelming loss. Given this approach to her work, it is helpful to understand the audience Julian had in mind when she was composing her text. For whom was she writing and what was her aim in communicating with them?

Julian herself provides information about her intended audience when in chapter 8 of the Long Text she states:

Everything I say about myself, that also goes for all my fellow Christians. For this is what I understood from our Lord, that this is his meaning. And so I beg you all, for God's sake, and I advise you for your own advantage, to ignore this wretch that it was shown to in the first place, and attend instead with all your might and wit and meekness to God. For it was by his courteous love and from his endless goodness that he wanted to show it to everyone, for the comfort of us all. Thus God truly wants you to receive it with every joy and gladness just as if Jesus himself had shown it to you all in person.[9]

Through both this statement and her subsequent elaboration of it, Julian indicates two things. First, in true humility, she notes that her revelation was not shown merely for her own sake, but that God intended it for the comfort of all. Second, Julian elaborates a theme that is central to her writing, namely, that she is not "special" or uniquely favored by God because of receiving the revelation. In fact, she says, "For in truth, I was never shown that God loved me more than the least soul that stands in his grace."[10] Instead, Julian perceived that she was in unity of love with all of her fellow Christians, and she wrote in the hope that those to whom she addressed her visions might receive comfort and find meaning through her experience. Thus, Julian's writing was an act of generosity directed toward her fellow Christians. Julian saw herself in union with them, and in reading the text, one is struck by the transparency of her reflection. She frankly narrates her struggles to comprehend the content of her revelations and in overhearing them we gain some insight into Julian's development as a spiritual counselor. It quickly becomes apparent how she drew on her own struggles in offering guidance and consolation to others.

My understanding of Julian's growth as a spiritual director has been greatly enhanced through Julia Gatta's description of Julian's work; she notes that Julian addresses herself particularly to "such men and women as for the love of God hate sin and dispose themselves to do God's will." Julian reveals this in chapter 73 of the Long Text, and Gatta uses the term "proficients" to describe those more mature Christians whose struggles especially occupied Julian. According to Gatta, Julian wrote to offer assistance with two kinds of struggles such souls face: the temptation to impatience or sloth and the tendency toward "despair or doubtful fear." The first temptation Gatta describes as "a spiritual malaise [that expresses] itself emotionally as despondency, listlessness and loss of heart."[11] The second temptation, to doubtful fear, arises from the first and results when the dispirited Christian embraces an "anxious pessimism" that undermines faith in God's love and saving work on our behalf. According to Gatta, the brilliance of Julian's work arises from the ways in which Julian is able to model through the medium of her own spiritual struggles the path toward greater faith and trust in God's love. As Gatta notes, Julian "does not categorically pronounce the *fact* of God's love as a proposition to be believed."[12] Rather, Julian, through her own intellectual honesty, confronts the struggles she and her fellow Christians faced, fully entertaining her own doubts and difficulties en route to her hard-won yet wholehearted embrace of God's love.

Julian offers her readers a pastoral theological approach, rather than an abstract intellectual analysis, of the thorny theological problems she addresses, and her mastery of her own doubts paves the way for her readers to share in the triumph of faith over depression and fear. I hypothesize that Julian's experience in counseling those who came to her for spiritual solace and strength had a hand in shaping the genre of her text.

Julian undoubtedly learned the value of aligning with those she counseled in addressing the problems they faced, rather than speaking to their concerns in a more detached way. Further, her experience of listening to those in need surely crystallized in her mind the theological concerns that most deeply troubled her fellow Christians. Julian's insights gained through pondering the content of her revelation alongside the pressing pastoral concerns of those she counseled clearly would have shaped not only the approach she developed but also the particular theological emphases she advanced in her text. Julian's authentic confrontation with her own doubts and fears in God's presence offers a courageous model to survivors today who struggle to find hope and meaning amid trauma and loss. They, like her, may find reassurance in openly disclosing all aspects of their struggles in heartfelt conversation with God.

Authority in Julian's Work

There are three aspects to the issue of authority as it relates to Julian's writing. The first describes the sources of authority Julian draws on in developing her theology. The second refers to Julian's perception of the authority of her religious experience, while the third refers to her own authority as a teacher in communicating it. Clearly, these three issues are interrelated.

Scholars who have studied the contents of both the Short and Long Texts uniformly comment on the growth in confidence and in authority that Julian demonstrates over time.[13] In the Short Text, Julian refers to herself both as a "wretched worm" and a "sinful creature," exhorting her readers to focus upon the content of the teachings rather than upon herself as the communicator of them. Further, she calls her readers' attention to Christ as teacher, and denies her own authority as teacher by saying, "But God forbid that you should say or assume I am a teacher, for that is not and never was my intention; for I am a woman, ignorant, weak and frail."[14]

However, in the Long Text, Julian removes most of these derogatory references to herself as well as her protestation that she is not a teacher, an indication that over time Julian grew in her sense of her own authority and worth.[15] I would speculate that this growth, which may be understood as a growth in compassion, arose from two sources. First, her prolonged reflection on her meditation with its themes of the honor accorded to sinners and the depth of God's love for her helped to convince Julian of her worth. Second, her attempts to communicate effectively God's love for her fellow Christians in counseling and in writing may also have helped her to grow in compassion, for it is often through extending love and forgiveness to others that we become more able to extend it to ourselves. Indeed, how could Julian effectively convince others of their worth in God's eyes when she continued to deny her own worth? I believe that through a process of mature theological reflection, Julian became more and more able over time to affirm her own God-given gifts.

Second, in developing her theology, Julian draws on three sources of authority, and she describes them in chapter 80 of the Long Text. They include the use of natural reason, the common teaching of the church, and what Julian describes as the "inward grace-giving operation of the Holy Spirit."[16] As Julian sees it, all three are grounded in the one God, and as such, there ought to be a unity of understanding arising from them.

Nevertheless, discerning this unity in practice was often a vexing problem for Julian. There simply were times when the teachings of the church did not seem to square with the revelations she had received. For example, when wrestling with the existence of hell and purgatory, Julian struggles with the apparent conflict between her visions, which provided no evidence of wrath in God, and the common teaching of the church:

Now one point of our faith is that many shall be damned —
such as the angels that fell from heaven on account of their
pride and are now fiends; or again a person here on earth
who dies without the faith of holy Church, that is to say,
those heathen people and also anyone that, having been a
Christian, lives an unchristian life and comes to die out
of charity — all these shall be condemned to hell without
end, for so Holy Church teaches me to believe.[17]

As we have seen, and as Grace Jantzen notes in her discussion
of Julian's authority, the church in Julian's day was clearly in
need of reform, and Julian knew it. Julian referred directly to the
troubles of the church when she said, "Yet God's servants, that
is to say Holy Church, shall be shaken in sorrow and anguish
and tribulation in this world, just as people shake a cloth in the
wind. . . . For [Christ] says: 'I will wholly break you of your vain
affections and your vicious pride; and after that I shall gather
you and make you meek and mild, clean and holy by oneing
you to me.' "[18] Grace Jantzen offers two possible explanations
for why Julian insisted on strict loyalty to the church's authority at the seeming expense of invalidating the authority of her
own visions. The first is fear: Julian may have worried about the
possibility of condemnation as a heretic, particularly in light of
the persecution of the Lollards, which was occurring in Norwich itself in her day. The second possibility Jantzen advances,
and one that she thinks is more likely, is that Julian may have
been making a deliberate distinction between the *teaching* of
the church and its actual *practice*, which Jantzen hypothesizes
she may have found both vain and arrogant.[19]

I believe that close study of Julian's text leads to a third explanation. In chapter 45 in the Long Text, Julian described the
existence of two judgments, a higher one deriving from God and
grounded in God's judgment and a lower human one, grounded

in changeable sensuality. The latter judgment she describes as mixed: sometimes it is good and lenient and at other times it is hard and painful. Julian believed that through the workings of mercy and grace, Jesus reforms human judgment through the power of the Passion, so that it could be reconciled with God's judgment. I believe that Julian likely held a similar view with regard to the discrepancies between the church's teaching and the contents of her vision. In the end, I think that Julian anticipated that these conflicts would ultimately be resolved through God's actions. Until then, rather than deny the authority of her visions or the church's teaching, Julian simply placed them in a somewhat uncomfortable juxtaposition. She never denies the authority of the church when it differs from the contents of her vision; at the same time, through frankly offering an account of her visions, she does not negate their authority either. Rather, she confidently awaits a resolution grounded in Christ's saving work that shall make all things well, including the seemingly irresolvable contradictions between her revelations and the teachings of the church.

In examining the texts, however, it does appear that Julian's epistemology is also an aid to her in living with these conflicts. On several occasions, Julian refers to the importance of general versus specific knowledge. In the case of the most serious conflict between her vision and the church's teaching, Julian notes that she was "strengthened and taught *in general* to keep my faith in every detail and in all I had understood before, hoping in this way that I was held in the mercy and grace of God, only wishing and praying in my every intention that I might continue in such way to my life's end."[20] I believe that in this statement and in other places in the text, Julian implies that there may be specific knowledge that would help to resolve the discrepancies between her vision and the church's teaching.[21] However, she assumes the position that knowledge of these specifics is not God's will at this time. For example, with regard to the great deed that will make all things well, Julian says:

> All the while we should leave aside our curiosity as what that great deed shall be. For we should seek to be like our brethren the saints in heaven who want nothing but the will of God; in this way we will delight only in God and be equally rewarded whether he shows himself or pleases to remain hidden. For truly I saw our Lord's meaning: *the more we busy ourselves to know his secrets now in this, now in the other, the further shall we be from knowing them.*[22]

Through these statements, Julian allows for the possibility that when it comes to specific aspects of the church's teaching, there may well be discrepancies between human knowledge and conclusions and God's way of understanding. To pursue knowledge of these specifics, Julian implies, will unsettle us and undermine true understanding. I believe that Julian's epistemology represents a healthy form of agnosticism that allows her to accept discrepancies between her vision and the church's teaching. Generally, they agree, and where they disagree, there may be another way of understanding the discrepancy, in God, the knowledge of which is closed to us at this time. I believe that through this stance, Julian affirms the value of her faith in God as both prior to the church's teaching and to what is and is not shown to her in her vision. The *general* knowledge she received as a result of her vision is that God loves us, is trustworthy, and does not blame us for sin. When faced with discrepancies regarding specific issues, Julian takes refuge in this general knowledge of God and trusts that in God the specific discrepancies will ultimately be resolved.

Thus, Julian's confidence in God's love and desire for human flourishing, derived from her vision, allows her to hold these seemingly contradictory views in tension, while patiently awaiting a gracious outcome to the apparent conflict between them.

From Desolation to Consolation: Julian's Critical Concerns

Before elaborating the grounds for Julian's ultimate acceptance of Christ's assurance that "all shall be well," it may be helpful to review the central theological problems with which Julian wrestles in her text. As the analysis of Julian's context has made clear, the problems that concerned Julian were undoubtedly shared by her contemporaries, who struggled to find comfort, meaning, and purpose in the face of the tremendous physical and spiritual suffering associated with the Black Death, the Hundred Years' War, the Great Schism, and the economic, social, and religious devastation arising from them.

Perhaps the greatest problem Julian faced in light of her vision was how to communicate the reality of God's love to a society that was steeped in shame, blame, guilt, and despair. At least two sources gave rise to these feelings: the traumatic grief associated with the plague and the dominant religious explanation for it, namely, that the plague arose as a punishment for human sinfulness. The problem of judgment for sin was central to these concerns, and as we have noted, Julian offers a very different view of God's judgment than that offered by the religious leaders of her day. Further, Julian's emphasis on God's immanence developed through her image of Christ as Mother counteracts the prevailing view of a transcendent and impassible God who offers judgment rather than compassion in the face of human limitations.

The second problem with which Julian wrestles is centrally related to the first, and that is the existence of sin and the suffering associated with it. As Gatta describes it:

> What [Julian] seeks is . . . a reconciliation of human sinfulness with faith in God's omnipotence. The question for her is: why does God permit not physical evil but moral evil? If "sin is the sharpest scourge with which any chosen soul can be struck," why does God allow Julian and others like her to persist in sin even when they want to be free of it? Why, in fact, does God tolerate the existence of evil at all?[23]

As Gatta indicates in her overview of Julian's theology, there are four aspects to this problem, each of which Julian confronts head on. They include these questions:

- If God is the ultimate cause of all things, if nothing ever happens by chance, is God also the author of sin?

- Given God's foreknowledge, why did God not prevent sin from the beginning?

- Can a God who allows sin be trusted?

- How can all be well when some, according to Holy Church's teaching, are condemned to eternal damnation?[24]

Julian's courage and unflinching honesty in addressing these questions to God provide an excellent model for faithful prayer. Further, the fact that Julian is ultimately able to achieve satisfaction in her search for answers testifies to the degree of trust she acquires through her confrontation with the vivid reality of God's love and acceptance. Her ability to move from doubt to hope through authentic confrontation with the divine reinforces the likelihood that contemporary survivors may find similar comfort through authentically wrestling with their own doubts and fears before God.

The final concern that Julian addressed is the loss of hope arising from the awareness of one's sin and the disappointments of life. As we have already noted, temptations to depression and despair torment even the most faithful Christians who seek to live faithfully in accordance with God's love and laws, yet find themselves defeated by the reality of their own sinfulness. Julian was particularly touched by these concerns as a result of her counseling ministry, and she devotes some space in the Long Text to addressing the "penance" associated with daily living. Further, through her eschatology, she directly addresses the ultimate grounds for Christian hope.

Let us turn, therefore, to Julian's theological reflection upon her vision, which provided her with grounds for her confidence that "all shall be well" even in the face of these very thorny problems.

Julian's Theology: Key Tenets

The starting point for Julian's theology is an understanding of God. In Julian's view, God is the ground of all existence, and God's nature is love. In fact, apprehending God's essential nature as love was one of the most surprising insights Julian received. In contrast to the religious teaching of her day, Julian realized that God is not angry, and that if God were to become angry and to withdraw love from us, we should not survive:

> This was a high wonder to the soul which was shown continually in all the revelations and beheld with great diligence: that our Lord God of his very nature, may not forgive since he may never be angry — for that would be impossible. This is what was shown: our whole life

is grounded and rooted in love, for without love we may not live.[25]

Love provides the foundation for life, therefore, and understanding God's essential nature as love undergirds Julian's development of all other doctrines.

As I see it, Julian's realization of God's loving nature constituted a form of conversion, for through it she moved from a stance of fear about her own salvation to the belief that she and all who would be saved were worthy in God's eyes.[26] Further, through her appropriation of God's love, Julian was able to master the depression, fear, and guilt that disturbed her prior to her vision. Profound experiences of transcendent love, such as Julian experienced in her vision, therefore, offer great promise for healing from loss. As Julian's experience indicates, surprising encounters with love are possible even in the midst of profound grief.

Besides being rooted in her understanding of God as love, Julian's ability to affirm that all shall be well despite the reality of sin appears to be grounded in five traditional Christian doctrines: creation, redemption, anthropology, incarnation, and eschatology.

Julian's view of *creation* derived from her vision of the "hazelnut":

At the same time, he showed me something small, about the size of a hazelnut, that seemed to lie in the palm of my hand as round as a tiny ball. I tried to understand the sight of it, wondering what it could possibly mean. The answer came: "This is all that is made." I felt it was so small that it could easily fade to nothing; but again I was told: "This lasts and will go on lasting forever because God loves it. And so it is with every being that God loves."[27]

Through contemplating this vision, Julian learned three things about the nature of God's creative work: first, that God has made everything that is made; second, that God loves everything that is made; and third, that God keeps everything that is made. Further, Julian learned that God's love is as strong for great things as it is for small and humble things,[28] and she experienced that we are kept whole and safe by God regardless of whether our feelings confirm this or not.[29]

Perhaps the most remarkable and praiseworthy aspect of God's creative work, however, is its efficacy. This quality was captured in Julian's use of the word "rightful" to describe God's creative work.

> Rightfulness is when something is so good that it may not be better than it is; and God himself is most rightfulness and his works are rightfully done as they are ordained from without beginning by his high might, his high wisdom and his high goodness. And right as he ordained it to the best, right so he works continually and leads it to the same end; therefore, he is always pleased with himself and all his works.[30]

Rightfulness describes the absolute efficacy of God's work, and it was her unshakable confidence in the rightfulness of creation that contributed greatly to the optimistic tone of her theology and to the facilitation of trust. Julian believed, for example, that the rightfulness of God's creative work embraced even those things that may appear evil to us: "While to us some deeds may seem well done, others evil, this is not so in God's sight. For since all things have their ground in God's making, so all that is done belongs to God's doing."[31] In Julian's view of creation, therefore, all that is done is well done, since God does all. Julian's view of creation's soundness rests not in the appearance of creation but in her trust in the Creator. Affirming the rightfulness of creation, therefore, is an affirmation of faith in the power of God's love in making "all things work together for good for those who love God."[32] Julian essentially admits that eyes of faith are required to affirm creation's soundness.

Two implications flow from this stance: first that the efficacy of creation is *not* self-evident, and second that with the growth of trust in God, one's ability to affirm creation's rightness grows. Given her frank expression of her own concerns, Julian would be unlikely to dampen the honest expression of doubt concerning creation's flaws. At the same time, I believe that she would urge contemporary survivors pained by them to move to faith in the Creator in two ways: through prayer for confident faith in God's loving care of all that is *not* well and through their efforts as co-creators to redress the wrongs observed.

Julian's affirmation of creation's rightness naturally raises questions about *sin and redemption*. Julian's views on sin include several key points. She believed, first, that sin has no being. While regarding the revelation about God's creative work, Julian did not see sin. Thus, she concluded that "sin is no-deed, for in all this sin was never shown."[33] Sin, therefore, is known mainly through its effects. Sin is "everything that is not good, and [includes] the shameful despising, the utter humiliation that [Christ] bore for us in this life, and his dying and the many pains that all his creatures also suffer; both in spirit and in body."[34] Sin, therefore, is the cause of pain. Julian also believed that sin is a source of rupture within human nature. Julian understood this rupture to exist between the higher and lower nature of humanity or between what Julian referred to as our substance and sensuality.

Julian used the term "substance" to describe the existence of divinity within the human soul.

And thus the human soul is made of God and in the same point is knit to God. And thus I understand that the soul is made of nothing, that is to say, it is made but not from anything that is made. It is like this: when God would make the body, he took the slime of the earth, that is material which is mixed and gathered of all material things, and in this way he made our body. But as to the making of our soul, he took nothing: he simply made it. And so is our made-nature rightfully oned with its Maker, who is substantial nature, unmade: that is God.[35]

Julian believed, therefore, that our soul is made of the very substance of God. It is this part of our being that Julian referred to as our "higher" nature. At the same time, however, humans also have a "lower" nature that Julian referred to as our "sensuality." According to Grace Jantzen, she used this term to describe "all of our psychology and physicality as individual human beings: our capacities for perception in sight, hearing, touch and so on, our whole sensory consciousness and our capacity for action. In other words, sensuality refers to our existence as psychosomatic beings in a physical world. . . . Our substance is the substance of being itself; our sensuality individuates us, making each of us one among many beings."[36] Jantzen also rightly notes that the distinction between substance and sensuality is not equivalent to a dualistic distinction between body and soul. Sensuality is an embodied quality, but it relates to the union between the body and soul and cannot be equated with the body alone. As she puts it, "sensuality relates to the union of consciousness with embodiment."[37]

The rupture within humans between substance and sensuality, between our higher and lower natures, came about through Adam's sin, which Julian understood as "the greatest harm that was ever done or ever shall be, until the world ends."[38] Despite the existence of this great harm, however, the rightfulness of God's creative work also applies to the work of the redemption. Julian believed that the work of redemption, "the re-making"[39] of humans through Christ's passion and death is "more pleasing to God and honors humankind's salvation more, without comparison, than any harm that ever came from Adam's sin."[40] Through the work of redemption, God "made well the greatest harm." Therefore, this knowledge provides a basis for Julian's faith that God shall make well all that is less.[41]

Through her vision, Julian also came to a somewhat startling conclusion for her time, namely, the view that God's love is never broken toward us when we sin: "Inasmuch as his love is never broken toward us when we sin, so does he will that it is never broken within ourselves or toward our fellow Christians; rather we should hate the sin itself but endlessly love every soul as God loves it."[42] Thus, God's love remains constant and can provide grounds both for self-love and love of neighbor.

On the basis of her revelation, Julian appeared to conclude that sin is an inevitable part of human existence. Speaking of sin, she stated, "In this life we may not keep ourselves from sin as holy and fully clean as we shall be in heaven."[43] Then, as Denise Nowakowski Baker notes, "given the fact of sin, she explores its function in the divine plan and God's disposition toward sinners now and at the end of time."[44] Julian concluded that sin purges us and "makes us know ourselves as we ask for mercy."[45] Sin provides us with knowledge of our limitations; it makes it possible for us to know "that we may not stand for a twinkling of an eye without being kept in grace, and reverently clinging to God, trusting only in him."[46] Further, despite the fact that sin is a great source of pain to us, through the efficacy of God's work in redemption, sins will be rewarded in heaven by joys that are proportionate to the pain they caused on earth.[47]

Therefore, the fact of sin cannot be a cause for despair. First, it does not diminish God's love for us. Second, we need not be ashamed because Christ has taken upon himself all of the blame for our sin.[48] Third, because of the rightfulness of God's creative work in the redemption, through Christ's passion "[there is] a great raising and fullness of bliss that mankind is come to, far surpassing what would have been ours had we never fallen."[49]

There are great grounds for hope for contemporary survivors in Julian's notion of sin. Julian believes that sin, though painful, is inevitable for humans. She also believes, however, that the effects of sin need not be crippling, since divine mercy and grace ensure that sin never has the last word. Like those in Julian's day, so too contemporary survivors who suffer from the crippling guilt arising from their own failed enactments in trauma may find peace in Julian's approach to sin. In affirming God's full acceptance of humanity's shortcomings, Julian relieves survivors from self-condemnation and frees them to open themselves more fully to God's love, which is available at their point of greatest need.

Despite the fact that sin exists, is painful, and remains as an inevitable part of our existence, Julian still believed that it is possible to experience hope. Hope results from Julian's belief that Christ's saving work makes even greater happiness possible, for humans and God alike, than existed prior to the fall. She believes, therefore, that the work of redemption more than compensates for the damaging effects of sin.

Julian's understanding of a twofold *anthropology*, expressed in her notion that humans are composed of substance and sensuality, also provided her with a basis for hope. Julian believed that "in every soul that shall be saved is a godly will that never assents to sin and never shall. Moreover, this will is so good that it may never will evil but evermore and continually it wills good and works only good in the sight of God."[50] Julian understood that this godly will is kept whole in Jesus; it resides in our higher nature. Julian experienced both her awareness of this godly will and its role in drawing the lower part of the soul toward God in the eighth showing when she refused to look away from the cross. It was through this experience that she learned of the superiority of the inward part, the substance, over the sensuality. Further, she developed faith in the power of the substance to draw the sensuality by grace toward salvation.

Julian's understanding of the goodness of creation and the efficacy of Christ's redemptive work came together in her understanding of the *incarnation*, which provided her with a means for explaining how God works both in human creation and in redemption.

Julian argued that in the incarnation, a necessary precondition for redemption, Jesus made possible the original union between substance and sensuality that characterized human nature in creation. In taking on human flesh, Jesus knit sensuality and substance together and, further, knit to him all those who shall be saved.

> For in that same time that God knitted [Jesus Christ] to our body in the Maiden's womb he took our sensual soul. In this taking, having enclosed us within himself, he oned it to our substance and in his oneing became perfect man. For Christ, having knit to himself all those men and women that shall be saved, is the perfection of humankind.[51]

This wedding of our substance and sensuality in Christ, according to Julian, makes humanity the pinnacle of creation, whose nature most fully reflects the nature of God:

> God is kind in his being, that is to say, that goodness that is kind [i.e., nature], it is God. He is the ground, he is the substance, he is the same thing as kindness and he

is the true Father and very Mother of Kind. And all kinds he has made to flow out from him to work his will shall be restored and brought again into him by the salvation of humanity through the working of grace. For of all the kinds he has set partially in the great variety of creatures, only in humankind is it set whole and in its fullness, by virtue, beauty, goodness, in royalty and nobility, and in all manner of celebration of refinement and honor.[52]

Goodness in creation, therefore, resides in the *imago dei* borne by God's creatures, and the *imago dei* is most fully known in humankind because of the union in humans of substance and sensuality achieved through Christ.

The work of redemption, which Julian described as re-making, also requires the incarnation. Julian used the image of childbirth to describe this re-making, the redemptive act. She envisioned Christ's passion as labor and his death as childbirth, for in his death, he brings us to life.

Our own true Mother Jesus, he who is all love, bears us to joy and endless living — blessed may he be! Thus he sustains us within himself in love and labour until the full time when he gladly suffered the sharpest throes and most grievous pains that ever were or ever shall be, and died at last.

And when he had done, and so borne us to bliss, yet all this still could not satisfy his marvellous love.... And therefore he is compelled to feed us, for the precious love of his motherhood makes him a debtor to us.[53]

Julian's use of childbirth as a metaphor for the passion is reflected both in the form and content of her vision. The description of Christ's passage from death to life on the cross in

the eighth showing parallels the movement from pain to celebration that accompanies the successful birth of a child. In the
moment of birth, the arduous pains of labor fade and awe at
the mystery of new life emerges. Julian captured the essence
of this experience in her description of Christ's death and his
consequent celebration of the fact that it has made life possible for those he loves. It is the vividness and aptness of this
description that suggests to me that Julian herself may have
experienced childbirth.[54] Further, the notion of the Passion as
childbirth is central to the development of Julian's theology; her
theology grew from the image organically. The centrality of this
metaphor shapes her unique development of maternal imagery
for Christ.[55]

In Julian's view, redemption required the incarnation because
in the maiden's womb: "Our high God, who is sovereign wisdom of all, arrayed himself in this low place, clothing himself in
our poor flesh, so that he might himself perform the service and
office of motherhood in all things."[56] It was in the incarnation,
therefore, that Christ assumed our sensuality, and according
to Julian, it was this act that made possible Christ's suffering
and death on our behalf. Just as humans are composed both
of substance and sensuality, so was Christ, and it was Christ's
sensuality, assumed in the maiden's womb, that suffered for
humankind's salvation.[57]

Julian fully developed the image of Christ's motherhood to
encompass the entire work of redemption. As Heimmel notes,
one gets the impression upon reading the text that Julian has
sought out earlier literary forms used to describe God as mother
and integrated them all in her treatment of this theme. Her
treatment of this metaphor does not just reiterate earlier works,
however, for Julian developed and elaborated their imagery into
a complete, connected cycle encompassing the entire passage
from birth to death.

Julian's majestic vision proceeds through all the various stages of: enclosure and growth within the womb, the trauma of labor and birth, the suckling of the infant and the feeding of the child, the care and education of the older child, the setting of examples and the disciplining of the child, the washing, healing, forgiving, and comforting of the child as it matures and the continual loving, touching and guiding of the child even to the point of its own death which becomes in turn a rebirth and return to the original womb.[58]

In short, Julian used this metaphor to describe a loving God who desires our salvation and accommodates to our needs at every stage of life to nurture us and bring us to fullness of life. Her development of this image provided a sharp contrast to the notion of a harsh and punishing God expressed during the plague. While Julian did not explicitly address God's role in disasters, her view of God's solicitous love seems contrary to the belief expressed by many in the plague that God abandoned humans and the earth as a result of sin. Julian's understanding of the incarnation and redemption both arose from and reinforced her belief in God's loving and rightful nature, thus providing a further basis for trust.

Julian's theology of the incarnation offers several resources to contemporary survivors. First, she proposes a solution to the inner split survivors experience in what Lifton describes as "counterfeit nurturance." In accepting that we are created in the image of God, our essential worth as persons is seen to endure even in the face of traumatic pain and loss. Second, in offering the accessible images of Christ as a loving mother, Julian communicates the possibility of loving intimacy with a God who draws near to us and longs to heal us and nurture our growth. Finally, Julian's treatment of the motherhood of God offers survivors the continual possibility of rebirth in the face of trauma, as Mother Christ is seen never to abandon those he loves. Rather, Christ is seen to continually guard, nurture, and heal them through the sacraments and the protection of mercy and grace.

The final basis for trust that Julian provided is her reference to a deed of the Holy Trinity:

> There is a deed which the blessed Trinity shall do on the last day, as I see it, and when that deed shall be and how it shall be done is not known to any creatures that are beneath Christ. . . . This is the great deed that God has ordained from without beginning, known only to himself, the deed by which he will make all things well.[59]

Julian believed that God has hidden this deed from us so that we shall be kept in peace. The context in which Julian revealed the deed suggests that it may be associated with universal salvation. Julian could not rest easily with the fact that many were to be damned. It was in the course of her reflection on this point that Christ revealed the deed and further indicated, even in light of the church's seemingly contradictory teaching on this point, that he most definitely had the power to make all things well. Christ said: "What is impossible to you, is not impossible to me. I shall keep my word in all things, and I shall make all things well."[60] Perhaps Julian herself may have profited most from the secrecy associated with the great deed. Since its nature was hidden, Julian was able to affirm both God's loving nature revealed in her vision and the church's stricter judgment, at least in principle. Further, she was freed from having to provide a concrete vision for how this seeming incompatibility might be resolved in the case of non-Christians and the lapsed.

Ultimately, the power of Julian's eschatological vision rests in her confidence in God's loving nature. Thus, it is grounded in the clarity of her vision of God's love. Julian recognized that her sight was extraordinary. I believe that Julian would not fault traumatized survivors who did not share the confidence of her hope. At the same time, however, I believe that she would exhort them to do what was necessary to increase their trust in a loving universe, namely, to face their doubts openly in the presence of God, to pass over their sufferings as lightly as possible while never denying their gravity, and to nurture their thirst for justice and love through dedication to prayer and charity. Further, because of her belief that Christ's suffering embraces all human pain, she would encourage survivors to empathize with all who have been traumatized, regardless of their particular pains, because all may be healed in the same way: through identification with the paschal mystery.

Julian's theological synthesis therefore provided a counterpoint to the prevailing theology of her day. It reaffirmed the goodness of God and creation and the efficacy of divine providence. Julian, who wrestled with the harmful effects of sin, came to realize that, although we may not keep ourselves from sin, we shall also not be punished for it. Instead, we shall be rewarded with joy for our repentance. Finally, Julian even hinted at the possibility of salvation for "heathen people" and Christians who abandoned charity.[61] She grounded her positive theological vision in the notion of a homely and courteous God who longs for our joy and salvation. Julian's encounter with God's unfailing love, expressed in her vision, provided the firm foundation for her affirmation that, indeed, all shall be well.

Julian's Theology as a Resource for Survivors of Traumatic Loss

Julian's theology is a valuable resource to survivors for the way in which it addresses four issues: the problem of suffering, the nature of God's judgment and justice, death and the ultimate fate of human beings, and the nature of human community.

The Problem of Suffering

The examination of historical accounts of the Black Death and work with contemporary survivors of trauma reveal a central concern with the problem of suffering. There are at least two aspects to suffering that are problematic for survivors: the first is the pain that it causes and the second is the isolation or self-absorption it engenders.[62] Those who are suffering frequently feel alone and abandoned in the experience of suffering. Julian grounds her response to these problems in her understanding of the crucifixion of Christ. As a result of her vision, Julian came to believe that the experience of suffering may be transfigured through the presence of love. Thus she understood *that suffering has meaning because love is present in suffering.* In Julian's view, the incarnation and crucifixion of Christ guarantee that God's love is present in all human suffering, since Christ's passion and death embrace all human pain.

In her analysis of Julian's theology, Julia Gatta describes how Julian's vision reveals the union of opposites that is key to understanding this view of suffering: "The vision of the Crucified (in Julian's writing) unifies conditions which are, to ordinary thinking, opposites: divine beatitude and human misery in Christ, joy and pain in Julian."[63] Gatta's analysis describes what I have learned from my work with survivors: that painful experiences of grief may also be experiences of transcendent love that offer tremendous potential for healing. For some individuals, grief becomes transfigured and they encounter within it the presence of the living God. Julian herself experienced such transfiguration at the moment of Christ's death:

And I watched with all my might for that moment when Christ would expire, and I expected to see his body quite dead; but I did not see him so, and just at the moment when by appearances it seemed to me that life could last no longer, and that the revelation of his end must be near, suddenly as I looked at the same cross, he changed to an appearance of joy. The change in his blessed appearance changed mine, and I was as glad and as joyful as I could possibly be. And then cheerfully our Lord suggested to my mind: Where is there now any instant of your pain or grief? And I was very joyful: I understood that in our Lord's intention we are now on our cross with him in our pains, and in our sufferings we are dying, and with his help and grace we willingly endure on that same cross until the last moment of life. Suddenly he will change his appearance for us, and we shall be with him in heaven. Between one and the other all will be a single era; and then all will be brought into joy.[64]

Through her vision, Julian discovered the inextricability of love and life for she came to appreciate that all aspects of life, even death and suffering, may be taken up into God.

My own pastoral research with survivors of traumatic loss reinforces Julian's insights concerning the transfiguration of grief through love. Between 1998 and 2001, I had the privilege of participating in and studying All Saints Episcopal Church in the Haight-Ashbury district of San Francisco. At that time, an average of ninety members attended worship at All Saints each Sunday. This church community sponsored a very active ministry of healing and pastoral care to members and non-members alike during the AIDS pandemic in San Francisco. Between March 23, 1987, and the end of 1997, the parish participated in the funeral or burial of thirty-four men who died of AIDS.

However, these figures do not tell the whole story of loss, as parishioners ministered to many more friends, church members, and acquaintances who were living with HIV disease. As part of my research, I interviewed fourteen lay and clergy members of the parish. Those I interviewed reported an average loss of 61.5 acquaintances to AIDS and an average loss of 8.8 close friends or partners to AIDS. Thus, the funerals within the parish represented only the tip of the iceberg of AIDS losses for many parishioners.[65]

In a very moving interview, the rector of the church, Kenneth Schmidt, described the death of a young parishioner, whom I shall call Stephen.[66] This parishioner's death could rightly be described as *the* overshadowing AIDS loss for the congregation.[67] Of all of the losses the parish had experienced, the loss of this young, talented, and popular parish leader came both to represent and to sum up for the congregation the onslaught of losses they had sustained. In ministering to Stephen, Father Schmidt described how he experienced a "conversion to love." When Stephen was dying, Father Schmidt's practice was to check on him from time to time to see if he needed pastoral support, for he knew that Stephen's death was drawing near. Most of the time, Stephen did not "need a whole lot of care," but then:

Schmidt: Finally, I did get a call from him, one Monday. I get choked up about it [he began to cry], and since he'd never asked for help before, I knew he needed it. I called Lucinda up [another parishioner scheduled to assist] because there was Mass, of course, and Lucinda's words were, "For God's sake, just go. I'll do Evening Prayer." Which was very important, as it were, because it gave me permission to do what I did. So I went and that was my week. Not that I was there all week, but he died that Thursday. So, he went from being passably well to dead in that short time.

And that visit was one of the strangest visits but it was one of the most wonderful visits, too, because it's the night that was in a way a real personal conversion for me, and it's a story I tell every now and again to the congregation because there's such turnover in the congregation. But I tell it because I think, well, it's part of the history of the place, but it's just an example of how conversion happens in very different ways and also happens in great pain. It's not overtly a conversion to God; it's a conversion to authenticity or in a way to yourself, but it's a transcendent conversion. It's transcendent because it's conversion to God whether you see yourself as already converted to God or not.

Interviewer: Is it a kind of conversion to faith, to a deeper level of trust?

Schmidt: Well, in this case to love, conversion to love. And . . . I was put in . . . just tremendous awkwardness. First of all, Stephen being Stephen, and being as popular as he was, he had too many people flocking around him that night. What he wanted to do was finally do his will and burial and he wanted to get that signed and wanted me there to witness it.

Schmidt goes on to describe how, as they talked, Stephen's sister, a massage therapist, began massaging him (Schmidt) and began undoing his shirt and collar, and he describes his discomfort in that moment.

So, suddenly I'm getting undressed and there, you know, you've got all this pastoral propriety, I mean, here I am on a pastoral call, so there I am shirtless. So, [laughing amid tears] finally Stephen says that he wanted everyone else to go. But he said, "I really want some time alone with you and once my family arrives tomorrow, you know, I don't know if that is going to happen." And he, he said, "Would you come into bed with me so I can hold you?" So, uh, D minus, F, whatever in pastoral care and counseling. So there I am not only shirtless but I'm crawling into bed.

Interviewer: Did it feel like the right thing?

Schmidt: Oh, I had no choice. For some reason, I didn't feel like I had any choice to have my shirt taken off me either. It was a real stripping. But you see, what was happening was a real stripping, too, because (crying) all my defenses were going. Professional role and everything else. So there I am lying next to this person. And he said, "I want to tell you why I love you. And it wasn't as if he had any secret romantic attachment, you know, it wasn't any of that and he began telling me just how I was the right person for the church and how much I was the right person for him and all the ways he was fond of me as a parishioner of his pastor and as a friend and colleague. I don't know about your life but in my life to have that said to me in that kind of directness, it doesn't happen very often.

Interviewer: Well, it sounds like he was really aware of what he was doing and why he was doing it.

Schmidt: Yeah. And then as a response, I then felt that I needed to tell him, and so that in itself was growth, because not only was I someone that people didn't say that to naturally, I also did not say that naturally to people. So I told him why I loved him. It was in some ways a holy week.

In the interview, Father Schmidt went on to describe the entire course of Stephen's death and funeral, the AIDS funeral that was repeatedly described in all the interviews as having the greatest effect on the parish.

Father Schmidt's experience of Stephen's death seemed to symbolize the parish's entire response to AIDS loss. Parishioners experienced great vulnerability in their experience of loss and yet, time and again, they reported how they encountered God's very presence amid the sadness and destructiveness of this loss. They noted, further, that it was their great vulnerability that opened them to discern God's presence so profoundly. This sense of vulnerability was captured in the "stripping of defenses" that Schmidt described so eloquently. The cause of vulnerability varies from person to person and occasion to occasion. For many in the parish, it resulted from loss. For others, it came about through an HIV diagnosis, while, for still others, it accompanied sobriety. But however it occurred, in opening themselves up or in being opened through life and loss, parishioners came to know and understand how God was with them even in moments of pain. The fruit of this encounter with God at All Saints was a concern with justice. Having experienced God's love and presence profoundly, members of the parish recognized that they and *everyone else* were enfolded within this embrace of love. Over time, through their experience of AIDS loss, the parishioners felt compelled to offer this embrace of love to others.

This understanding of the inextricability of love and loss was expressed theologically in the parish's understanding of resurrection life. In preaching and in conversation, the clergy and laity of the parish described this encounter with the immanent and incarnate God in the midst of pain and loss as resurrection life. We have already noted that vulnerability opened them to resurrection. Other prerequisites for experiencing resurrection life included the willingness to face death and to be surprised by God. In their view, living a resurrected life also required courage and forgiveness. They experienced resurrection in the context of suffering, but also through worship and in relationship. Having experienced resurrection life, the people of All Saints valued justice, which they understood as the extension of this life to all, including all those on the margin, such as gays and lesbians, the homeless and hungry, children and youth, the sick, women, persons of color, animals, and the parish's beloved dead with whom members understood themselves to be connected in the light of God's love.

Father Schmidt summarized his understanding of resurrection through the words of Andrew, the fourth-century bishop of Crete. According to Schmidt, "he referred to the cross as both the sign of God's suffering and the symbol of God's triumph, and so for him, crucifixion and resurrection are one and the same thing. It's not that we wait for something to happen afterward. [Resurrection] is the way we go through the crucifixion."[68] Further, in Schmidt's view, resurrection does not depend upon a denial of death. As he put it: "If there is a resurrection it has to be a resurrection that comes through the willingness of being able to face the stark reality of what you are experiencing."[69] So the transformation that is resurrection is effected through facing the reality of suffering, yet finding within it transcendent love which makes it bearable.

These sentiments echo Julian's experience of participating in Christ's crucifixion and resurrection. However, while Julian believes that suffering can be transformed through love, Julian in no way glorifies or seeks suffering. Instead, she believes that life itself is a form of suffering that must simply be endured. In speaking to her God says: "For I tell you that whatever you do, you will have woe. And therefore I want you to understand the penance you are continually in, and to accept that meekly, for your penance. And then you will truly see that all of your life is profitable penance."[70] Julian responds: "This place is prison, this life is penance, and he wants us to rejoice in the remedy. The remedy is that our Lord is with us, protecting us and leading us into the fulness of joy."[71] Julian believes that when faced with suffering one must pass over it as lightly as possible and keep one's focus, in faith, on Christ's love.

Gatta's analysis helpfully illustrates how, in choosing to stay with the suffering Christ and not to look away from the crucifix, Julian chooses an incarnate God who is fully engaged with suffering humanity rather than a transcendental religion which would rise above human pain and misery and "attain detached tranquility."[72] Through choosing to suffer with Christ, Julian embraces the suffering of all humanity that is summed up in the crucifixion — and it is only in making that choice that she is able to attain the healing that is communicated through the resurrection. Thus her view squares quite nicely with the beliefs articulated at All Saints.

Judgment and Justice

A second problem with which survivors often contend is the issue of judgment and justice. Julian struggled mightily with issues of judgment. After realizing that sin was inevitable for humans, Julian worried over the fate of those whose sins the church perceived as unforgivable. In understanding God's essential nature as love, Julian puzzled over how it could be that anyone would be excluded from God's saving embrace. Julian resolved this concern through faith in three ways: first, through her understanding of the difference between divine and human judgment; second, through her distinction between general and specific knowledge; and finally, in her faith that Christ would make all things well through a final great deed.

Parishioners at All Saints also grappled with issues of judgment in the midst of an epidemic. The Christian church as a whole was not particularly accepting of persons living with

AIDS in the early days of the epidemic, a fact that has become easier for us to lose sight of over time.[73] Christians who were living on the front lines of the epidemic in the earliest days of AIDS struggled to make sense of the losses they witnessed and the stigmatization of gay men that resulted from the initial patterns of HIV infection in this country. Over time, however, in facing the reality of death, All Saints parishioners found their understandings of God and God's judgment transformed. One parishioner, Lucinda Grey, described the effects of AIDS loss on her relationship with God as follows:

> I think this loss has gotten me away from thinking of God as being very judgmental and gotten me away from thinking that there are standards for behavior and belief that people need to follow to get God's approval and go to heaven. It's gotten me more to a conviction that whatever the life of the world-to-be may be, that we'll probably all be there and that I don't think that God sweats the small stuff.[74]

In her response to follow-up questions, Lucinda described how she came to believe that she, also, would be among those who will be with God. When I asked her how she had come to greater acceptance of herself and others, she said, "I've seen so many very good people that the vast majority of people would consider undesirable die in the church and have been to the funeral services with those hymns, those readings. I cannot imagine that God would not accept Stephen, that he would not be pleased with Mike or Hank or any of those people" (naming young gay men who had died of AIDS.)[75] Thus, through her experience of traumatic loss, Lucinda came to an understanding of God as more accepting and, finally, of herself as no more or less worthy than others. Julian, also, came to this same stance and through it, she truly opened herself to love and care for her "even Christians."

Contemporary survivors of trauma are often vexed by the injustice of their suffering. Why is it that they must live with such suffering, while others do not? How may human suffering and oppression be reconciled with the existence of God?

Julian does not explicitly address the issue of why some individuals or groups suffer more than others. In her treatment of sin, she focuses on the sin of individuals versus structural sin. However, Julian does concern herself indirectly with the issue of justice through her eschatology. As the theologian Krister Stendahl notes, the biblical doctrine of the resurrection, rather than being centrally concerned with the immortality of the soul, is concerned instead with whether God's justice will win out. As Stendahl puts it, "Resurrection answers the question of theodicy, that is the question of how God can win, the question of a moral universe. Does crime pay? Will evil win? Where is God's promise and power? Will God ultimately come through?"[76] In this regard, although Julian does not explicitly address issues of justice, I think we may confidently assert that she does believe in the ultimate triumph of good over evil. However, she adopts a decided agnosticism about the means to this end. Yet that agnosticism was neither passive nor disengaged. Julian communicated her vision and reflections upon it at some personal risk. She demonstrated a clear willingness first to serve as advocate with God for those viewed as hopelessly lost in her day and second to engage herself with her "even Christians," offering them hope and meaning through her writing. These factors underscore Julian's desire to live a compassionately engaged life and to work to create a climate in which justice might flourish.

All Saints parishioners struggled with issues of justice no less than Julian. While they did not resolve these concerns in exactly the same way, two viewpoints prevailed. First, some survivors of AIDS loss dedicated themselves to working for justice as a way of redressing the deaths of those whose deaths to AIDS could have been prevented through a more vigorous political agenda in the early days of the epidemic. Their faithfulness to the memories of their loved ones compels them to seek justice so that their friends will not have died in vain. Second, other parishioners look beyond the present life to the afterlife as a place where justice may be achieved. As one parishioner put it, "I think a lot of AIDS patients have paid a very high price for their lives and I mean death is rarely a painless experience for anybody, but I think especially for AIDS patients, it can really be excruciating. I always pray to God that God will honor the trials of these people and draw them close and give them the peace and the lack of pain and the wholeness and the lack of struggle. I really wish that for them in whatever form it takes."[77] Thus, individuals experiencing loss resolved issues of justice differently, yet their solutions also inspired hope and healing and upheld the memories of their beloved dead.

Death and the Ultimate Fate of Human Beings

One of the greatest issues with which contemporary survivors of trauma struggle is their need to face the inevitability of their own death. Interestingly, Julian does not appear to struggle with questions of immortality; as a woman of her day, she adopts an otherworldly eschatology more naturally than do most twenty-first century believers. However, in her reflection on the ultimate fate of humans, Julian strikes me as truly contemporary in her thinking. The agnosticism of her final solution to the problems of sin and suffering, associated with faith in Christ's great deed that shall make all things well, squares well with contemporary feminist solutions to questions of ultimate meaning. Let us compare Julian's response to eschatological concerns with that offered by Rosemary Ruether in her book

Sexism and God-Talk. In considering the question of personal eschatology, Ruether writes

> What of the sad insufficiencies of human finitude and the consequences of social evils that take the lives of little children and cut off adults in the prime of life before they can make their contribution? What of the vast toiling masses of human beings who have had so little chance to fulfill themselves? What of the whole tragic drama of human history where so few have been able to snatch moments of happiness and fulfillment in the midst of toil and misery? What even of those worthies who have made good contributions and lived a full life? Do their achievements live on only in our fading memories, or is there some larger realm where the meaning of their lives is preserved? The appropriate response to these questions is an agnosticism. We should not pretend to know what we do not know or to have "revealed" to us what is the projection of our wishes.[78]

Ruether goes on to conclude that, in her view, our individual beings are gathered up and assimilated into the fabric of being and carried forward into new possibilities. Yet she concludes that understanding our fate in this way is beyond the power of our imagination. While we cannot understand the "immortal" dimensions of our life, we can concentrate on using "our temporal life span to create a just and good community for our generation and for our children."[79]

In reading Ruether's conclusions, I was struck by the similarity between them and Julian's. Julian's solution to the problem of death and immortality is to trust in the goodness of creation and God's love, which, through her vision, became the most real and vital presence she knew. While her reflections on human destiny may not completely satisfy contemporary survivors' questions and concerns, Julian's forthright acceptance of human limitations offers a healthy model in an age when seeming attempts to achieve human invulnerability through the proliferation of deadly weapons and endless cycles of violence provide temptations to despair.

In addressing questions of immortality, All Saints parishioners also displayed a striking agnosticism about the ultimate fate of their loved ones. When pressed for their views, most parishioners said, rather simply, "They are with God," without attempting to specify their fate more concretely. However, despite the tangible absence of their loved ones, through the power of remembrance, their loved ones remained very much alive to them.

Human Community

A crucial spiritual need of survivors of trauma is to achieve an empathic connection with human community. We have already noted Julian's concern for the welfare of her community; in fact, it became a primary motivation for Julian, who wrote to address the needs of her fellow Christians for meaning and solace. However, Julian's concern was not limited to her fellow Christians, for we have already seen that she extended her care to those understood in her day to be beyond salvation, including Jews and apostate Christians. As a result of her vision and her reflection upon it, Julian came to a crucial understanding about human community: she learned that all are gathered in unity of love with God: "The love of God creates in us such a unity that when it is truly seen, no man can separate himself from another. And so each soul ought to think that God has done for him all that he has done."[80] Thus in her text, Julian suggests the possibility of salvation for all. Through the power of her vision, she advances the notion that all of us are "oned" to God, and she hints that no individual is beyond the reach of Christ's saving embrace. Julian's passion to communicate the power of God's love for all motivated and vivified her theological reflection.

All Saints parishioners developed a concern to reach out to and embrace those ordinarily marginalized through their experience of AIDS loss. However, perhaps the most striking effect of loss within the parish was the sense of connection parishioners felt to deceased members. Through sharing stories and honoring memory, the congregation retained a strong communal bond to those who had died. The parish built an AIDS memorial garden and then eventually a memorial chapel with a columbarium in honor of their deceased. These cherished spots served as concrete reminders of dearly departed parishioners. The presence of many beautiful memorial gifts also brought to mind their friends. Through cultivating beauty and narrative as forms of remembrance, the theological understanding of the communion of saints came to life at All Saints as a result of AIDS. Further in the Eucharistic liturgy that was so central to the parish's life, past, present, and future came together in a sacredly constituted moment that made absent loved ones seem at times to be tangibly present. Re-membrance of loved ones combined with the Christian eschatological hope expressed in the prayer of Great Thanksgiving endowed the unity between living and dead with a transcendent power. It is the power of this holy union that fuels the parish's thirst for justice and serves as a reminder, for them as well as for Julian, that "all shall be well."

FIVE

Julian's Spirituality of Trust and Longing

But when our courteous Lord shows himself by grace to our soul, we have all our desire; in that time, we see fit to leave aside prayer as all our attention, all our might is set wholly on beholding him. But this is a high and unknowable prayer, as I see it. For now our reasons for praying come together in the sight and contemplation of him to whom we pray, marvelously enjoying him with reverent dread and such great sweetness and delight that our prayer is nothing anything more: instead it is he that stirs within us.
— Julian of Norwich, *Revelation of Love*[1]

According to Julian, God draws us forward to himself by fulfilling our hunger for him only partially. We seek him because we desire him. Once our craving is eased, satisfaction is withdrawn, so we might burn for him ever more strongly. . . . But the sense of loss is in fact purely subjective. Although Julian regards this inevitable impression of incompleteness as "our ordinary undertaking in this life," it is not objectively true. Though we feel a loss of God emotionally, God is in fact always near us. . . . God is in all our experience, even our experience of his absence.
— Julia Gatta, *The Pastoral Art of the English Mystics*[2]

Life following traumatic loss poses a tremendous challenge to survivors. Perhaps the greatest struggle they face is attempting to integrate the new understandings of life and God wrested from their traumatic experience into their everyday human experience. In doing so, survivors inevitably face many questions. Will my life have meaning despite these losses? Can I heal, and

142

if so, how? Will I ever relate normally to others again? Is it possible for me to retain or regain my faith in life and in God?

As we have seen, Julian herself was a survivor, of traumatic loss, and she, like other survivors undoubtedly wrestled with these questions. Further, through her counseling ministry, she would have encountered many others who were attempting to understand and integrate the losses they had sustained.

One of Julian's most remarkable contributions is the very positive and life-affirming spirituality that she developed in response to her vision. This spirituality, based on her affirmation that "all shall be well," may be characterized as a spirituality of trust and longing. It was a distinctive spirituality that grew out of her experience of the loving God she encountered in her vision. Through this experience and her reflection upon it, Julian moved from self-deprecation toward greater self-acceptance. In addition, through her wholehearted participation in the crucifixion and resurrection, Julian appeared to move from a view of life as drab and sorrowful to a more positive and hopeful stance grounded in the certainty of God's love.

In light of this experience and her reflection upon it, what manner of life did Julian propose for believers? How could believers both develop and maintain a relationship with the loving God she had come to know? What beliefs and practices would enable them to transcend day-to-day concerns, doubts, and limitations and live with the confidence that all shall be well? As we examine Julian's responses to these critical questions, we shall explore how contemporary survivors may find strength through the insights that she developed and how they, also, may find spiritual meaning through grief.

Addressing questions of meaning arising in trauma is essential in developing an appreciation for Julian's spirituality and in understanding the practical counsel she would have offered to survivors of traumatic loss. In considering the help afforded

through Julian's approach to spirituality, we shall particularly
attend to three aspects of her thought: Julian's understanding
of the purpose of life and the human condition; the possibility of self-transcendence and the means to it; and living a life
informed by the knowledge that "all shall be well."

The Purpose of Life and the Human Condition

Julian's vision indelibly influenced her understanding of the
purpose of life. Through it, she clearly came to a deeper
knowledge of God, of herself, and of life's meaning.

In reflecting on the reality of her vision, Julian came to several
conclusions. First, she realized that she had received her vision
for the benefit of all Christians.[3] Second, she concluded that the
revelation was made for several purposes, specifically so that
we might come to know God; that we might come to know
ourselves; that we might know ourselves as we are in our sin
and feebleness;[4] and finally, because God wanted to give people
light and solace with the contemplation of heavenly joy, so that
they might experience relief from the sorrow and darkness of
this life.[5]

One of the greatest difficulties Julian faced following her vision was how to live with the lack of clear sight she had known.
Interestingly, a major consequence of this struggle was the emphasis Julian placed upon sight in her theology and spirituality.
Seeing became a central metaphor in her work, and her stress
upon this notion was most directly reflected in her views regarding the purpose of life and the human condition. After receiving
her revelation, Julian reached the conclusion that we were created for two ends: union with God and union within ourselves.
In one particularly inspiring and expressive passage, Julian described the former union as a total sensory experience in which
after death "we will be hidden in God without end, seeing him

truly, feeling him fully, hearing him in spirit, and smelling him delectably and swallowing him sweetly."[6] Yet, even here, Julian gave priority of place to vision. For, in the next breath, she stated that "we will see God face to face, homely and fully; the creature that is made shall see and behold God who is maker without end."[7] Perhaps inevitably, therefore, Julian, the visionary, expressed the end of our existence in terms of sight: we shall achieve fulfillment and bliss when we have clear sight of God and clear sight of ourselves as God sees us: "And I know full well, when these two may be seen wisely and truly, we shall get rest and peace here, at least in part, and by his plentiful grace know its fulfillment in the bliss of heaven."[8] With this clear vision will come the union of our will with God's will.[9]

In reflecting upon her vision, Julian concluded that the degree of sight she had experienced in it was extraordinary indeed: "I knew in this showing of God that such a way of seeing him cannot be continuous in this life, by reason of his dignity and so that our endless joy may grow. And therefore we often fail in his sight, and presently we fall into ourselves."[10] Thus, Julian believed that the absence of sight in this life causes us sorrow. In contrast, she believed that the perfect sight of God, reserved for us in heaven, would bring us bliss, peace, and rest.

Julian's choice of blindness as the central metaphor for the human condition flowed directly from her understanding that we do not have clear sight of God in this life. She described our state of life as follows:

> I understood that we are changeable in this life: overcome by frailty, we fall into sin. We lose all our strength, all common sense — also our will is overlaid; in these moments we feel nothing but tempest, sorrow and woe. And the cause of all this is blindness; we cannot see God. For if we were to see God continually, then there would be none

of this mischief, nor any manner of stirring[,] that yearning to enslave us in sin.[11]

In Julian's view, therefore, *the essence of the human condition is deprivation of the clear sight of God.* The consequence of this deprivation is that "we may never cease from mourning and weeping nor longing until the time we can see [God] clearly in his blissful countenance."[12] Through these words, therefore, Julian the visionary reinforces her view that human happiness is dependent upon the clear sight of God. Survivors of traumatic grief are at great risk of sadness, for as we have already observed the experience of loss blocks the awareness both of God's goodness *and* human kindness, and many survivors wrestle mightily with a sense of God's absence in loss.

For Julian, human blindness, however it arises, invariably leads us to sin, the cause of our pain. As we have seen, the inevitability of sin led Julian to characterize this life as a prison and penance, for she believed that whatever we do in this life, we would have sorrow.[13] Nevertheless, Julian believed that sin serves a useful purpose because it increases our knowledge of our human limitations, leading to meekness, and it increases our awareness of God's love. Julian prized the meekness resulting from knowledge of our sin, for in her view, it makes us like children, dependent on Mother Christ: "And I took it that in this life there is no higher state than childhood, that feebleness and failing both in capacity and understanding that shall last until such time as our gracious Mother has brought us back to our Father's bliss."[14]

Julian described the gracious way in which a courteous God reveals our sin to us, creating this meekness so that we may benefit from the self-knowledge we gain without losing heart.

For in his courtesy, he measures the sight for us, for indeed it is so vile and horrible that we could not endure to see it as it really is. And by this humble knowledge, through condition and grace, we shall be broken from all those things that are not our Lord; and then our blessed Saviour will heal us perfectly and make us one with him.[15]

The sight of our sin, therefore, is mercifully tempered by God's goodness.

In her treatment of the effects of sin, Julian expressed a final helpful effect of it in her belief in the fruits of spiritual conflict. According to Julian, the conflicts between right and wrong that we encounter in this life increase our strength and future blessedness, "for if our faith [had] no conflict, it would deserve no reward."[16]

Contemporary survivors of traumatic loss struggle as Julian did to make sense of their lives and to find within them not merely pain but purpose. While the survivors of AIDS loss at All Saints Church did not use the language of sin to speak of their limitations, they did describe their attempts to come to terms with the enhanced knowledge of human vulnerability that accompanied their grief. Three aspects of this experience captured their sense of heightened vulnerability: their willingness to accept the limited nature of human life, their increased ability to live in the present, and the authenticity of their encounter with HIV/AIDS. Through these characteristics of their experience, parishioners developed greater self-acceptance and demonstrated a growing wisdom regarding the human condition, both powerful fruits of their loss.

The experience of traumatic loss clearly intensified the spirituality of the members of All Saints. The AIDS epidemic was a crisis, and in coping with it, members inevitably found themselves wrestling with spiritual concerns. For example, when I asked Jerome about the effects of AIDS loss on his spiritual life, he stated, "It kind of put it in my face. I had to deal with it. I could be begging God or angry at God, but it was always there. I couldn't just coast and relax. I mean, I could choose to ignore God, but I think my response usually was to deal with the spiritual dimension because it was forced on me."[17] The experience Jerome recounts seems typical for the members of All Saints, for many described the way in which their attempts to come to terms with AIDS precipitated a spiritual search. This search continued to dominate the lives of a number of members for some time.

In my interviews with parishioners, several commented on the premature encounter with death they had experienced in AIDS. With that encounter came an increased appreciation of their vulnerability. As Michael Wallace put it, "I think the deaths had a huge impact. You know living through pain like that and prematurely living through it when we're not supposed to be at that point in our lives. I think it changed a lot of people's lives and the way they acted. I think a lot of people realized how vulnerable they were and that they don't really control their lives."[18] For some parishioners, this increased awareness of their vulnerability and mortality led ultimately to a greater acceptance of death in general. Tom's response may be considered representative. When asked how AIDS had affected his life, he stated, "It has caused me to think a lot more about death. I have been to so many funerals that I can't help thinking about my funeral. Being in a period of plague and seeing so many funerals makes you think about life and death differently."[19] He went on to describe a somewhat dangerous vacation he had taken and the way in which he matter-of-factly prepared for the small probability of death before he left. Despite the risk, "I was very at peace because I really wanted to do this and I felt if I die, this is okay. I mean, I am almost fifty years old. Ever since I've gotten to the age I am now, I just feel a little bit less afraid than I used to be. I don't want to die. I want to live, but I'm not as afraid of death."[20] Life with AIDS increased Tom's degree of comfort as he anticipated his own death.

An increased ability to live in the present and to live with gratitude constituted a second aspect of self-acceptance present despite human frailty. Jan talked about how AIDS increased his ability to appreciate the present: "You know, we put too much emphasis on what's going to happen five years down the road. I'm worried about retirement, I'm worried about am I going to have enough money. And yet, damn, we just need to live. This is an important day, and it's a hard thing to do. My parents had this Depression mentality. I really want to break that. I mean, I know I can live and I know I can make money and I know that I can survive and I've got to learn how to be happy with that instead of being a crusty old unhappy guy with lots of money. It's definitely changed my whole outlook on life."[21]

A third interviewee, Leona, described how the awareness of AIDS deaths in the parish increased her gratitude and appreciation for life. "When an eighty-year-old person passes away, you say, well, they lived a good life and God bless them. And you know they're on their journey elsewhere, but when you're losing people thirty years old and forty years old and twenty years old, it really makes you stop and think. You have to be grateful and thankful that the Lord allows you to get up and smell the fresh air in the morning and say, "Thank you, Lord, for helping me get up and smell the fresh air and be in my right mind, because everybody is not able to get up and say that and we're in a church where you hear about another funeral and another funeral and it does, in fact, affect you."[22]

For these parishioners, an important fruit of their encounter with AIDS lay in a greater acceptance of their own mortality and an increased ability to live in the present moment. For other members, the encounter with AIDS was an incentive to

embrace sobriety: this also provided an enhanced appreciation
of vulnerability that was quite healing.

For some members, the acceptance of mortality — their own
and others — was not achieved without conflict or struggle. At
least one lay member of the parish dramatically experienced
his limits in coping with a friend's plan to end his own life
prematurely. This occurred when the suffering his friend anticipated from his AIDS-related opportunistic infection was more
than he could bear. His friend was told, "Your pneumocystis
keeps recurring, and we can't treat it anymore. You've got about
two weeks to live and the last week of your life is not going to
be pleasant."[23] At that point, his friend called his family and
began to formulate a suicide plan. Despite his own reserva-
tions about suicide, the parishioner helped his friend to obtain
the information he needed to die with dignity. He said:

> I suppose that felt to him like I was condoning what he
> was doing, and I guess I was. This was a matter that I
> have conflicted feelings about as a result of my religious up-
> bringing and attachments. You understand that there are
> certain teachings of the church that I value about human
> life, but I also don't understand sticking around for two
> weeks' worth of agonizing dying. I had seen other folks
> do that.[24]

This parishioner made himself available to his friend's family
members both before and after the suicide. Several members
of All Saints faced similar very difficult decisions during the
height of the epidemic, and inevitably there was no easy resolution to the quandaries they faced. Certainly, confronting these
difficult situations heightened their awareness of their human
limitations and the fragility of life.

Experiencing AIDS loss also enhanced the parishioners' appreciation of authenticity in grieving. In the course of the

epidemic, they learned the value of facing the pain of AIDS head on. Michael described the importance of "talking about it, being open" in sharing about AIDS and about the losses he had experienced. This lesson was reinforced when a close friend of his died. Michael attributed his friend's premature death, in part, to his denial. As he put it, "One of the things that made AIDS difficult was that it started out having to be such a secret. That caused a lot of people to want to hide and deny it and that paralyzed a lot of the feelings associated with it."[25] Secrecy and dishonesty were difficult because, in the end, they robbed people of the emotional support that was so essential in coping with loss. At All Saints, people felt free to be themselves. The value the church placed on authenticity bore fruit in the AIDS epidemic, because it allowed members to mourn in a genuine way. Some parishioners had the unpleasant experience of attending funerals in other churches in which important aspects of the deceased's identity and lifestyle were hidden. This was not the case at All Saints, and it is part of what facilitated healing in the parish.

Both Julian's writings and the experience of All Saints parishioners highlight the confrontation with human limitation central to traumatic loss. Julian used the image of blindness to characterize human limitations and describes their association with sin. While All Saints parishioners do not *inevitably* connect their enhanced vulnerability with the notion of sin, they do emphasize how coming to terms with death and loss involves both pain and sadness. Neither Julian nor All Saints parishioners, however, believe that painful awareness of human limitation prevents human growth and flourishing. We have already seen how such knowledge in All Saints parishioners increased their capacity for self-acceptance, just as Julian moved through awareness of her own sin to greater self-love through her faith in Christ's redemptive work on her behalf.

In light of the increased knowledge of human limitation that accompanies loss, how did Julian understand our ability to move through loss toward the union with God that we desire and that is our rightful end? The answer to this question resides in Julian's twofold understanding of self-transcendence, to which we now turn.

Self-Transcendence and Its Achievement

If we accept Julian's characterization of humans as limited by sin, yet destined for union with God, we must confront the question of how we are able to transcend our limitations in this life and move toward the end for which we were created. Does our lack of clear sight of God prevent us from experiencing God's presence? Julian's response to this question would be a resounding no! Instead, she affirms our need to trust in the reality of God's presence in our lives at the same time as we seek God as an expression of our longing for God. According to Julian, the basis for self-transcendence resides in this dynamic tension between trust and longing which may also be understood as a tension between our sense of God's presence and God's absence. In other words, Julian believes rather paradoxically that we must both trust that God is with and in us, at the same time as we seek signs of God's life within us and around us. In our movement toward wholeness, Julian also emphasizes that we must seek the virtue of our higher nature, or our substance, which draws our lower nature toward the integration God intends for us. Thus, trusting that we are created in God's image also contributes to our healing.

The necessity for trust, of course, arises from our blindness. Because we do not see God face to face in this life, and because we do not see ourselves as God sees us, we must learn to have faith in common sense, the teaching of the church, and the grace of the Holy Spirit working in our souls.[26] These allow us to know of God and of our value as God's creatures. As Julian noted, all of these are gifts and "all work us to God."[27]

While we cannot see God face to face in this life, on the basis of her revelation Julian stated that Christ wants us to trust that he is always with us. His presence is known in three ways: he is with us in heaven in his spiritual thirst that draws us to him, he is with us on earth leading us on, and he is with us in our souls through his unceasing care for us.[28]

Confidence in the third point, that God dwells within our soul, allows us to have faith that we, like Julian, shall not be overcome by temptation, fear, depression, or despair. Thus, confidence in God's indwelling enables us to trust in God's salvific work on our behalf. As Julian noted repeatedly, this work begins with the gift of our substance and ends with the perfection of our sensuality through the workings of mercy and grace. Trusting also enables us to pass over our sufferings lightly. In doing so, we live into our anticipation that God will take us from our pain. According to Julian, God wants us to find comfort even in our death and in our passing through the knowledge that following death, there will be no more pain of any sort, no more discomfort, or nothing to want, since all will be joy and bliss without end. In revealing this to her, Christ said, "Why [then] should it seem hard for you to suffer awhile since that is [God's] will and does [God] honor?"[29]

In elaborating these aspects of Julian's spirituality, it is important to note that such emphases in her writing reveal her mature vision and are the fruit of long years of reflection. Julian was no stranger to doubt or to the difficulties inherent in suffering as her own writings and Christ's words above reveal. Julian wrestled quite authentically and painfully with her own lack of clear sight.[30] Thus, the serene spirituality she articulated developed over time, and survivors seeking solace in her writings may per-haps find comfort in witnessing the strengthening of her faith that came with greater maturity and enhanced wisdom.

In developing her spirituality, therefore, Julian postulated a dynamic tension between trust and longing. On the one hand, trust manifests our certainty that God is with us; on the other hand, our longing for God manifests our awareness that we do not yet fully possess the union with God we desire. In speaking of our longing for God, Julian notes that our longing for God is a mirror image of Christ's longing for us. Julian describes Christ's longing as a spiritual thirst that will persist until all destined for salvation are united with him in heaven.[31] As a further elaboration of faith, Julian noted that our seeking for God in this life is as good as finding God, for it is God's will that we seek God. The act of seeking is itself an expression of trust.[32] In fact, Julian noted that the longing we have for God might be understood as a form of penance, for this longing, which often arises from our sense of God's absence, causes us pain throughout this life and never leaves us until we come to final union with God in heaven.[33] The principal value of longing, therefore, is that it draws us toward heaven. Our longing for God leads us so deeply into God that we come "verily and truly to know our own soul."[34]

Given that the experience of suffering and limitation is inherent in the human condition, what allows us to tran-scend it? Julian describes two main resources that foster self-transcendence: prayer and repentance. Prayer is valuable for two reasons: first, it provides a means by which we may experience union with God in this life.[35] Second, prayer helps to make our will supple to the will of God, that we may be joined to God in all things.[36] Prayer is a concrete expression both of longing and trust, for it arises "from a right understanding of the fullness of joy that is to come, as well as a longing and sure trust that it will be ours."[37] Repentance, in contrast, arises from contrition, compassion, and longing.

> By contrition we are made clean, by compassion we are made ready, and by true longing for God we are made worthy. These three are the means by which, as I understand, all souls come to heaven; that is to say, those who have sinned on earth and shall yet be saved, for by these medicines it is fitting that every soul be healed.[38]

According to Julian it is through acts of prayer and repentance that we are able to express our trust in God's love for us and realize the object of our longing, namely, union with God. These two activities provide powerful vehicles that enable us to overcome the limitations imposed by the human condition and to further our movement toward our ultimate destiny in God.

In the experience of survivors today, self-transcendence as an aspect of survivor spirituality manifested itself in several ways. Parishioners at All Saints described how living through a period of great loss caused them to reevaluate their existing beliefs and to look for new meaning, particularly as their existing sources of security were shattered. In describing their experience they identified several sources of self-transcendence, including the intensification of emotion in loss; the heightened appreciation of relationships in loss; the growth derived from caregiving; the richness of liturgy, prayer, and music; and the hope of justice in loss.

Members of All Saints who encountered enormous loss spoke of the tremendous emotional impact of this experience. Jerome noted that in the period of greatest loss there was both a sense of personal connection with those who had died and a sense of personal distancing. "For me, it was always a balance between wanting to embrace the whole world and then wanting to shut it all out. And all the distancing, I think, was because of the fear of being totally overwhelmed, totally crushed by the whole."[39] At the same time, he also remembers a heightened perception of emotion during that time:

> *Jerome:* Thinking back to that period when AIDS was so much a part of everyone's life, it just elevated everything to a new level. It was such a profound experience to be in the presence of so much loss that was unexplainable that every person became more precious.
>
> *Interviewer:* Uh huh. And pain became more painful. And joy was more joyous.
>
> *Jerome:* Yeah. That was my experience. And I think also, especially being a gay man, the added edge knowing that, you know, this cold I am catching, is this the last disease I get? Is this the beginning of the end?[40]

This heightened perception of life and its fragility encouraged parishioners to expand their horizons of meaning and to reach out in new ways to God and each other. An increased sense of community, a second form of self-transcendence, resulted from this search for many parishioners. The spirituality of AIDS at All Saints was, first and foremost, a spirituality of friendship. For example, Jerome notes: "One thing I want to mention that is important is the sense of support. I can remember a close friend that was dying in the hospital, and I would always go with a group to visit. You know, go with two or three other people, never alone, and he was just surrounded by love. There was so much caring, love, and support and people showed up, people were present for their friends."[41]

Thus, a major effect of AIDS was to deepen the ties among friends. Referring specifically to this phenomenon in the parish, Silas said:

> I think the HIV epidemic did a lot to strengthen the communal ties because people were grieving and let each other grieve and were good about providing support and giving people freedom to mourn. I think that the AIDS epidemic was bad enough that guys particularly had to, were pushed into letting their grief show and that formed a much stronger communal bond than would have happened otherwise.[42]

Besides strengthening individual friendships, the experience of AIDS loss also helped to strengthen bonds across constituencies: between men and women and straight and gay members of the parish. As a consequence of his experience of HIV, one parishioner's understanding of God as the cohesive force in relationships was strengthened. In his view,

> it reinforced my understanding of God as this relationship force because of the relationships that I've developed through the disease and through involvement with people in general. AIDS being what it was, it caused people to get in relationships a little more readily than just the normal day-to-day life. In the gay community, of course, it was something that everyone identified with, everybody identified with the loss. So it had this effect of just developing that relationship aspect.[43]

Thus, an important effect of life with HIV/AIDS at All Saints was to increase the members' appreciation of those with whom they shared the experience of loss.

The increased authenticity accompanying life with AIDS, besides contributing to greater self-acceptance for parishioners, yielded another important benefit to the community: it allowed the parish to embrace openly those who were suffering, and the members grew in caring for them. Thus, caregiving provided a third form of self-transcendence. As Jerome noted,

> I was talking to a woman a few years ago who goes to a fundamental black church in Oakland, and there were a few people with AIDS and they just kind of dropped out of the church and dropped out of the community because that was what was expected to happen. They stayed home and they missed out on the support of the church and the church missed out on the experience of supporting them.[44]

All Saints parishioners learned of the transformation that comes through providing care, and during the epidemic they particularly supported their members who heroically provided care to the dying.

A fourth source of transcendence at All Saints arose from the parish's rich liturgical life. One of the overwhelming impressions I formed during my first Holy Week at All Saints was the way in which the rich heritage of Anglo-Catholic liturgy provided a strong container for the many and varied emotions associated with loss. The nonverbal richness of the liturgy and its sheer beauty facilitated experiencing and expressing the heightened joy and sadness that were a part of life with AIDS. The robustness of the parish's liturgical life provided a tremendous buffer in the face of AIDS losses. The liturgy was rich enough both to hold and to help parishioners interpret the overwhelming emotions associated with grief. Further, several parishioners described the importance of the parish's practice of intercessory prayer to their own healing amid sickness and loss. When asked how membership in the parish had helped to facilitate the individual experience of grieving, Jerome noted the importance of having a place where he could talk about his losses and where he could have others join him in praying for his friends. He found it helpful to add the names of his loved ones to the prayer list and to know that the community was praying for them, even though they did not know the people for whom they were praying.[45] Intercessory prayer, therefore, provided a concrete way in which the community could help to share the individual burden of pain.

When members of the parish were asked to describe the religious and spiritual resources most important to them in coping with AIDS loss, the resource mentioned most frequently was the psalms. Psalm 91 was particularly important to many during the AIDS crisis. Father Schmidt's powerful teaching about the psalms of lament helped the members of All Saints to move toward a more honest expression of their feelings toward God. Other forms of prayer that seemed helpful were repetitive prayers, such as the rosary, the Jesus prayer, and the use of mantras, which had a calming effect in times of crisis.

Music in the liturgy provided another vital aid to transcendence in the parish. For a church of its size, All Saints was blessed with an amazing depth of musical talent. Singing certain hymns facilitated the expression of emotion. One of the most important was a hymn used at Stephen Wilson's funeral and included in the parish's AIDS memorial services:

> I'll praise my Maker while I've breath;
> and when my voice is lost in death,
> praise shall employ my nobler powers.
> My days of praise shall ne'er be past
> while life and thought and being last,
> or immortality endures.
>
> How happy they whose hopes rely
> on Israel's God who made the sky
> and earth and sea with all their train;
> whose truth forever stands secure,

who saves the oppressed, and feeds the poor
And none shall find his promise vain.

The Lord pours eyesight on the blind;
the Lord supports the fainting mind
and sends the laboring conscience peace.
He helps the stranger in distress,
the widowed and the fatherless,
and grants the prisoner sweet release.

I'll praise him while he lends me breath;
and when my voice is lost in death,
praise shall employ my nobler powers.
My days of praise shall ne'er be past
while life and thought and being last,
or immortality endures.[46]

This hymn expressed the hope felt by many in the congregation in the continuity of life. It also summarizes the confluence of hope and desire expressed in the parish's resurrection theology.

A final source of transcendent hope for All Saints parishioners resides in the hope of God's justice. This hope appears to be both present and eschatological in nature. It is most vividly expressed in the makeup of the community itself. All Saints was and is comprised of people who, though marginalized by the wider church and society, tenaciously cling to a vision of wholeness grounded in the love of a God who embraces all. The ravages of AIDS served to impress more deeply upon the members of All Saints the depth of that love and the wideness of God's embrace. The inspired vision of an inclusive church birthed in them through the pain of loss constitutes the eschatological expression of hope.

Living as If "All Shall Be Well"

It is fair to say that Julian's view of life realistically captures the ambiguities and sorrows experienced by survivors. Further, the themes Julian explores in her approach to life, including living with limitation and transcending pain in hope, continue to have meaning for contemporary survivors. In the end, Julian concluded that, although this life is difficult, the most honor that we can pay to God comes as we live "gladly and merrily for love of him in our penance."[47] God's unfailing love for us makes joy in this life possible and this love "keeps [us] full surely."[48] Despite the fact that we must fall, as Julian noted, "in falling and rising we are always preciously kept in one love. For in the beholding of God we do not fall, in the beholding of ourselves we may not stand; and both these are true as I see it. But the beholding of God is the highest truth."[49] It is this truth that provides the basis for hope.

Perhaps the most remarkable effect of Julian's revelation is the confidence it instilled within her in God's loving nature. Through her vision, Julian came to understand that "we have been loved and known in [God's] endless purpose without beginning"[50] and, further, that God's love for us "was never slaked, nor never shall be."[51]

In the final analysis, it is Julian's recognition and appropriation of this love, concretely manifested in her vision, that is the source of her healing, confidence, and triumph over the fear of death. Her belief in God's love and goodness produces a confident faith in the efficacy of God's actions on our behalf. As she notes, "When the doom and judgment is given and we have all been brought up above, then we will see clearly in God those secret things that are hidden from us now. Then will none of us be stirred to say: 'Lord, if only it had been thus, then it had

been full well'; but we shall say all with one voice: 'Lord, blessed
may you be! For it is thus, it is well."[52]

For Julian, love is the source of light, the foundation of goodness, and the basis for hope. God's unfailing love ensures that
all shall be well, and her unshakeable confidence in God's love
is both her most powerful and enduring legacy and her greatest
gift to contemporary survivors.

SIX

Exploring Traumatic Loss through Terrorism, Tremors, Wind, and Waves

> Thus I was taught that love was our Lord's meaning. And I saw full surely in this and in all, that before God made us, he loved us; which love was never slaked, nor never shall be. And in this love he has done all his work; and in this love he has made all things profitable to us; and in this love our life is everlastingly fixed.
>
> — Julian of Norwich, *Revelation of Love*[1]

> This seems to me to be the challenge to theology, to do theology in a way that recognizes it as a kind of performative knowledge, which is what Christian understanding is meant to be. . . . I would alter theology's definition from *fides quarens intellectum* (faith seeking understanding) to *fides quarens mundum agendum propter Deum* (faith seeking the kind of world that should be acted out, because of who God is).
>
> — Bernard Lee, "Pastoral Theology as Phronetic"[2]

Julian's awareness of God's love became the most potent and integrating force in her life. She understood that God's love was the cause, meaning, and consequence of her vision. Further, she understood God's love as enduring: it was the source of life and would lead at life's end to unending union with God. Thus, as Julian would undoubtedly conceive of it, care for survivors of traumatic loss would begin and end in love, the same love she knew in God, the love that animated all of human existence, including the experience of human suffering.

This chapter explores more specifically how God's love may be extended to survivors of various kinds of traumatic loss. We shall consider the particular needs of survivors who have experienced three different forms of loss: loss due to the terrorist attacks in New York City and elsewhere on September 11, 2001; loss due to the Southeast Asian tsunami of December 2004; and loss due to Hurricane Katrina's devastation in 2005. These accounts, in conjunction with our analysis of the effects of AIDS loss in San Francisco, shall enhance our understanding of the survivor's experience of traumatic grief.

In considering the recent experiences of trauma that have challenged the global community in new and painful ways, we shall specifically explore theological insights arising from them concerning the relationship between the nature of God and the quality of human connections we seek. We shall also consider how Julian's insights about God's loving nature may provide a resource in this conversation.

September 11, 2001: "It Is All One"[3]

At 8:46 a.m. on Tuesday, September 11, 2001, American Airlines Flight 11, commandeered by five young Arabic hijackers, crashed into the North Tower of the World Trade Center. Seventeen minutes later, at 9:03 a.m., United Airlines Flight 175 crashed into the South Tower, an event viewed simultaneously by millions of people on national television. Unfortunately, these disastrous crashes were only the beginning of the day's horror. At 9:37 a.m., American Airlines Flight 77 plowed into the offices of the U.S. Department of Defense at the Pentagon in Virginia. Finally, the downing of United Airlines Flight 93 in Somerset County, Pennsylvania, an action attributed to the heroic initiative of the plane's passengers trying to avert an even greater tragedy, served as the culminating blow to the American people's sense of invulnerability to foreign attack.[4]

The death toll for the day was staggering: 2,993 people lost their lives. This figure includes the deaths of 2,738 U.S. citizens and 255 foreign nationals, including the 19 perpetrators. The vast majority of these casualties occurred in New York at the World Trade Center. The death toll at the Pentagon was 125, while 256 people died on the four planes.[5]

The 9/11 attacks were planned and coordinated by Islamist terrorists sponsored by Al Qaeda, an organization led by Osama bin Laden, a former Saudi national whose citizenship was revoked in 1994.[6] This was not the first attack against U.S. interests sponsored or supported by Al Qaeda. Other attacks with which the terrorist group is associated include the downing of U.S. helicopters in Somalia in October 1993; the 1998 truck bomb attacks upon the U.S. embassies in Nairobi, Kenya, and Dar es Salaam, Tanzania; and an attack on the USS *Cole* in October 2000. These attacks led to the deaths of nearly fifty Americans and several hundred foreign citizens and the injury of many others. When considered along with attacks perpetrated by other Islamist groups, such as the 1993 bombing of the World Trade Center and the 1995 and 1996 attacks in Riyadh and Dhahran, Saudi Arabia, it is clear that throughout the 1990s, terrorist threats to American citizens were on the rise.[7]

Despite this history, however, Americans seemed unprepared for the assault that occurred on September 11, 2001. On the one hand, in hindsight, the American emotional response to the attacks seemed naïve. How could Americans have sustained a sense of invulnerability in the wake of increasing attacks on U.S. targets? On the other hand, how many citizens could have imagined the deadly and calculated intent that led to the coordinated series of attacks on U.S. soil? Further, while

U.S. intelligence had considered the possibility that commercial planes might be used as weapons, who could have predicted the extent of destruction that would be wrought by a small group of young men determined to exploit the deadly power of jet fuel as incendiary bombs?

That religion was central to the attacks is indisputable. In February 1998, Osama bin Laden and four associates issued a fatwa in the name of the "World Islamic Front." In this statement, they insisted that America had declared war against God and his messenger. Thus, they called for the murder of any American anywhere on earth, as "the individual duty for every Muslim who can do it in any country in which it is possible to do."[8] A fatwa is normally an interpretation of Islamic law signed by a religious authority, but in this case, the signatories to the fatwa were not religious authorities. The religious motivation of the 9/11 attacks, so destructive of human lives, complicates the process of recovery from the pain of grief associated with them. It is simply inconceivable to believers of all faiths that such devastation was wrought openly and deliberately in the name of God. Yet other people, especially many who devote their lives to the study of religion, immediately recognized in these attacks the power of religious passion and the demand for absolute faith that gave rise to them.[9]

The emotional burden borne by 9/11 survivors was staggering. As Robert Lifton writes in his analysis of the aftermath of the day, all Americans are survivors of 9/11. This includes those who were far removed geographically from the World Trade Center and the Pentagon, since as a nation we were immersed in "death-linked" television images, and also felt ourselves to be participants in a powerful and dangerous ordeal that threatened both the future of the country and our own futures.[10] It is also clear, however, that those closest to the attack, whether at the Pentagon or at the World Trade Center, suffered the most through their exposure to the violence of death and the grotesque death images that threatened to annihilate them.

The circumstances of some survivors caused them to be particularly overwhelmed with grief, death guilt, and anxiety. Among them were employees of businesses in the World Trade Center that suffered disproportionate loss, such as those who worked for the bond information firm Cantor Fitzgerald. This employer lost 658 of its one thousand Trade Center employees.[11] Employees of Windows on the World, a first-class restaurant in the World Trade Center, also suffered the loss of many colleagues who, along with countless guests, were unable to evacuate from their location on the 107th floor of the North Tower.[12] Further, first responders died in large numbers: 343 New York City firefighters lost their lives, along with 23 NYPD personnel and 37 Port Authority police officers.[13] Others who bore particularly heavy burdens were the so-called "miracle survivors," including sixteen people who survived inside the collapse in Stairwell B of the North Tower.[14]

As the wife of one of these survivors has said, "Everyone else feels like 9/11 was a long time ago. I still feel like we are stuck on September 12, not really able to move beyond it."[15] These survivors were completely immersed in images of death and destruction and thus struggled with the persistent guilt and anger they felt for having survived in a situation where so many others died. They have learned that survival is not an end in itself; instead, they must work hard to integrate the images of death and destruction in a manner that gives meaning to their survival and peace to their souls.

Lifton has provided a powerful psychological analysis of the aftereffects of 9/11. In his book *Superpower Syndrome: America's Apocalyptic Confrontation with the World*, Lifton built on his earlier work with survivors to describe the various emotional aftershocks associated with the terrorist attacks. Death anxiety on 9/11 derived from the shocking images of suffering and destruction associated with the event, including the grotesque images of people leaping from the top floors of the tower. Along with the indelible imprints associated with these images, Americans as survivors also struggled with the fear of recurrence of the attacks. Once our vulnerability to attack was exposed, the fears of recurrence became quite plausible. The discovery of anthrax contamination in Washington, D.C., one month after the attacks on 9/11 only served to heighten the nation's sense of vulnerability. Those who lived through the attacks, as well as those responsible for the nation's failed defense, also clearly suffered from death guilt that resulted from their powerlessness to help those in danger and from their inability even to feel the appropriate emotions of compassion and horror in the face of the day's overwhelming suffering.[16] Those who have studied survivors of 9/11 have also described what researchers call "zones of sadness" in its aftermath, with the most intense numbing and grief in those closest to Ground Zero.[17] A study cited in *New York* magazine indicates that 17 percent of the U.S. population outside of New York reported symptoms such as nightmares, sleeplessness, and anxiety in the days after 9/11. However, for every non–New Yorker who suffered, almost three New Yorkers reported symptoms. Further, the incidence of symptoms increased in proportion to one's proximity to Ground Zero, with those below Canal Street reporting symptoms at three times the rate of those below 110th Street.[18]

In exploring the political implications of 9/11, Lifton offers both a helpful and disturbing framework. First, as he rightly notes, our political leaders are themselves survivors who face the same need to integrate their experience of loss and the dark side of the grief they have witnessed. In the case of 9/11, Lifton has described President Bush's response as proceeding

from a sense of failed enactment, from his inability to anticipate the events or to mitigate them. Further, Lifton suggests that
the President suffered from professional numbing. In choosing
to move the United States toward a unilateral and aggressive
military response, Bush clearly underestimated the effects of
this aggressive reaction on Islamist minds and the potential
for increased terrorism they posed, effects that are now clearly
being witnessed in the insurgency movements in Iraq. Further,
in choosing an aggressive military response, the United States
numbed itself to the high numbers of civilian casualties that
would result from the wars, first in Afghanistan and then in
Iraq. Lifton labels Bush's response a "survivor mission" that
has, at times, been described religiously as a "crusade" against
terrorism.[19] In speaking of the political aftereffects of 9/11,
Lifton describes the dangers that have proceeded from American intolerance of vulnerability and the impulse to annihilate
whatever is perceived as a threat to us.[20] He dubs these tendencies the "superpower syndrome," and describes the way in
which this absolutist response to the terrorist acts seems only
to encourage an unending cycle of violence. In a profound sense,
what he describes as an "all or none" political mind-set mirrors
the unyielding religious mind-set of the terrorists who seem
willing to kill large numbers of Americans to achieve an absolute form of religious purity. In reflecting on Lifton's views, I
have sensed that the president's belief in an omnipotent deity
may be guiding his desire to create an invulnerable nation,
one whose power reigns supreme throughout the world, thus
mirroring the power of his God.

Religion was indeed a central force in the events of 9/11.
Osama bin Laden framed the terrorist attacks upon U.S. cit-
izens in religious terms, assailing the moral corruption of
Western society. He also blamed Americans for the unrest and

attacks upon Muslim societies [21] and condemned their military presence in Saudi Arabia as a desecration of two principal Islamic holy places, Mecca and Medina. In declaring a holy war upon Americans, bin Laden called upon his followers to embrace martyrdom since "the walls of oppression and humiliation cannot be demolished except in a rain of bullets."[22] In addressing Americans, Al Qaeda's leaders frankly admitted that the organization "desires death more than you desire life."[23] Thus, the confrontation between the Islamist warriors and their opponents was framed in ultimate terms.

In fashioning a religious and spiritual response to the events of 9/11, we must confront three questions: Where was God on 9/11? How was/is God involved in our loss? and Why did God allow this to happen? These are the religious questions on the hearts and minds of those who experienced the trauma of this day and those who have lived since then with the memories of departed loved ones.

In addressing these questions, the response I have personally found most helpful is that of Conservative Rabbi Irwin Kula featured in the Frontline investigation of September 11 entitled *Faith and Doubt at Ground Zero*. After enumerating the questions raised by the event, Rabbi Kula notes that rather than answering the questions, we must live with them. Providing quick answers, he says, is too easy. Those of us who lived through the horror of the day will live with the questions for the rest of our lives. Perhaps the most profound religious insight that emerged from the events of 9/11 for Rabbi Kula is the awareness that "it is all one." 9/11 has taught us that we are absolutely connected to one another. When we refer to God, he believes that we are pointing to the seamlessness of reality. His experience of religion is not that there's something "out there" against which he must define himself. Instead, he said, "my genuine experience is that there is nothing out there — this is all there is." He goes on to describe how, since he was a child, he has recited the Shema three times a day, "Hear O Israel, the Lord our God is One." He said that 9/11 helped him to realize the truth of that prayer. He says it's not "that there's some guy out there who has it all together who is one, but that it is all one." Each and every one of us in his view has experiences of unity that testify to this truth, whether we are looking at our child in a crib, appreciating our spouse or partner, or enjoying a sunset.

The events of 9/11 helped him to appreciate the underlying connection in all relationships and all of reality. This connection, in his view, is the essence of the divine. As Rabbi Kula so poignantly notes, it is hard to hold on to the awareness of these deep connections in our lives, and when we lose sight of them, we experience loneliness and alienation. Nevertheless, in his view, 9/11 helps us to understand that the core human experience constituting religion is love, the binding force in relationships. The experience of human grief, particularly the very painful psychological effects of traumatic loss, serve to reveal the deep ties that unite us.[24] Thus, loss is transfigured through our awareness of oneness.

What kind of religious/spiritual response is evoked by the events of 9/11? If 9/11 teaches us anything, it is the danger of religious absolutism — the belief that any person or group is able to speak absolutely in the name of God. In my view, a faithful response to the day's events calls forth a more humble religious viewpoint. As Professor Khaled Abou El-Fadl, a scholar of Islamic law cited in the Frontline video notes, a religious response suited to 9/11 would emphasize tolerance, God as beauty, the autonomy of the individual, the importance of conscience, and the necessity for morality always to question the law rather than for the law to embody morality.[25] In a similar way, Lifton describes the importance of embracing ambiguity, which includes accepting vulnerability as a core human experience. Death is inevitable, and the shock of 9/11 for many lay in their stark confrontation with this inescapable reality. In his sustained study of situations of massive death, Lifton has brought to the forefront the many ways in which immortality may be imagined symbolically through "significant engagement with ideas and communities that extend beyond one's limited life span."[26] Surviving 9/11 does not require that we destroy life in order to preserve an illusory sense of our own immortality. Instead, we must embrace our vulnerable humanity so that we may be freed truly to live life in all of its wonderful fragility.

Many survivors grappling with the horror and loss of the day's events have asked themselves: Where is hope to be found in the experience of 9/11? Following Lifton, I would say that hope is found in an empathy that is willing and able to embrace both sides of the suffering that leads to such horrific acts as 9/11.[27] One must understand the suffering that has given rise to the extreme acts of Islamist terrorism, just as one must probe to understand the pain suffered by those grieving in New York, Washington, and Pennsylvania. To view the pain of one or the other side as absolute is to fall short, to fail to make way for a more humane response to the events. As Lifton wisely notes, the pain of survival often leads directly to violence. He says, "There is a widespread psychological tendency for people experiencing death anxiety to become aggressive, and in some cases engage in violent rhetoric or action. When threatened with individual annihilation, one may lash out at others as a means of reasserting one's vitality, of simply *feeling* alive."[28] Yet to succumb to violence as a way of assuaging one's pain is to perpetuate the cycle of violence and victimization that gave rise to 9/11 and, in its aftermath, to war in Afghanistan and Iraq.

The events of 9/11 raise the issue of formulation: How may one make meaning from the indelible images of grotesque death that emerged from the day? For survivors in New York, perhaps the most psychologically troubling imagery was that of persons who chose to leap to their death rather than to burn to death in the towers. Yet, even in this imagery itself, there was a testimony to the power of connection, as survivors witnessed victims reaching for one another and holding hands as they leapt to death below. Some find no hope in this scene, yet Monsignor Lorenzo Albacete interviewed in the Frontline investigation finds in it "an inescapable provocation." He says:

> This image embodied what September 11th is all about. The image confronts us with the need to make a judgment, a choice. Is it an affirmation of the greatness of our humanity itself, that somehow shines in the midst of that darkness and that contains a hint, the possibility of a power greater than death itself? Or does it show the ultimate hopelessness of human attempts to survive the power of hatred and death? Which of the two? It's a choice. It's *the* choice of September 11th.[29]

The image speaks to me of the power of human connection in love that enables us to face life's darkest hour together, a connection that transfigures and transcends death. The events of September 11 reveal the power of this connection and fiercely oppose the devaluation of human life that gave rise to them. I write of these events in the hope that we will learn to affirm the existence of the bonds that unite us across nations and religions through empathy and compassion, so that we may conquer the suspicion, anger, and alienation that threaten our future life together, so evident in the events of 9/11.

"The One Face of Grief":
The Southeast Asian Tsunami

On Sunday, December 26, 2004, at 7:58 a.m., the India tectonic plate shifted beneath the Burma plate along a 750-mile
seam near the island of Sumatra. The largest earthquake in
forty years resulted from this shift, along with the displacement of billions of tons of water in a tsunami, a series of giant
waves. According to the U.S. Geological Survey, the energy released with this quake was the equivalent of 23,000 Nagasaki
bombs.[30] The earthquake and its tsunami killed more than
157,577 people and displaced more than 1,075,000 people. An
additional 26,763 people were reported missing.[31] The tsunami
wrought devastation throughout the lands surrounding the Indian Ocean, including Indonesia, Sri Lanka, South India, and
Thailand. In May of 2005, scientists reported that the quake
triggering the tsunami lasted ten minutes; other major earthquakes have their duration measured in seconds.[32] The effects
of the earthquake were felt as far away as Alaska and Africa,
with a death in Port Elizabeth, South Africa, five thousand miles
from the epicenter, considered the furthest casualty.[33] While experts disagree concerning the intensity of the quake, it is now
estimated to have measured 9.0 on the Richter scale.[34]

As Barry Bearak reported in a November 2005 study of the
tsunami's aftermath published in the *New York Times Magazine*, more than two-thirds of the quake's victims came from
a single place, the Indonesian province of Aceh.[35] Nearly half
of those casualties were suffered in Banda Aceh, a city on the
northwestern tip of Sumatra that sits at the intersection of
sea lanes from the Malay Peninsula, India, and Arabia. This
city was only 155 miles from the earthquake's epicenter, and
the tsunami overpowered it within thirty minutes of the earthquake. Thus, while people in many lands suffered as a result of

this powerful natural disaster, the Sumatran people were particularly hard hit. Tragically, the lack of a tsunami warning system prevented advance notice of the disaster, and residents of the affected regions were unprepared for the tragedy that overtook them.

Certainly, the breadth of the region affected by the earthquake and tsunami, as well as the intensity of the disaster measured both in human and natural terms, makes this disaster unique. There is another aspect to the tragedy, however, that is unusual: the international scope of those affected by the events. The quake's arrival during the holiday season, combined with its effects on coastal resort areas frequented by vacationers, intensified its devastation. Data reported in the online encyclopedia Wikipedia indicate that citizens of some forty-two countries, in addition to those physically affected by the quake and tsunami, lost their lives.[36] An editorial in the *New York Times*, published on December 30, 2004, emphasized the international nature of the event. Not since the end of World War II, it reported, had the world witnessed a nearly global catalog of woe. Despite the diversity of nationalities affected, however, the *Times* captured the unifying factor, namely, the pain of grief. "Out of all that diversity," the editorial writer noted, the tsunami created a single, simple division, between the living and dead." After highlighting the need for worldwide relief effort, the *Times* summarized the tragedy, describing it as "the one face of grief."[37]

The multinational nature of the tragedy was not without its complications for relief workers. In his book *Wave of Destruction: The Stories of Four Families and History's Deadliest Tsunami*, the writer Erich Krauss described how doctors at the Takuapa hospital in the Pangnga Province in Thailand made a collective decision to treat their Western patients as quickly as possible so that they could discharge them. As a result of cultural differences, the Western patients were demanding the attention of the physicians in the crisis because the doctors were recognized authority figures. The doctors, unable to respond to their patients' many and varied cries for help, judged that discharging these foreign patients more quickly would allow them to provide better care to their Thai patients. As a result, many foreign patients with insurance were transferred to private hospitals for care, while local Thai patients were not.[38] In addition, Burmese patients in this hospital, while treated as well as Thai patients, were not treated as frequently because, historically, the Burmese were enemies of the Thais. In the end, given the overwhelming scope of the tragedy, the doctors had to make very difficult decisions about whose lives they would save, and clearly, a variety of complex cultural factors influenced these decisions.[39]

Each form of trauma has its own "signature" loss, summarized in the death imprint. For many affected by the tsunami, the loss of children provided the most poignant image of loss. Roughly one-third of those who died in the tsunami were children.[40] Speaking in Indonesia, less than a month after the tsunami, Dr. Didier Laureillard, an infectious disease specialist from Doctors without Borders, put it bluntly: "On the west coast," he said, "there are no children." The children died because they couldn't swim and also because they were on the beaches looking for fish as the ocean receded in the aftermath of the quake prior to the arrival of the killer waves.[41] In addition, a large number of surviving children were orphaned. Since the tsunami, tens of thousands of parents have struggled with their guilt and grief because of their inability to protect their children from death. While grieving parents know rationally that they could not have prevented these deaths, they nonetheless struggle with split-second decisions they made, wondering if things might have turned out differently had they made another choice as the waves approached. An important resource for healing for these tormented parents are other parents who have also experienced loss.[42]

Other populations disproportionately affected by the tsunami included women and the elderly. According to Oxfam, four times as many women as men died in the tsunami in some regions. Women may have been on the beaches looking for their fisherman husbands. In addition, a large number were in homes caring for children.[43] Elderly survivors are facing particular challenges in the aftermath of the tsunami, as Erich Krauss reported one year following the tsunami.[44] Many older people lost the children upon whom they depended for their survival. Weakened and in poor health, many are unable to advocate for their own needs, and they are particularly affected by the corruption that undermines the equitable distribution of relief supplies and financial aid. As a result, the frail elderly whom Krauss interviewed in Thailand reported a shortage of monetary assistance, housing, and food. Many are in desperate need of meat and vegetables to supplement their supply of rice. Further, they lack medical supplies and a means of obtaining income.

In the immediate aftermath of the quake, survivors were hampered by their own physical injuries, as many were battered and bruised by their rough ride on the giant waves. Many also struggled desperately to find lost family and friends, even as they suffered severe disorientation from the complete and utter devastation they witnessed following the tragedy. It took many survivors days, weeks, and even months to receive an answer to the most pressing question: "Did my husband, wife, child, or parent survive?" The process of recovering bodies was both grim and lengthy, and relief workers were overwhelmed by the sheer number of dead. In the end, DNA specialists were needed to identify the remains of many victims, and survivors were haunted by the memories of the physical corruption their loved ones experienced following their death. In many cases, survivors were denied the opportunity to mourn properly for their deceased loved ones. This was particularly true in Banda Aceh, where some 53,835 bodies were buried behind a short red-and-white picket fence in a field along the road to the airport.[45] Attending to the huge number of corpses undermined the usual mourning rituals that mark the care of the dead. For example, in Banda Aceh, the dead were not buried in the usual shrouds, and local imams interrupted the burial in mass graves because of the lack of dignity with which the dead were treated. As Bearak noted, "The bodies were crudely tumbled off dump trucks into their final resting places."[46]

Those who survived the tsunami continued to experience suffering, not only from the displacement, disorientation, and grief that accompanied the wave, but also from the aftershocks that followed upon the original quake. In a report published in the *International Herald Tribune* on July 9, 2005, Seth Mydans noted that there had been four thousand aftershocks in the six months since the original quake. Some of these aftershocks were of considerable strength. For example, on March 28, 2005, an earthquake of magnitude 8.7 was reported at approximately the same location as the Sumatran quake, and it is viewed as an aftershock of the original quake. It ranks as the seventh largest earthquake since 1900.[47] These powerful reminders of the original quake keep survivors on edge, and many report stress-related ailments, such as dyspepsia and recurring headaches.[48]

Besides coping with the physical devastation that accompanied the quake, survivors also struggled with looting and corruption, each of which intensified the pain of survival. In his study of the quake's effects in Thailand, Erich Krauss describes how quake survivors returned to their homes, only to find that looters had preceded them, robbing them not only of their valuables, but also of such necessities as rice cookers, radios, shoes, and clothes.[49] The police in Nam Khem, Thailand, arrested seventy looters within forty-eight hours of the quake and found that the robbers had come from all over Thailand to profit from the misfortune of the villagers. Laborers stripped construction sites, hotel staff members stole guests' valuables, while others robbed the dead of watches, jewelry, and wallets.[50] The complete breakdown of governmental structures contributed to these unfortunate results. Moreover, governmental corruption itself intensified suffering during recovery, as greed and the hoarding of supplies interfered with the equitable distribution of relief.[51] For example, Krauss reports that Thai people from non-affected regions traveled to Nam Khem so that they could receive a share of the donated items being distributed to survivors. Unfortunately, some survivors also experienced religious exploitation. Krauss described how one couple he interviewed was convinced to "convert" to Christianity to obtain access to the bricks, cement, and tiles needed to repair their home.[52]

Survivors of the tsunami faced many difficult questions in the aftermath of the tragedy they had experienced. The most perplexing question, of course, was Why? Why did this happen to me, to my family, my neighborhood, and my business? Equally troubling was the question that tormented many survivors: Why did I survive while others died? In the context of the Southeast Asian tsunami, these difficult questions were confronted by survivors of many different religious groups, as Hindus, Buddhists, Christians, Muslims, agnostics, and atheists were all directly affected by the disaster. Responses to these questions of meaning ranged widely throughout the affected region. As three reporters from the *New York Times* found in a series of interviews following the tsunami: "Some [survivors] discern[ed] a lesson that humanity should unite, citing the bodies of people of all religions tumbling together into mass graves, while others see affirmation of the rightness of their own path. Amid sympathy, there [was] judgment; beneath public compassion, a private moralizing."[53] Hence, in Sri Lanka, Buddhists blamed Christians. In Indonesia, Muslim leaders accepted the tragedy as "a sign of God's disapproval and a divine examination to test their faith." Hindus in India interpreted the disaster as a divine reaction to the corruption and greed of society. Some survivors felt that the dead, rather than being punished, were returned to paradise, whereas those who had survived had been left to struggle with suffering in the quake's aftermath. The tsunami, like other disasters, has demonstrated the great variety of religious explanations that are offered in the wake of tragedy. In the face of the pluralistic religious response to the quake's physical and human destruction, two facts stand out. The first is the unity of human experience, the common pain and suffering that all affected peoples experienced. The second is the possibility of human agency, of action and compassion in the face of suffering. These points, emphasized by Buddhist Professor Asoka Bandarage of Georgetown University in an interview on NPR's *Talk of the Nation*, remind us both of the need for humility and of community in the aftermath of tremendous loss.[54] The scope of the tsunami, which affected people of so many faiths in such a devastating manner, at its best led to an outpouring of generosity and love from people of many nations. Like other disasters this tragedy revealed both the best and worst of human response to suffering. It has also raised the possibility that the uniquely multicultural and multireligious character of this event may create openings for interreligious dialogue and cooperation. In the wake of such widespread and indiscriminate suffering there is at least the possibility that greater tolerance, rather than judgment or divisiveness, may guide our interpretation of and response to these painful events.

Hurricane Katrina:
"The Big Uneasy"[55]

At 10:11 a.m. central daylight time on Sunday, August 28, 2005, the National Weather Service issued an urgent hurricane warning for New Orleans and the Gulf Coast. This missive predicted the disastrous effects that were anticipated with the arrival of Hurricane Katrina, described as "a most powerful hurricane with unprecedented strength."[56] The NWS Bulletin predicted the damage and destruction of homes and apartment buildings; power outages; danger to pets and livestock; the uprooting and destruction of trees and crops; and the significant hazards associated with hurricane force winds. Dr. Jeffrey Halverston from NASA described the storm as "a doomsday scenario." "Very rarely," he said, "have we ever seen nature conjure up a storm this powerful in the last 100 years."[57]

Six years prior to the arrival of Katrina, Dr. Ivor van Heerden, director of the Center for the Study of Public Health Impacts of Hurricanes at Louisiana State University, predicted with uncanny accuracy the devastation that a hurricane such as Katrina would pose.[58] Further, in June 2002, the *New Orleans Times-Picayune* ran a five-part series entitled, "Washing Away," which described in painful detail the threats New Orleans would face if a Category 4 or Category 5 hurricane hit the area.[59] This article graphically described nearly all of the effects that did, in fact, occur with Katrina, including the levee breach, the flooding, and the numbers of people stranded and dead. The tragedy of Katrina is that these predictions, while known, remained unaddressed. When the worst-case scenario arrived, not only were governmental agencies unprepared; they were nonresponsive to initial reports from the scene. Marty Bahamonde, the first FEMA official to arrive in New Orleans, sent regular missives to agency leaders that were ignored or rebuffed.

In evaluating the governmental response to Katrina, a report issued by a U.S. House of Representatives Special Investigative Committee stated: "Our investigation revealed that Katrina was a national failure, an abdication of the most solemn obligation to provide for the common welfare." The report continues: "At every level — individual, corporate, philanthropic and governmental — we failed to meet the challenge that was Katrina. In this cautionary tale, all the little pigs built houses of straw."[60]

The specific failures that compounded the suffering and death experienced by New Orleans residents, according to the report, included failing to create an interagency leadership team to ensure that sufficient emergency supplies and rescue teams were in place; failing to procure sufficient vehicles — boats, buses, and planes — to evacuate the Gulf Coast; failing to respond in a timely manner to eyewitness accounts of breaches in New Orleans levees, which further delayed evacuation of hurricane victims; waiting too long to issue an evacuation order for the city, and finally, failing to check information coming from the city and to substantiate, analyze, and act on it. In short, a lack of leadership and initiative at all levels characterized the government's poor response to Katrina.[61]

As a result, weaknesses in the public sector's response to Katrina only exacerbated the human suffering resulting from the storm's natural terrors. In the wake of Katrina, the Red Cross estimates that 350,000 homes were destroyed, 146,000 homes sustained major damage, 850,791 housing units including apartments were damaged, 40,000 households lacked adequate plumbing, and 50,000 households receiving federal aid were displaced. In addition, 60 percent of the counties that were declared disaster areas had poverty rates above 20 percent.[62] Katrina exposed the extreme vulnerability of the nation's poor and marginalized. These were the citizens who lacked the means to evacuate the city and were left behind without food, water, medical care, secure shelter, or adequate sanitation.

The human toll associated with Katrina is devastating: the official death toll associated with the storm now stands at 1,277. As late as February 16, 2006, nearly five and a half months after the storm, the *New York Times* reported that dozens of unrecovered bodies still lay buried in the mud in the shattered remains of New Orleans homes.[63] Their recovery awaited adequate funding for the search and rescue teams required to remove them. A bureaucratic snarl between FEMA and the city's fire department was responsible for the delay in rescue operations, and as a result, families continued to live with fear and uncertainty about the fate of their loved ones.[64]

The extent of loss associated with Katrina is virtually unprecedented for a natural disaster in the United States. In addition to the loss of lives and property, over one million residents of Louisiana, Alabama, and Mississippi evacuated the areas devastated by the storms and large numbers had to await adequate housing. A *New York Times* article published during Christmas week 2005 described the "Tent Village" that sprang up in Pass Christian, Mississippi, where nearly a hundred Katrina survivors live in tents. Other survivors along the Gulf Coast took up residence in FEMA-provided trailers, where they awaited the outcome of insurance company investigations and disputes about the cause of destruction of their homes, whether wind or waves.[65] And in New Orleans and elsewhere hurricane survivors engaged in a delicate dance with FEMA to ensure continuance of temporary housing arrangements in hotels as late as February 2006. Survivors in New Orleans faced particular difficulties in developing a permanent housing plan given the extreme housing shortage that plagued the city in the aftermath of the storm.[66]

Following Katrina, we observed many of the same difficulties arising from trauma that we have already explored: survivors who have experienced tremendous loss have suffered depression and post-traumatic stress. Late in 2005, mental health statistics indicated that the rate of suicide in the immediate aftermath of Katrina was double or more the national and local averages.[67]

These statistics capture the anxiety and despair that some survivors faced in the aftermath of the storm's damages. As Dr. Denise L. Dorsey, president-elect of the New Orleans Psychoanalytic Center, reported, for many the devastation was beyond their ability to cope. "Looking down a street where it's house after house, and the garbage and the innards of the houses, there's something about it that people in general can't grasp," Dr. Dorsey said. "It's not within the realm of any experience anyone's ever had. Your ordinary American doesn't have that in their repertoire of experience."[68]

The children of New Orleans were a particularly vulnerable population following the hurricane. A child psychiatrist in New Orleans found children as young as five years of age who talked about wanting to die after Katrina.[69] A report issued by the American Academy of Pediatrics, composed in the wake of 9/11 and released in September of 2005, delineated the potential deleterious effects of trauma and its aftermath on children and adolescents. These included the potential for post-traumatic stress disorder, bereavement, anxiety, and depression. In the aftermath of Katrina, such symptoms may have reflected the multiple losses associated with the storms, including the loss of homes, neighbors, pets, friends, and, in some cases, parents and grandparents. In addition, since many parents were themselves experiencing these symptoms, their ability to attend to the needs of their children was compromised, thus undermining further their children's care. Consequently, the most important priorities were attending to the parents' concerns to obtain housing and employment and to enroll the children in school, where they would have a greater sense of normality and an expanded range of potential caregivers.[70]

As one might expect, based on the study of other disasters, even those who fared relatively well in the aftermath of Katrina were not exempt from suffering. According to a report in the October 18, 2005, *New York Times,* survivors in the Gulf Coast area who emerged from the storm relatively unscathed confessed to Catholic priests, that really, they did all right. Their sin, in effect, was the guilt they sustained from surviving well. As a result, they felt disconnected from the huge tragedy unfolding around them, and many experienced a crushing burden of guilt. They debated whether they should return the disaster money they received from FEMA and wrestled openly with whether and how to help those who were less fortunate. As one survivor put it, "I see those palm trees that have fallen on my front lawn and know that they could have fallen on my roof, not on my lawn," she said. "Whenever I go out and see the tremendous devastation, the places that were completely destroyed, all I want to do is come home. Then you come home and ask why didn't other people do better." As a way of assuaging her guilt, this survivor mobilized her prayer group to pray for the survivors who had not fared as well. In addition, they planned to bring food and supplies to shelters. Thus, we observe in Katrina's aftermath similar emotional and spiritual dynamics to those we have encountered in other traumatic events.[71]

In the same way that all Americans are survivors of 9/11, all are survivors of Katrina. To the credit of the American people, the outpouring of financial assistance they have provided in the wake of the hurricane has been truly generous. On February 3, 2006, the American Red Cross announced that current financial donations and pledges would fully cover the $2.116 billion estimated cost for its response to Hurricanes Katrina,

Rita, and Wilma.[72] Private donations to Katrina relief totaled
$2.7 billion just eleven weeks after the hurricane reached U.S.
shores.[73] This figure compares with total private donations of
$2.8 billion for 9/11 relief. This outpouring of donor generos-
ity is particularly impressive since it occurred less than one
year after the record-breaking charitable giving for the Southeast
Asian tsunami.

Katrina, like 9/11 and the tsunami, have underscored the
tremendous vulnerability that is a part of the human condition. Further, Katrina unmasked the high incidence of poverty
in New Orleans and exposed the plight of the nation's poor, who
are woefully lacking in resources when large-scale disasters hit.
In the aftermath of Katrina, the nation has learned of its responsibility to be prepared to evacuate the ill, the elderly, and
the poor and to meet their needs for sanitation, rescue, food,
water, and medical care until they can be removed from the
disaster scene. Katrina has also exposed the effects of racism
in U.S. society. This exposure has created opportunities for the
presidency. "Katrina has posed a challenge to the White House
and the country regarding the great divide, which is race and
class in America," said Rev. Eugene F. Rivers III, the president
of the National Ten Point Leadership Foundation, a coalition
that represents primarily black churches. "It's a challenge and
an opportunity which can be won or lost, and ultimately it is
the decision of the White House as to which way it goes."[74]
Spokespersons for the African-American community are particularly hopeful that blacks will be included in contracts to
rebuild New Orleans, so that the hurricane will not be a disaster for the poor and a windfall for the rich, as Jesse Jackson
fears it has become.[75]

The aftermath of Katrina, like other disasters we have considered, has also revealed both the best and worst of human nature.
Those on the scene did experience moments of tremendous

grace in addition to pain and desperation. While the government failed miserably in its disaster relief efforts, neighbors
saved neighbors in powerful expressions of charity. These final
words from a CNN report focused on the Katrina disaster testify once again to the power of loss and calamity to reveal the
connections between us:

> Whether it was a sympathetic neighbor taking in house-
> holds of people and serving dinner, or a reporter who
> listened and tried to help, the real silver lining wasn't that
> New Orleans could rebuild again better, without its poverty
> or feeble infrastructure or that hard lessons were learned
> about survival and preparation. The real silver lining in the
> aftermath of Hurricane Katrina was in people reconnecting
> with one another. . . . What [we took] from the tragedy in
> New Orleans was some of the spirit of the Big Easy itself:
> the community, the fragile openness of a poor neighbor-
> hood that also allows bonds to develop; the outrage of its
> citizens at being neglected and unprotected; the connected-
> ness of its families and history and love for the city. . . . The
> lessons really learned from this are ones few [of us] will
> ever forget. They remain in the heart which only recently
> got a whole lot bigger.[76]

Those on the scene in this tragedy were moved by the "holding,
hugging, human connections that were strengthened by this
storm." This was the grace of Katrina and a powerful sign of
the ability of Spirit to transfigure tragedy and allow love to shine
through.

What Kind of World?

Bernard Lee's observation about the phronetic nature of pastoral theology offered at the beginning of this chapter provides

a challenge to all who seek to live faithfully in the aftermath of the recent traumatic events we have surveyed. What kind of world do these events challenge us to create? What values, expressed in traumatic situations, are true to the theology of love and compassion Julian has articulated?

I believe that recent events have helped to highlight our need as a global community to value:

- our diversity and unity, and the grounding of this unity in the empathic connections we discern between our own pain and that of others

- humility in articulating our religious and spiritual understandings, recognizing the wisdom all faiths offer for elucidating human fragility, mortality, and hope

- care for the most vulnerable in our midst, who are often unable to help themselves when trauma strikes

- strength that results from shared acts of compassion and service to those in need

- human dignity that is strengthened when the dead are mourned and buried with dignity

- the power of forgiveness and reconciliation, rather than condemnation, in shaping the response to traumatic loss

- the wisdom of responding, rather than reacting, to insults and the need to anticipate in advance the emotional dynamics that support reconciliation rather than revenge

- remembrance as a source of hope, fueling work for justice and peace in the name of those who have died

- the inevitability of death and the need to imagine the continuity of life, which provides a sense of purpose following loss

Seeking to live out these values, which help to communicate the nature, mercy, and grace Julian knew in God, makes God's

love more concretely present in the world and strengthens survivors coping with traumatic loss. Our research on traumatic
loss has clearly revealed the common denominator in experiences of trauma: the explicit awareness of the bonds that unite
all people. Simply put, we have learned that we are all survivors.
May our growing awareness and acknowledgement of this bond
empower us to create a world that more nearly reflects the diversity and community of love that Julian experienced in her
compelling vision of God as Trinity. This love, faithfully disclosed in the compassion of those who minister with love and
tenderness to survivors' needs, humanizes the experience of
loss and draws us into the very heart of a God who works in
partnership with people everywhere to make all things well.

SEVEN

A Pastoral Theology and Praxis for Survivors of Traumatic Loss

What we may hear when we listen through pain is the promise of a presence that transcends our limited efforts at care. Human pastoral care is sustained by its participation in the healing care of God. Before God there are no hierarchies of difference; the ones giving care and those receiving care are all "broken-hearted," women and men alike. What we hear when we listen is "the voice of God as that voice speaks silently and mysteriously through all other voices to which our ears give attention" and that voice invites our participation in making all things new.
— Bonnie J. Miller-McLemore and Herbert Anderson,
"Gender and Pastoral Care"[1]

Our analysis of traumatic loss has clearly illustrated the promise and the perils that survivors face following the experience of trauma. On the one hand, survivors may come away from the experience of trauma with a newfound sense of connection and an enlivened sense of meaning. On the other hand, they may find themselves suspended in time, unable to move through the pain of their loss to recover vitality, purpose, and a capacity for intimacy. Fearing the pain of new loss, and suspicious of those who offer help and hope, they may choose to live a half life of dread and fear.

Our exploration of Julian's theology has demonstrated that, despite overwhelming loss, it is possible for survivors to recapture a sense of hope and goodness through the power of God's love expressed in human connection and experiences of transcendent grace. From my own pastoral work with survivors I have learned that *loss is transfigured when the presence of God is revealed within it*. Further, transfigured loss provides healing, for it represents resurrection from death in life and empowers survivors to enact the love they have encountered in grief. I believe that the power of traumatic loss resides in its ability to reveal the deep connections that exist among humans and the responsibility that we feel for one another's survival. A key contribution in pastoral work with survivors — which includes all of us — is making these connections explicit.

Here, then, is an anatomy of traumatic loss based upon our earlier analysis of survivors' experiences. I summarize the key theological and spiritual concerns inherent in them and indicate how Julian's text might serve as a resource in addressing them. I then explore praxis and describe concrete strategies for the alleviation of pain that are revealed through the experience of survivors and through the literature on traumatic bereavement. Finally, I explore the implications of this analysis for life in an increasingly fragile and vulnerable world.

Survival Is Just the Beginning: An Anatomy of Traumatic Loss

As the wife of one of the last survivors to be pulled alive from the World Trade Center noted following the events of September 11, 2001, surviving trauma is just the beginning.[2] In other words, survival, while important, does not guarantee that those who escape death in situations of trauma, disaster, or pandemic will necessarily emerge with a sense of vitality or meaning from the trials they have endured. Instead, as we have seen throughout this study, trauma survivors must work to wrest meaning from the horrors they have witnessed or personally experienced.

In reviewing the traumatic situations explored in this research, a number of key themes arise. The compilation of them provides an "anatomy" of survival, if you will, and summarizes the core issues with which survivors grapple in coming to terms with their painful experiences.

The first theme arising in this investigation is *the human tendency to deny or minimize the possibility of life-threatening events.* This theme is particularly evident both in the exploration of 9/11 and in the analysis of the response to Hurricane Katrina. Each of these tragedies, which clearly took by surprise those affected by it, had been anticipated. This was especially true of the devastation associated with Katrina, whose horrors had been predicted in advance with surprising accuracy. Because of the capacity for denial, those responsible for the care of society's most vulnerable were simply unprepared for the extent of suffering the events posed. This failing was observed particularly in the lack of preparation for relief evident in the aftermath of Katrina and in the vulnerability of U.S. airways to the actions of the hijackers on 9/11.

Second, we have learned from each of these events that *our denial or minimization of the possibility of disaster masks human vulnerability and especially impedes the care of those most dependent on others for their survival,* including the very young, the very old, and the sick. Much of contemporary life, it seems, conspires to heighten our denial of human fragility and limitation, including our mortality, the ultimate expression of our vulnerability. However, once the sense of invulnerability has been shattered, survivors experience heightened anxiety about their physical and emotional integrity and forfeit their sense of personal safety and well-being. Even those who were rescued miraculously in traumatic events failed to find joy in their survival as they were burdened by their sense of guilt and grief for those who did not make it. Frequently, they felt that their survival came at the cost of others' deaths.

Third, analysis of these three recent disasters also reveals to us the *death immersion to which we are exposed through such media as television and the Internet.* Each of the recent disasters we have explored received extensive coverage by the media, and as a result many Americans experienced secondary traumatization through their exposure to disturbing images. In addition, the "edited" nature of the exposure the media offered created a sense of unreality. Thus, those at a distance experienced difficulty in integrating the experience, since much of the human content of the events was absent. For example, as Lifton observed, media coverage of 9/11 featured endless replays of the planes striking the towers, offering viewers de-humanized and de-personalized images of the horrors unfolding at Ground Zero. Such emaciated coverage only served to heighten the emotional numbing associated with the unfolding tragedies.[3]

Fourth, *we are beginning to appreciate the fact that the humanly caused suffering associated with trauma is perhaps the most difficult form of suffering to absorb and to forgive.* This is patently evident in the events of 9/11, which resulted directly from treachery, but it was also true in Katrina and the tsunami, which were in the first instance natural, rather than humanly caused traumas. While many Katrina and tsunami survivors could come to terms with the suffering caused by the ravages of nature, it was much harder for them to forgive the inhumanity they experienced in the delayed governmental response to their need. A sense of betrayal by others clearly magnifies the suffering associated with trauma.

Fifth, *we have learned the importance of observing the parallel process in the response of both governments and individuals.* Lifton's brilliant analysis of the effects of 9/11 on President

Bush's rush to war illustrates this important principle. In situations of massive violence and death, leaders, as well as the citizens they govern, are trauma survivors. Thus, their emotions and problem-solving skills are vulnerable to the same temptations to violence and all-or-none thinking as those accompanying acts of aggression. This reality underscores the need for insight, humility, and advanced preparation for disaster on the part of those who govern.

Sixth, *we have learned that structural evils such as classism, racism, poverty, and xenophobia have the potential to intensify greatly the suffering resulting from trauma and disaster.* The effect of Hurricane Katrina on the poorest residents of New Orleans was the most painful aspect of the hurricane's suffering to witness and assimilate. It highlighted the dehumanization of prejudice, for it illustrated the ways in which the needs of the city's most vulnerable residents were either overlooked or systematically discounted, both in planning for and in response to the disaster. Further, analysis of the Thai doctors' response to the tsunami has also demonstrated how complex cultural factors may affect the process of triage in situations of trauma, particularly when resources are limited. Thus, prejudice and cultural difference affects decisions about which groups ultimately receive priority in care.

Seventh, analysis of recent disasters has again illustrated how *survivors' suffering may be heightened when the normal rituals associated with death are impeded.* When loved ones remain missing for months after the disaster, mourning is complex and unsatisfying. Likewise, the creation of mass graves and the inability to keep up with the pace of death that was experienced both in the tsunami and in the aftermath of Katrina inevitably lead to a dehumanization of the living and the dead. Ultimately, lack of care for the dead seems to make survivors themselves feel less than fully human through their inability to respond to and honor their dead in customary caring and ritual ways.

Having explored the key social and psychological themes emerging from our analyses of recent traumatic events, let us now consider the spiritual and theological themes they raise and the contributions of Julian's work in addressing them.

"All Shall Be Well":
The Triumph of Love over Death and Suffering

Our consideration of three recent traumatic events — 9/11, the tsunami, and Hurricane Katrina, along with the experience of AIDS loss — has reminded us once again of the terrible pain associated with suffering and trauma. Survivors struggling to find meaning in the wake of these tragedies appear to wrestle with a number of key theological and spiritual issues. These include the nature and presence of God in suffering, the nature of humans and their capacity for evil, the experience of human vulnerability and limitation, and the nature of immortality.

As our analysis of Julian's life and times revealed, Julian is fully cognizant of the reality of human suffering. Nevertheless, she does not resort to despair; rather, she articulates a hopeful view of life, a view that is grounded in the reality of God's love. Julian's understanding of God's nature consistently emphasizes God's all-embracing love and eschews any notion of God's wrath or judgment in the face of human limitations. In Julian's view, God's love for us is so creative and vital that it has the power to redeem all suffering and pain. Through her vision, Julian came to believe that the power of God's love is unquestionably greater than the power of sin and suffering. She came to this awareness through compassionately entering into the pain of Christ's crucifixion and experiencing within it the triumph of the resurrection, which trumped the pain of suffering and death. Thus, Christ's love for humanity transfigured the pain of the cross, which, in Julian's view, was the greatest pain a human had ever experienced. In other words, her reflection communicates her understanding that the presence of love amid suffering provides an experience of resurrection, of triumph over pain and death. Furthermore, since in her view the crucifixion encompassed all human suffering, which is attributable to sin and its effects, all of us are drawn to union with Christ through it, and we share in the triumph over pain and death that Christ revealed on the cross.

We have already noted that contemporary survivors of trauma experience in human connection a transfiguration of the pain of loss. We witnessed this transfiguration in the loving exchange between a dying parishioner and his pastor in the case of AIDS. We noted its presence in the deep experience of community that was articulated among those present in New Orleans during the hurricane. In that case, it was described as a "holding, hugging, human connection that was strengthened by the storm." In 9/11, it was present in the selflessness of the first responders and ordinary citizens who gave of themselves in crisis to help the vulnerable evacuate the Twin Towers. Each tragedy, besides revealing the pain of suffering and loss, also offers opportunities to glimpse the indomitable love and interconnection that are undeniably part of the human experience.

Thus, Julian's response to the question: "Where was God on 9/11, in the tsunami, or in the hurricane?" would be that God was present in each case as love. God was present in the acts of compassion that were everywhere observed amid the very real pain of these events. Julian's understanding of the nature of God is that God is pure love and is known in the triumph of creativity, compassion, and communion over the pain of sin, suffering, and death.

Second, we have seen that Julian spent much of her own life wrestling with the existence of evil in the form of sin. Through her reflection on the events of her own day, Julian came to the conclusion that suffering and evil, in the form of sin, are unavoidable realities of human existence. As humans begin to appreciate and experience the power of God's love, the power of sin diminishes as we seek to avoid it. Nevertheless, in Julian's view, sin is inevitable. As God's lovers, it is incumbent on us to dwell in God's love and to attempt to live in love rather than in sin, yet Julian believed that even saints would never be completely free of sin. Sin results from our blindness, from our inability to dwell in God's love. In this regard, Julian's views were very similar to those of Rabbi Irwin Kula, who in the wake of 9/11 expressed his belief that human alienation and loneliness result when we lose sight of the connectedness and oneness that are at the heart of reality and human community.[4]

What can survivors glean from Julian's theology to enable them to comprehend the disregard for human life that was a part of 9/11 or the evils of poverty and racism that contributed to the suffering of Katrina? I believe that Julian would find in them an expression of the human blindness that leads to such woes. These events grew out of the distortions, pride, and misplaced loves that are part of human existence. At the same time, she would encourage us to draw on the power of God's love to respond to the insults in these situations, not out of anger or judgment, but out of humility and compassion. As Julian herself became an advocate for those who were perceived as excluded from the knowledge of God's love and acceptance, so she would encourage us to find ways to communicate the concrete realities of God's love to those suffering from the pain of these events.

It is in learning to treat our adversaries with empathy and compassion, rather than wrath or condemnation, that we begin to transmute the reality of evil experienced amid trauma.

Third, despite the fact that Julian experienced a very vivid and personal encounter with Christ through her vision, what strikes me above all in my encounter with Julian's text is her humility and acceptance of her vulnerability. Through her theology and spirituality, Julian models a grounded wisdom and accceptance of all of life viewed through the lens of God's love. Julian's balanced appraisal of the joys and difficulties of human life is one of the most attractive aspects of her theology. It serves as a wholesome example to other survivors who wrestle with the same vexing questions that Julian explored. Julian frankly admits that "this place is a prison, this life is penance, and [God] wants us to rejoice in the remedy."[5] The remedy, in her view, is that rather than condemning us for our blindness and weakness, God protects us and leads us to fullness of joy. It is her unshakeable confidence in God's love that enables Julian to affirm that all shall be well. As we noted in our exploration of her theology, Julian's faith in God's goodness allowed her ultimately to accept God's affirmation of this fact, even though not all of her questions were fully resolved. Further, her trust in God's love enabled her to take very real risks in communicating her understanding of this fact to her fellow Christians. Nevertheless, despite the fact that Julian's vision was extraordinarily clear and compelling, she did not attempt to speak for God in any absolute way. Her reflections were always grounded in humility, and she was well aware of the limits of her understanding and expression. Thus, we see in Julian the humility of one who has suffered but who has learned to remain open to inquiry, ambiguity, and even outright contradictions between her experiences, the content of her vision, and the teaching of her church. Her confidence in God enabled her to adopt this humble stance, for her faith in God's love transcended her need for certainty. In the end, Julian's grounded wisdom and trust, along with her open and inquiring spirit and willingness to question God, remain as a model for survivors who struggle to understand God's nature and action in trauma. It also provides a powerful contrast to the absolutism that has characterized much religious discourse and conflict amid the trauma of our time.

Finally, Julian's writing helps to address the need survivors have encountered to embrace human mortality and affirm the continuity of life. Through her vision, Julian anticipated an unending life in God. The power of this vision fueled her imagination and enabled her to envision this blissful and enduring union with God. Nevertheless, Julian does not speculate about the exact nature of this fate. She is simply content to rest in God's assurance that she would not be overcome by life and its trials and chose to dwell in the certainty of God's love.

Analysis of the trauma and death due to violence, war, and pandemic in the twentieth and twenty-first centuries emphasizes both the need and urgency that we have to imagine the triumph of life and justice in the face of the many growing threats to both. Since the United States unleashed the power of nuclear weapons, people everywhere have faced the real possibility of the annihilation of life. Further our fear of the death of life has also been fueled through the images of massive death we have witnessed through genocide, war, and disaster in recent years.

Such experiences cry out for a revitalized theological treatment of death and immortality. How may we find hope in the face of our undeniable mortality? Our lack of compelling images and understanding of our ultimate fate only serves to fuel our anxiety about death and destruction amid the onslaught of death images to which we are exposed.

In this arena, Lifton's work on survivors offers both great promise and provocation to theologians. Lifton's notion of the continuity of life in the face of death envisions multiple avenues through which humans may imagine and re-create a sense of life's vitality. In a similar manner, Krister Stendahl's affirmation that resurrection is about the ultimate triumph of God's justice rather than individual survival offers us a stimulus for reinterpreting and revitalizing older and more individualistic understandings of traditional doctrines.[6] Contemporary survivors, overwhelmed by images of death and suffering, need robust theological resources to enable them to reinvigorate both their threatened vitality and their sense of life's purpose. Such resources, at their best, will not ask survivors to accept a diminished view of their present life in this world in favor of a more robust life in a world to come. What survivors need instead is a religious imagination that powerfully transfigures our view of present reality through compelling images of re-creation and salvation. Julian's articulate testimony to the power of love at the heart of the universe provided her with hope for life in this world and the life to come. Her unshakeable faith in the power of this dynamic and enduring love is her greatest contribution to contemporary survivors. Further, it provides contemporary theologians with an example of how religious imagination and vision may serve as a vital resource when confronting the inescapable fact of human mortality.

Making All Things New: Pastoral Praxis for and with Survivors of Traumatic Loss

Based on my experience with survivors of AIDS loss and on my reading and reflection on other forms of trauma, what can I now suggest with regard to pastoral praxis for survivors of multiple loss? The literature addressing the intersection of trauma and bereavement has been growing exponentially in recent years, and caregivers will find many excellent guides to help those afflicted by traumatic bereavement. The work particularly of Charles Figley, Therese Rando, Robert Neimeyer, and Robert Lifton offer help and hope to those working regularly with the traumatically bereaved.[7] Given these resources, I focus instead on the three important tasks I identified in chapter 1 as facing the bereaved, namely, to experience symptom relief; to reconstruct meaning and identity in a manner true to the suffering one has experienced; and to promote spiritual wholeness.

As regards symptom relief, I have already mentioned the variety of techniques that psychologists have developed to address this need. They include cognitive and behavioral therapies, grounding techniques, EMRD,[8] and group therapy. When considering symptom relief, pastors who have experience with soothing forms of prayer, including the use of breath prayer, the rosary, centering prayer, and other forms of meditation, have important tools for offering care and hope. Pastors may work as partners with psychologists in contributing knowledge of resources that offer peace and a calming sense of God's presence amid loss. Pastors may also assist in offering what the World Health Organization describes as "psychological first aid" to survivors."[9] This includes listening; conveying compassion; assessing physical, emotional, and spiritual needs; ensuring that basic physical needs are met; not forcing survivors to talk; providing company, preferably of family, friends, and significant others; encouraging social support; and protecting survivors from further harm. It is important for pastors, also, to acknowledge the limits of their own knowledge and care and to know when and how to refer survivors for additional care. Andrew Weaver, Laura Flannelly, and John Preston have prepared a useful handbook for pastors and other professionals who counsel survivors of traumatic events, and this book includes a helpful chapter on referring to a mental health specialist.[10] Throughout their care for survivors, it is critically important for pastors to "normalize the abnormal" by communicating to survivors that many of the troubling symptoms experienced in the aftermath of grief and trauma, such as sleeplessness, agitation, and nightmares, are a common consequence of the distress they have experienced.

A second need of survivors is to reconstruct their meaning and identity in a manner that is true to the suffering they have experienced. We have already explored the psychological approaches that Neimeyer and Sewell and Williams have developed to assist in this task. Pastoral psychotherapists have also developed narrative approaches that may aid survivors in the process of reconstructing meaning. Andrew Lester, in his important book *Hope in Pastoral Care and Counseling*, describes how pastoral psychotherapists can help clients to explore and construct future stories that provide them with hope following experiences of pain. With the help of tools such as dreams, free association, guided imagery, storytelling, and "as if" conversations, clients may be empowered to develop a narrative about their own future that counteracts the depression or despair they are experiencing in the present. By helping clients to more consciously connect their stories to sacred stories pastors can also help to provide a sense of meaning and incorporate theological content that is life-affirming. This work builds on the understanding that human crises and emotional suffering result not only from disturbances in the present, but also from lost, distorted, or dysfunctional future stories.[11]

The third task that survivors face is addressing the need for spiritual wholeness. Pastors have a wide array of resources that may be helpful in this task. First, the ritual care that they provide both for the living and for the dead is an important source of comfort in times of loss. Ritual particularly helps to orient survivors toward a religious and spiritual context in which they may engage the trauma and losses they have experienced. My work at All Saints Church taught me how important sacramental, musical, and liturgical resources can be in alleviating grief. These resources allow for the expression of emotion in a multisensory context. They also provide a rich symbolic context, thus addressing the need Lifton has found in survivors for reviving the capacity to create symbols. Pastors can draw on rich scriptural, liturgical, and artistic resources in their ministries of healing care to the dying and bereaved.

Second, pastors and religious communities have at their disposal a plethora of community resources that can help survivors to overcome a sense of isolation and to experience the power of shared memory as a resource in healing. My research at All Saints demonstrated how helpful it was for a grieving community to have the opportunity to gather together in times of loss. Parishioners at All Saints commented on the usefulness of "wakes" in the rectory and the shaping of a "second" requiem on Sunday for the parish family when faced with the death of significant loved ones. Further, annual services of remembrance focused on important anniversaries (such as the anniversary of 9/11) provide a chance for parishioners and community members to come together around their loss. These communal events help to facilitate the honest sharing of feelings, including sadness and grief, and help those mourning to feel connected rather than isolated in their loss.

The power of remembrance grounded in a sacred space also provides a key resource in healing from loss. At All Saints, the community profited from the construction of a garden dedicated to the memory of the departed. Further, the presence of beautiful memorial gifts also aided remembrance. The ability of the pastor to tell warm, personal stories about the departed also proved to be an important resource for this congregation in healing from the loss of dear loved ones. The sharing of stories facilitated remembrance, but more important, it allowed celebration of the uniqueness of each and every deceased parishioner. Projects such as the Names Quilt have demonstrated the value of creating a ritual way in which to remember deceased individuals in situations of overwhelming loss.

The parish setting also provides many opportunities for education and support that may be particularly helpful to survivors of traumatic loss. All Saints offered an AIDS support group, and it provided parishioners with an opportunity to share feelings and strategies for coping with illness and loss. Support groups for the bereaved, for caregivers, and for other vulnerable populations can help those struggling to cope with trauma and grief. Further, pastors have important opportunities to educate communities about the dynamics of grief and its healthy resolution. In framing educational programs, pastors should attend to individual differences in the grief process, the particular challenges posed by multiple loss and cumulative loss, the varied beliefs and schemas that are altered by traumatic loss and their implications for theology and spirituality, the varieties of strategies that help to resolve grief, and the importance of achieving closure with the dying. Psychological research has helped to dispel a number of myths surrounding the grief process, and exposure to these findings may improve the care pastors and communities offer to those who mourn.[12] Further, helping survivors to identify the particular burdens they bear and the specific impediments to coping they experience may foster greater healing and wholeness.

Pastors also have at their disposal important ritual resources that can help survivors to begin to lighten the burden of guilt they may carry in situations of traumatic loss. The rite of reconciliation provides an important ritual way of helping survivors come to terms with the guilt they are experiencing and to forgive themselves for what they were unable to do in times of trauma. The work of James Pennebaker suggests that providing parishioners and other mourners with opportunities to write and talk about the suffering they have experienced may also help to alleviate survivor guilt.[13] Assisting parishioners in expressing their anger toward God and in openly articulating fears they may have about losing their faith because of trauma can help survivors to move beyond crippling doubts and to forge increasingly effective theological worldviews that are robust enough to sustain them in times of traumatic loss.

Lifton's writing, in conjunction with my experience at All Saints, has also taught me how valuable advocacy can be as a tool in recovery. Advocacy requires the ability to build bridges of empathy and compassion to others who suffer. In situations where oppression has contributed to the suffering of mourners, as in Katrina and the AIDS pandemic, survivors can gain strength and power from directly addressing the injustices that have led to the deaths they witnessed. As Lifton notes each of us has resources drawn from our everyday life experience that can be offered to alleviate suffering and to address injustice. One way to overcome the sense of meaninglessness and despair that can threaten to engulf us as survivors is to contribute our gifts and energy to improving the world, by helping those who suffer or by working for political and social change. Artists can offer imagery that fosters a healthy sense of transcendence, and religious communities can offer both practical help and the witness of prayer for healing and peace. In such ways, we may strengthen Julian's sense that "all may be well" by adding our creativity, agency, and love to that which we experience in God through faith.

"To Embrace the Whole World": *Transfiguring Loss, Celebrating Love*

In his book *Superpower Syndrome: America's Apocalyptic Confrontation with the World*, Robert Lifton recounts an important story that offers guidance to survivors and to those who would assist them. He was describing the early stages of his work with Nazi doctors. He had completed a first set of interviews in Germany and then went to visit a friend who was an Auschwitz survivor with a keen interest in Lifton's research. Lifton notes:

> As we sat over coffee, I said to him in a tone that was not without a bit of self-pity: "I appreciate your encouragement, but the truth is that I've begun to have terrible dreams. In my dreams, I'm behind barbed wire in some kind of camp. Worse than that, my wife, and at times my two children, are there in the camp with me." My friend looked directly at me and answered in a matter-of-fact tone that was neither unkind nor especially sympathetic, "Good, now you can do the study."[14]

Lifton concluded that his friend was telling him that unless he took in some small part of the victims' pain, his work would have little significance.

Throughout this book, I have struggled to describe the way in which Julian's theology of hope was forged in a crucible of struggle and loss. While it may be easy to conclude from the optimistic tone of her theology that she was untouched by grief, this is far from the truth. Julian, a survivor herself, struggled mightily to offer her fellow Christians a more hopeful and loving view of God than the religious authorities of her day propounded. Clearly, she was touched by the suffering of those who sought counsel from her in coping with the pain of the losses they and she had endured. From what we know of her time, it seems likely that she risked either censure or persecution for sharing her views on these subjects in writing. Nevertheless, Julian wrote about her visions because she believed in the message of comfort and reassurance with which she had been entrusted.

Our world is in need of both comfort and courage. When I began this work in May of 2001, I did not realize the tremendous suffering that lay just around the corner for many in our nation and world. The events of September 11 soon followed, and these led, in turn, to the wars in Afghanistan and Iraq. As I labored on, new and equally devastating forms of suffering arose in Southeast Asia and on the U.S. Gulf Coast. Like many Americans, I have watched with horror the tremendous loss of lives that may be attributed to our nation's military strategies, and I have also grieved over the lives lost through tremors, wind, and waves.

My review of research on traumatic loss, however, has helped to remind me of the power of the human spirit to prevail in desperate times. I have learned two important lessons from my work that offer hope. First, I have learned that the power of transcendent love can transfigure grief. When viewed through the lens of love, grief becomes the doorway to a profound emotional and spiritual awakening that softens the heart and enables a degree of intimacy that heals. Nevertheless, this transformation is often hard won. As an AIDS survivor at All Saints commented: "For me, it was always a balance between wanting to embrace the whole world and then wanting to shut it all out. And all the distancing, I think, was because of the fear of being totally overwhelmed, totally crushed by the whole." Nevertheless, he continued, "thinking back to that period when AIDS was so much a part of everyone's life, it just elevated everything to a new level. It was such a profound experience to be in the presence of so much loss that was unexplainable that every person became more precious."[15]

His insight leads me to the second important lesson I have learned: that grief provides a tangible reminder of the interconnection between human beings, of the responsibility we feel for one another, and of the union we share in love. Why else does grief cause such pain? As John Donne wrote centuries ago: "No man is an *Island*, entire of itself; every man is a piece of the *Continent*, a part of the *main*; if a *Clod* be washed away by the *Sea*, *Europe* is the less, as well as if a *Promontory* were, as well as if a *Manor* of thy *friends* or of *thine own* were; any man's *death* diminishes *me*, because I am involved in *Mankind*."[16] Through this meditation, Donne reminds us of the underlying truth revealed in survivor guilt, perhaps the most painful and debilitating aspect of traumatic loss, namely, that we are indeed connected to our neighbor and responsible for his or her welfare. This truth is no less evident in plague, in war, or in natural disaster. We grieve when we cannot prevent the suffering or death of our fellow human beings. The union between us seems writ on our very souls as an expression of the *imago dei*, for just as the Godhead is a diverse and interpenetrating community, so are we.

Given the power of these lessons, I hope and pray that we will find ways to overcome the tendencies toward the denial of death and the numbing we experience through constant exposure to war and suffering and to reach out to those around the world who need our empathy, compassion, and care. Many forces in the world today conspire to mask the essential connection that binds us one to another in a web of love and care. Our own experience as survivors, when it remains unexplored and unaccepted, may blind us to the economic, social, political, and religious forces that encourage us to emphasize our differences rather than our interdependence.

As a testimony to the power of Julian's life and ministry to remind us of these bonds of unity and to offer peace and reconciliation, I conclude this book with a story first shared by Robert

Llewelyn in his book *With Pity Not with Blame: The Spirituality of Julian of Norwich and The Cloud of Unknowing*. For many years, Robert Llewelyn, an Anglican priest, served as a chaplain at the Julian shrine in Norwich. He reports that early in the summer of 1974, a blind man and his friend made their way to visit the Julian Cell. This man had been a prisoner of war in the custody of the Japanese. During this captivity, he had been mistreated and his blindness had resulted from this treatment. While he and his companion were kneeling in prayer in the Julian shrine, Julian herself appeared to the man and brought with her the Japanese soldier who had mistreated him. According to Llewelyn, this dead man had come to seek forgiveness from his war-time victim, who had not yet been able to release the bitterness that he had felt toward his own captor. The blind man was heard to speak in Japanese to his captor. Following this conversation, he was released from his resentment and experienced tremendous joy and peace. The two visitors then retired to the adjacent guest house for tea, and in the course of this visit, the vision was repeated. Once again, the visitor engaged in an animated conversation in Japanese with his unseen companions. Obviously freed from the burden of resentment and pain through his visionary encounter, the man went on his way in great happiness and peace.[17]

Llewelyn's story testifies to the ongoing power of Julian's revelations of love to produce healing and communion. While those who seek inspiration from her work may not experience a dramatic personal revelation, nevertheless, they may find solace and hope through her work. Through both the vibrancy of her prose and the compelling character of her theology and personality, Julian continues to reach out to survivors who search for meaning and the courage to live anew in the knowledge that "all shall be well." May you find in her work healing, hope, and the continued assurance of God's unfailing love.

Notes

Preface

1. These details about Julian's life and visions are disclosed in her written accounts of these events. See *Julian of Norwich: Showings,* trans. Edmund Colledge and James Walsh (New York: Paulist Press, 1978) for translations from Middle English of both the Short and Long Texts. Julian used the term "even Christians" to refer to her fellow Christians. It is derived from a word meaning "hold together," and thus, it suggests the unity she shares with fellow believers.

2. Lifton introduced the concept of the "survivor mission" in his book *Death in Life: Survivors of Hiroshima* (New York: Basic Books, 1967). See especially the discussion on 302–5.

3. Julian of Norwich, *Revelation of Love,* ed. and trans. John Skinner (Evesham, Worcestershire: Arthur James, 1996; New York: Doubleday, 1997), 38–39. For future reference, all chapter citations from the Skinner translation refer to the Long Text. This translation is based upon Marion Glasscoe's critical edition. Page numbers are drawn from the Arthur James Edition.

4. Lifton's descriptive term "death in life" describes an entire complex of psychological characteristics of those who survive death encounters. However, his description of psychic numbing particularly captures the essence of this experience. See *Death in Life,* 500–510.

5. Rebecca S. Chopp, "Theology and the Poetics of Testimony," *Criterion* 37 (Winter 1998): 2–12.

6. Ibid.

Chapter One: The Experience of Traumatic Loss

1. Fenton Johnson, *Geography of the Heart: A Memoir* (New York: Scribner, 1996), 233. The quotation is from a letter of Wendell Berry to Johnson.

2. JW, interview by author, October 12, 1999. The initials reflect a pseudonym given to the interviewee to maintain his privacy. This and all other interviews by the author may be found in Jane Maynard, *Finding Religious and Spiritual Meaning in AIDS-Related*

Multiple Loss: A Comparative and Constructive Theological Analysis of Communal Bereavement (Ann Arbor, Mich.: Proquest, UMI Microform 3123956, 1994).

3. The experiences summarized in this account may be accessed at *www.sharedexperience.org/wtc/experienceedit.lasso?VisitorRole=* *&CommentGeneral=Annette%20Juneau&Oper=And&Skip=0.*

4. This account draws on material accessed at *www.livejournal .com/users/coolprasad.* The entry is dated January 4, 2005.

5. This account is based on an interview published in Steve Perry, "New Orleans Survivor Stories" in *City Pages* 26, no. 1294 (September 20, 2005): 11, online at *www.citypages.com/databank/26/1294/article13694.asp?page=11.*

6. Kathleen R. Gilbert, "Traumatic Loss and Grief," Unit 12 in an online course entitled "Grief in a Family Context," Fall 2005, and accessed at *www.indiana.edu/~famlygrf/units/traumatic.html.*

7. Ibid.

8. Jeannette Ambrose, "Traumatic Grief: What We Need to Know as Trauma Survivors," *www.ctsn-rcst.ca/Traumaticgrief.html.*

9. Erich Lindemann, "Symptomatology and Management of Acute Grief," *American Journal of Psychiatry* 101 (1944): 141–48, and Mardi J. Horowitz, *Stress Response Syndrome* (New York: Jason Aronson, 1976).

10. Charles R. Figley, Brian E. Bride, and Nicholas Mazza, eds., *Death and Trauma: The Traumatology of Grieving* (Washington, D.C.: Taylor and Francis, 1997).

11. Therese Rando, *Grief, Dying and Death: Clinical Interventions for Caregivers* (Champaign, Ill.: Research Press, 1984), and *Treatment of Complicated Mourning* (Champaign, Ill.: Research Press, 1993); Beverly Raphael, *The Anatomy of Bereavement* (New York: Basic Books, 1983), and *When Disaster Strikes: How Individuals and Communities Cope with Catastrophe* (New York: Basic Books, 1986); Colin M. Parkes and Robert S. Weiss, *Recovery from Bereavement* (New York: Basic Books, 1983).

12. Therese Rando, "Foreword," in Figley, Bride, and Mazza, *Death and Trauma*, xvii.

13. This work is cited in Gilbert, "Traumatic Loss and Grief."

14. Ibid.

15. Robert J. Lifton, *Superpower Syndrome: America's Apocalyptic Confrontation with the World* (New York: Thunder's Mouth Press/Nation Books, 1993), 138.

16. Gilbert, "Traumatic Loss and Grief" and Ambrose, "Traumatic Grief."

17. Ambrose, "Traumatic Grief."

18. Ibid.

19. Rando, "Foreword," xvii.

20. B. Green, M. Grace, and G. Leser, "Identifying Survivors at Risk: Long-Term Impairment Following the Beverly Hills Supper Club Fire," *Journal of Clinical and Consulting Psychology* 53, no. 5 (October 1985): 672–78.

21. Rando, "Foreword," xvii.

22. Ambrose, "Traumatic Grief."

23. Robert A. Neimeyer, "Traumatic Loss and the Reconstruction of Meaning," *Innovations in End-of-Life Care* 3, no. 6 (2001), *www.edc.org/lastacts.*

24. Ibid.

25. The research of Holly Prigerson and her associates is described in Neimeyer, "Traumatic Loss and the Reconstruction of Meaning."

26. Neimeyer, "Traumatic Loss and the Reconstruction of Meaning."

27. Andrew J. Weaver, Laura T. Flannelly, and John D. Preston, *Counseling Survivors of Traumatic Events: A Handbook for Pastors and Other Helping Professionals* (Nashville: Abingdon Press, 2003), 100.

28. Lifton, *Superpower Syndrome*, 40.

29. David Baldwin, "Trauma Information Pages," available online at *www.trauma-pages.com*, February 8, 2006, version.

30. Neimeyer, "Traumatic Loss and the Reconstruction of Meaning."

31. Robert J. Lifton, "The Concept of the Survivor" in *The Future of Immortality and Other Essays for a Nuclear Age* (New York: Basic Books, 1987), 235.

32. Ibid., 236.

33. Lifton, *Death in Life*, 480–81.

34. Robert J. Lifton, *The Broken Connection: On Death and the Continuity of Life* (New York: Simon & Schuster, 1979), 171.

35. Ibid., 172

36. Ibid.

37. Ibid., 175.

38. Lifton, "The Concept of the Survivor," 241. This phenomenon was particularly troubling for concentration camp survivors who "on entering the camp in the morning would have been dead by nightfall if they had adhered to all the ethical and moral standards of civilian life." See William G. Niederland, "Psychiatric Disorders among Persecution

Victims," *Journal of Nervous and Mental Diseases* 139 (1964): 458–74, 468; cited in Lifton, *Death in Life,* 487. The relationship between life and death often seemed random in the camps.

39. Ibid.

40. Lifton, *Death in Life,* 367.

41. Baldwin, "Trauma Information Pages."

42. Thomas Attig, "Relearning the World: Making and Finding Meanings," in *Meaning Reconstruction and the Experience of Loss,* ed. Robert A. Neimeyer (Washington, D.C.: American Psychological Association, 2001), 35.

43. This description draws on Sandra M. Schneiders's widely accepted definition of spirituality. See Schneiders, "Christian Spirituality: Definitions, Methods and Types," in *The New Westminster Dictionary of Christian Spirituality,* ed. Philip Sheldrake (Louisville: Westminster John Knox, 2005), 1–6.

44. Kenneth Sewell and Amy Williams, "Construing Stress: A Constructivist Therapeutic Approach to Posttraumatic Stress Reactions," in Neimeyer, *Meaning Reconstruction,* 299.

45. Dennis Klass, "The Inner Representation of the Dead Child in the Psychic and Social Narratives of Bereaved Parents," in Neimeyer, *Meaning Reconstruction,* 77–94.

46. Neimeyer, "Preface," in Neimeyer, *Meaning Reconstruction,* xii.

47. Attig, "Relearning the World," 33–53. See also Thomas Attig, *How We Grieve: Relearning the World* (New York: Oxford University Press, 1996).

48. Ronnie Janoff-Bulman, *Shattered Assumptions: Towards a New Psychology of Trauma* (New York: Free Press, 1992); Colin M. Parkes, *Bereavement: Studies of Grief in Adult Life* (New York: International University Press, 1972); P. Marris, "Attachment and Society," in *The Place of Attachment in Human Behavior,* ed. C. M. Parkes and J. Stevenson-Hinde (New York: Basic Books, 1982), 185–204; and F. R. Epting and R. A. Neimeyer, eds., *Personal Meanings of Death: Applications of Personal Construct Theory to Clinical Practice* (Washington, D.C.: Hemisphere, 1984).

49. Charles Figley, *Helping Traumatized Families* (San Francisco: Jossey-Bass, 1989).

50. See the work of Mardi Horowitz, "Psychosocial Responses to Serious Life Events," in *Human Stress and Cognition,* ed. Vernon Hamilton and David M. Warburton (New York: Wiley, 1979), and Horowitz's *Stress Response Syndrome.* I am indebted to Kathleen Gilbert for her discussion of this material. See her chapter, "Couple

Coping with the Death of a Child," in Figley, Bride and Mazza, *Death and Trauma*, 101–21.

51. Sewell and Williams, "Construing Stress."

52. Lifton, *Death in Life*. See especially chap. 9, "Formulation: Self and World," 367–96.

53. See the beautiful description of this process in Stephen Levine, *Unattended Sorrow: Recovering from Loss and Reviving the Heart* (Emmaus, Pa.: Rodale, 2005).

54. Lifton, *Superpower Syndrome*.

Chapter Two: The Fourteenth Century and Its Perils

1. James Tait, ed., "Chronica Johannis de Reading et Anonymi Cantuariensis, 1346–1367," in *The Black Death*, ed. and trans. Rosemary Horrox, Manchester Medieval Sources Series (Manchester: Manchester University Press, 1994), 74.

2. Barbara W. Tuchman, *A Distant Mirror: The Calamitous 14th Century* (New York: Ballantine Books, 1978), xiii–xiv.

3. Julian, *Revelation*, chap. 27, 48.

4. T. S. R. Boase, *Death in the Middle Ages: Mortality, Judgment, and Remembrance*, ed. Joan Evans and Christopher Brooke, Library of Medieval Civilization (London: Thames & Hudson, 1972), 9.

5. Tuchman, *Distant Mirror*, xix.

6. Julian, *Revelation*, 4. However, as Grace Jantzen notes in *Julian of Norwich: Mystic and Theologian* (London: SPCK, 1987), 13, n. 10, variant readings in the manuscripts of Julian's work have yielded some uncertainty about this date. According to Jantzen, Colledge and Walsh, editors of the critical edition of Julian's work, follow the Paris manuscript and set the date at May 13 (xiij), whereas other authorities, including Skinner and Jantzen, follow the Sloane manuscript's viij. According to Brant Pelphrey in *Love Was His Meaning: The Theology and Mysticism of Julian of Norwich* (Salzburg: Institut für Anglistik und Amerikanistik, Universität Salzburg, 1982), 1, n. 1, Julian's reference to the Passion and to Easter implied in her visions yields a preference for the May 8 date, as this fell on the third Sunday after Easter in 1373.

7. Julian of Norwich, *A Shewing of God's Love*, ed. Anna Maria Reynolds (London: Sheed & Ward, 1958), lviii. For future reference, quotations from Reynolds are from the Short Text.

8. However, as Jantzen, *Julian of Norwich*, 20, correctly observes, this evidence is not definitive, since "Julian" was a common name at this time. In addition, it was the practice for anchoresses to adopt

their name from the church in which their cell was located. Therefore, it is theoretically possible that this bequest was for another
anchoress named Julian who resided at the Church of St. Julian at
Conisford, a Saxon-Norman church on the Wensum River. However,
most scholars, given the dates associated with the manuscripts and
Julian's vision, assume that it is indeed plausible that this bequest
was made to the anchoress we know as the author of the *Revelations.*

9. Jantzen, *Julian of Norwich,* 21.

10. Margery Kempe, *The Book of Margery Kempe,* trans. B. A.
Windeatt, rev. ed. (New York: Penguin, 1994), 77.

11. See, for example, Pelphrey, *Love Was His Meaning,* 12.

12. Denise Nowakowski Baker, *Julian of Norwich's Showings:
From Vision to Book* (Princeton, N.J.: Princeton University Press,
1994), 4.

13. Minority opinions are offered by Nicholas Watson and Julia Bolton Holloway. Watson believes that the Amherst manuscript
reflects the greater anxiety of the period closer to 1413, when Arch-
bishop Arundel of Norwich, in response to the Wycliffites, was
prohibiting lay people, especially women, from teaching theology. He
suggests that the Long Text was written later than the Short Text
when Julian would have been eighty-five or ninety. In contrast, Holloway agrees that the Short Text is late, but argues that the Long
Text's traditional date of approximately 1373 is right, thus revers-
ing the order of composition and assuming that the Short Text is
composed after the Long Text. See Nicholas Watson, "The Composition of Julian of Norwich's *Revelation of Love*," *Speculum* 68 (1993):
637–83, and "Censorship and Cultural Change in Late-Medieval
England: Vernacular Theology, the Oxford Translation Debate, and
Arundel's Constitutions of 1409," *Speculum* 70 (1995): 822–64; and
Julia Bolton Holloway, "Anchoress and Cardinal: Julian of Norwich
and Adam Easton, O.S.B.," lecture delivered at Norwich Cathedral,
Norwich, England, December 1, 1998.

14. For a lively account of Julian's background see Sheila Upjohn,
In Search of Julian of Norwich (London: Darton, Longman & Todd,
1989). Theories about Julian's level of education, in particular, abound.
On the one hand, Colledge and Walsh believe that Julian was "a master of rhetorical art to merit comparison with Chaucer" who was well
versed in the Latin Vulgate and familiar with the foundational texts
of the monastic contemplative tradition of the Western Church. See
Julian of Norwich, *Showings,* trans. Edmund Colledge and James Walsh
(New York: Paulist, 1978), 19–21. On the other hand, Brant Pelphrey

suggests that Julian may have been uneducated, possessing only rudimentary literary skills, and may have composed her text with the help of a scribe. Like Jantzen, *Julian of Norwich*, 15–20, I would argue that the truth falls somewhere between these two extremes.

15. I am indebted to Pelphrey, *Love Was His Meaning*, 41, for this list of figures.

16. Tuchman, *Distant Mirror*, 69.

17. Jantzen, *Julian of Norwich*, 7.

18. Norman P. Tanner, *The Church in Late Medieval Norwich, 1370–1532* (Toronto: Pontifical Institute of Medieval Studies, 1984); Roberta Gilchrist and Marilyn Oliva, *Religious Women in Medieval East Anglia: History and Archaeology*, Studies in East Anglian History, 1 (Norwich, England: Centre of East Anglian Studies, University of East Anglia, 1993).

19. Tanner, *Church in Late Medieval Norwich*, 167.

20. Ibid, 168.

21. Ibid., 169.

22. Tuchman, *Distant Mirror*, 25.

23. Ibid., 25.

24. Ibid., 26.

25. Ibid., 28.

26. Ibid., 250.

27. Ibid., 30.

28. Julian of Norwich, *Revelation of Love*, chap. 28, 56.

29. Tuchman, *Distant Mirror*, 403.

30. Ibid., 402.

31. Ibid., 403.

32. Jantzen, *Julian of Norwich*, 10, provides three possible origins for the term "lollard": she notes it is a term "derived from a combination of a Middle Dutch word meaning 'a mumbler of prayers,'" and a Middle English word meaning "loafer," and made even more abusive by a pun with the Latin "lolia" which means "tares."

33. See Tanner, *Church in Late Medieval Norwich*, 165–66.

34. Julian of Norwich, *Shewing of God's Love*, 17.

35. Julian of Norwich, *Revelation of Love*, 57.

36. Tuchman, *Distant Mirror*, 195.

37. Richard Butler, ed., "Annalium Hibernae Chronicon," Irish Archaeological Society, 1849, 37, in Horrox, *Black Death*, 84.

38. Horrox, *Black Death*, 229.

39. J. M. W. Bean, "The Black Death: The Crisis and Its Social and Economic Consequences," in *The Impact of the Fourteenth Century Plague*, ed. Daniel Williman (Binghamton, N.Y.: Center for

Medieval and Early Renaissance Studies, 1982), 23; quoted in Philip Lindley, "The Black Death and English Art: A Debate and Some Assumptions," in *The Black Death in England*, ed. Mark Ormrod and Phillip Lindley (Stamford, Lincolnshire, England: Paul Watkins, 1996), 136, n. 51.

40. Horrox, *Black Death*, 234.

41. Norman Cantor, *In the Wake of the Plague: The Black Death and the World It Made* (New York: Free Press, 2001; New York: Perennial, 2002). Citations are to the Perennial edition.

42. Graham Twigg's research, which may be found in *The Black Death: A Biological Reappraisal* (London: Batsford, 1984), is described in Cantor, *In the Wake of the Plague*, 14.

43. Cantor, *In the Wake of the Plague*, 15–16.

44. Tuchman, *Distant Mirror*, 93. Robert S. Gottfried gives a full account of the hypothesized origin of the plague in the East and its spread through Eurasia in *The Black Death: Natural and Human Disaster in Medieval Europe* (New York: Free Press, 1983), 33–42.

45. A. W. Henschel, "Document zur Geschichte des schwarzen Todes," in *Archiv für die gesammte Medicin*, ed. Heinrich Haeser, II, Jena, 1841, in Horrox, *The Black Death*, 17.

46. Gottfried, *Black Death*, 50.

47. Ibid., 55.

48. Ibid., 65.

49. Ibid., 66.

50. Ibid., 77.

51. Jim Bolton, " 'The World Upside Down': Plague as an Agent of Economic and Social Change," in *The Black Death in England*, 30.

52. See T. S. R. Boase, *Death in the Middle Ages*, 98–103, for depictions of these tombs.

53. As Tuchman notes, the "Black Death" received this name only in later recurrences. It was known during the first epidemic as "The Pestilence" or "Great Mortality." See Tuchman, *Distant Mirror*, 101.

54. Horrox, *Black Death*, 3.

55. Giovanni Boccaccio, *The Decameron*, trans. G. H. McWilliam (Harmondsworth: Penguin Classics, 1972), in Horrox, *Black Death*, 32.

56. "Continuation Novimontensis," *Monumenta Germaniae Historica — scriptorum* IX, ed. G. H. Pertz (Hanover, 1851), in Horrox, *Black Death*, 59.

57. William Dene, *Anglia Sacra* (London: Henry Wharton, 1691), British Library, Cottonian MS, Faustina B V fos 96v–101, in Horrox, *Black Death*, 70.

58. Boccaccio, *Decameron*, in Horrox, *Black Death*, 32–33.

59. Gilles li Muisis from J.-J. de Smet, ed., *Recueil des Chroniques de Flandre II* (Brussels, 1841), in Horrox, *Black Death*, 46.

60. Bishop Ralph of Bath and Wells, cited in Francis A. Gasquet, *The Black Death of 1348 and 1349*, 2nd ed. (London: Bell & Sons, 1908), 94.

61. Boccaccio, *Decameron*, in Horrox, *Black Death*, 30.

62. Gabriele de Mussis, *Historia de Morbo*, in Horrox, *Black Death*, 22.

63. Ibid., 23.

64. Ziegler, *Black Death*, 54.

65. Horrox, *Black Death*, 108.

66. The sense of "loss of community" is one of the most significant effects observed in twentieth-century accounts of multiple loss. See, for example, Kai T. Erikson's account of this phenomenon in the Buffalo Creek disaster in his chapter entitled "Collective Trauma: Loss of Communality" in his book *Everything in Its Path: Destruction of Community in the Buffalo Creek Flood* (New York: Simon & Schuster, 1976), 186–245.

67. Boccaccio, *Decameron*, in Horrox, *Black Death*, 29.

68. Cortusii Patavina Duo, sive Gulielmi et Abrigeti Contusiorum Historia de Novitatibus Paduae et Lombardiae ab anno MCCLVI usque as MCCCLXIV, in L. A. Muratori, ed., *Rerum Italicarum Scriptores XII* (Milan, 1728), in Horrox, *Black Death*, 34–35.

69. Horrox, *Black Death*, 224–26.

70. Besides the dominant religious explanation, contemporary accounts provide a number of scientific explanations for the plague. These include the famous astrological explanation offered by the faculty of the University of Paris that attributed the plague to the 1345 conjunction of Mars, Saturn, and Jupiter. More sophisticated explanations attempted to wed this astrological phenomenon with the belief in humors to explain why some grew ill and others did not. Other scientific explanations implicated a corruption in the air that was, at times, attributed to the release of foul vapors from earthquakes that preceded the plague. The popularity of this explanation explains why fourteenth-century art shows doctors ministering to plague victims with pomanders before their faces to protect them from foul odors. It was also known that the plague could be contracted through contact with the dying and their possessions, although the exact means of infection was obviously unknown. In addition, some thought that worry or brooding on the plague could bring on its symptoms. Finally, the explanation that has been most ridiculed, but one that made sense

given the theories of vision prevalent in the day, was the belief that the plague could be contracted through sight, through looking at those who were infected. For a survey of these interesting pseudo-scientific explanations, see Horrox, *Black Death*, 158–206.

71. Horrox, *Black Death*, 14–26.

72. De Mussis, *Historia de Morbo*, in Horrox, *Black Death*, 14.

73. Ibid., 15. Note how de Mussis's description of God's judgment captures the principal failings of the fourteenth century that we have already observed.

74. This accounts for the allusions to the story of Jonah that occur, for example, in the pastoral letter of Ralph of Shrewsbury, bishop of Bath and Wells. In it he calls upon the faithful to confess their sins, recite psalms, and perform works of mercy so that they may be rescued from destruction as the people of Nineveh were in the days of the prophet. See Horrox, *Black Death*, 112–13.

75. For sins associated with tournaments, see Henry Knighton's account in Horrox, *Black Death*, 130. For a critique of fashion, see especially the chronicle of John of Reading in Horrox, *Black Death*, 31–34.

76. William Langland, *Piers the Plowman*, in Horrox, *Black Death*, 136.

77. Horrox, *Black Death*, 98.

78. Ibid., 146.

79. Ibid., 95. Interestingly, St. Michael the Archangel also became a patron in a San Francisco parish during the AIDS epidemic, as this same saint was viewed as a source of strength and protection for parishioners.

80. Tuchman, *Distant Mirror*, 99–100.

81. Horrox, *Black Death*, 147–48.

82. John B. Friedman, "He hath a thousand slayn this pestilence': The Iconography of the Plague in the Late Middle Ages," in *Social Unrest in the Late Middle Ages*, ed. Francis X. Newman (Binghamton, N.Y.: Medieval and Renaissance Texts and Studies, 1986, 75–112), 85.

83. Ibid.

84. Horrox, *Black Death*, 97.

85. Friedman, "Iconography of the Plague in the Late Middle Ages," 85–88.

86. Philip Ziegler, *The Black Death* (New York: Harper & Row, 1971), 97.

87. Ibid., 97–98.

88. Cantor, *In the Wake of the Plague*, 150.

89. Ibid., 151.

90. Ibid., 160.

91. Ibid., 163.

92. Ibid.

93. Tuchman, *Distant Mirror,* 110.

94. Ibid., 110–13.

95. Chronicle of Gilles li Musis, cited in Tuchman, *Distant Mirror,* 109.

96. Tuchman, *Distant Mirror,* 115.

97. Ibid., 116.

98. As Ziegler notes, a number of European rulers did attempt to protect their Jewish subjects. The town councilors of Cologne urged their colleagues at Strasbourg to deal with the Jews more moderately, although their efforts were unsuccessful. Casimir of Poland, under the influence of his Jewish mistress, Esther, was able to prevent persecution there. Finally, Pedro IV of Aragon intervened on behalf of Jews whose homes had been attacked by the residents of Barcelona. He also intervened on behalf of several leading Jews in Tarragona who had been ruined by the loss of their homes and documents. When the plague returned in 1361, the Jews appealed to him for protection and he set an armed guard at the gates of the ghetto. See Ziegler, *Black Death,* 106–8.

99. Ibid., 109.

100. Horrox, *Black Death,* 236.

101. Christopher Harper-Bill, "The English Church and English Religion after the Black Death," in *The Black Death in England,* ed. Ormrod and Lindley, 83.

102. Ziegler, *Black Death,* 260.

103. Ibid.

104. These aspects of clergy behavior are noted by a number of observers. See, for example, Horrox, *Black Death,* 241–42, 310–12.

105. Horrox, *Black Death,* 242.

106. Ziegler, *Black Death,* 272.

107. Ibid., 274.

108. Horrox, *Black Death,* 244.

109. Ibid., 245.

Chapter Three: Julian as Survivor

The phrase "You Are My Heaven" is taken from Skinner, *Revelation of Love,* chap. 19, 37. Julian utters these words in making her decision not to turn away from the vision of Christ's passion despite the pain she is experiencing.

1. Lifton, *Death in Life*, 253.
2. Julian of Norwich, *Revelation of Love*, chap. 73, 145.
3. *Wikipedia*, the online encyclopedia, attributes 34 million deaths to the European Black Death pandemic. This compares with a total of 66 million deaths for World War I (which includes the death toll from the Spanish flu epidemic) and 62 million deaths for World War II. See *www.en.wikipedia.org/wiki/List_of_wars_and_disasters_by_death_toll*. If one includes figures for related outbreaks in Asia and the Middle East, the death toll for the plague pandemic is considerably higher, perhaps as great as 200 million.
4. There are some readers who may question the advisability of applying twentieth- and twenty-first-century research on survivors to Julian's experience of plague in the fourteenth century. I would argue that this comparison is appropriate based on the striking similarities I have observed between twentieth-century accounts of multiple death experiences and the accounts of plague loss. Even within the twentieth century, survivors of widely varying disastrous situations, such as the holocaust, Hiroshima, the Vietnam War, AIDS loss, and natural disasters, like the Buffalo Creek flood, appear to experience very similar effects. It would appear that post-traumatic stress and its symptoms seem fairly consistent across time. However, we must be careful to note, as Lifton does, that *"To observe common psychological responses of survivors . . . in no way suggests that the historical events themselves can be equated"* (original emphasis). It will be important in the present study, therefore, to observe both the similarities and differences that characterize the forms of multiple loss we shall explore. See Lifton, "Concept of the Survivor," in *Future of Immortality*, 232.
5. First, it is important to note that the rite for becoming an anchoress mimicked a requiem. The bishop led the anchoress by the hand into her cell and the door was bolted from without. In many practical respects, therefore, the anchoress was understood to be "dead to the world." Second, I agree with the position of a number of scholars that Julian may have been a mother who lost a child in the plague. I base my support for this view on several facts. It seems quite likely that Julian may have married before the onset of the second plague epidemic and given birth to a child. She would have lived to a marriageable age after the first epidemic, and one result of the first epidemic was an increase in the number of marriages and births. Second, it also seems likely that Julian may have lost a child and possibly a

spouse in one of the subsequent epidemics. The plagues of 1361 and 1369 were known to cause particularly heavy deaths among young men and children. Third, I do not find compelling evidence in the text to support the view that Julian was a nun. Fourth, I believe that the descriptions of the motherhood of Christ that occur in the text are quite compelling. I find it quite conceivable that they may reflect Julian's experience as a mother. However, it is important to note that there is no external evidence to support this view, nor is there likely to be any. Therefore, each reader must decide for himself or herself how to interpret the textual evidence on this point.

6. Lifton, "Concept of the Survivor," in *Future of Immortality*, 236.

7. Julian of Norwich, *Revelation of Love*, chap. 2, 3.

8. Ibid., 3–4.

9. In light of this, it is important to recall that the association of the plague with unprepared death was, as Horrox notes, "one of its particular terrors" (Horrox, *Black Death*, 245). This fear is addressed in the literature of the day, including the famous *Ars Moriendi*, a fifteenth-century French treatise on the art of dying well.

10. Julian of Norwich, *Revelation of Love*, chap. 8, 15.

11. Ibid., chap. 3, 4.

12. See the discussion of the death imprint, p. 25, above.

13. Julian of Norwich, *Revelation of Love*, chap. 7, 12.

14. Ibid., chap. 10, 18.

15. Ibid., chap. 10, 18, and chap. 16, 31.

16. Ibid., chap. 16, 31.

17. Ibid., chap. 17, 33. It would also appear that Julian's memories of her vision were characterized by the same vividness of recall that accompanies other survivors' descriptions of their death imprints. See Lifton, *Death in Life*, 482.

18. Lifton, *Death in Life*, 480.

19. Julian of Norwich, *Revelation of Love*, chap. 17, 34.

20. Ibid., chap. 18, 36.

21. Ibid., chap. 20, 38.

22. Ibid., chap. 17, 34.

23. We shall return to this issue of her efficacious interaction with the vision immediately below in our discussion of death guilt.

24. Ibid., chap. 21, 39.

25. Ibid., chap. 68, 137.

26. On the term "even Christians" see note 1, p. 211.

27. Lifton, *Future of Immortality*, 237.

28. Julian of Norwich, *Revelation of Love*, chap. 19, 37.

29. Ibid.
30. Ibid.
31. Ibid.
32. Ibid., chap. 22, 40.
33. Ibid., chap. 24, 44.
34. Ibid., chap. 37, 63.
35. Ibid., chap. 38, 64.
36. See n. 22 above.
37. On the former, see especially chap. 64. For the latter, see chap. 77, 152. "This place is a prison; this life is a penance. Yet it is a remedy that he wants us to enjoy. For the remedy is that our Lord is with us, keeping and leading us into the fullness of joy."
38. Julian of Norwich, *Revelation of Love*, chap. 64, 129.
39. Lifton, *Death in Life*, 367, describes the sense of connection, the sense of symbolic integrity, and the sense of movement as aspects of formulation.

Chapter Four: Julian's Theology of Wholeness

1. Julian of Norwich, *Revelation of Love*, chap. 20, 38, emphasis mine.
2. Julia Gatta, "Passion and Compassion in Julian of Norwich," in *The Pastoral Art of the English Mystics: Julian of Norwich, The Cloud of Unknowing, Walter Hilton* (Eugene, Ore.: Wipf & Stock, 2004), 87–88.
3. David Tracy, *Blessed Rage for Order: The New Pluralism in Theology* (New York: Seabury, 1975), 51.
4. Tracy describes the task of interpreting the meaning "in front of the text," the referent of the text, as a truly hermeneutical task. He notes that interpreters seeking to understand a text must attend both to the "sense" of the text and the "referents" of a text. The sense refers to "the internal structure and meaning of the text as that structure can be determined through the ordinary methods of semantic and literary-critical inquiry." The referent, in contrast, is "that way of perceiving reality, that mode of being-in-the-world which the text opens up for the intelligent reader." For religious texts, the referent expresses a religious way of looking at reality. For example, the referent or existential meaning of the New Testament affirmation that "Jesus is the Christ" is that "one can now live as though in the presence of a gracious God." Tracy borrows this particular interpretation of the New Testament affirmation from Herbert Braun. In elaborating his distinction between the sense and the referent of the text, he cites an

unpublished manuscript by Paul Ricoeur. See Tracy, *Blessed Rage for Order*, 52.

5. Ibid., 134 (original emphasis).

6. Ibid.

7. Ibid.

8. Julian of Norwich, *Revelation of Love*, chap. 27, 48.

9. Ibid., chap. 8, 16.

10. Ibid., chap. 9, 16.

11. Gatta, *The Pastoral Art of the English Mystics*, 54.

12. Ibid., 56.

13. See, for example, Grace Jantzen, *Julian of Norwich: Mystic and Theologian* (London: SPCK, 1987), 80; Ritamary Bradley, *Julian's Way: A Practical Commentary on Julian of Norwich* (London: Harper-Collins Religious, 1992), xii; and Denise Nowakowski Baker, *Julian of Norwich's Showings: From Vision to Book* (Princeton, N.J.: Princeton University Press), 137–41.

14. Colledge and Walsh, *Showings*, chap. vii, 135. This excerpt is from the Short Text.

15. Even in the Long Text, however, Julian continues to characterize herself as a "wretch." Ibid., chap. 8, 191.

16. Ibid., 335.

17. Julian of Norwich, *Revelation of Love*, chap. 32, 55.

18. Ibid., chap. 28, 49–50.

19. Grace Jantzen, *Power, Gender and Christian Mysticism* (Cambridge: Cambridge University Press, 1995), 183. In establishing her argument, Jantzen also refers to her earlier book *Julian of Norwich*, 96.

20. Julian of Norwich, *Revelation of Love*, chap. 33, 57.

21. See, for example, chap. 35 in the Long Text, in which Julian inquires about the fate of a specific "creature" that she loved. Christ responded that God is honored more through knowing all things in general rather than by taking delight in one thing in particular, that is, in knowing that "All shall be well." Julian of Norwich, *Revelation of Love*, 59.

22. Ibid., chap. 33, 57, emphasis mine.

23. Gatta, *The Pastoral Art of the English Mystics*, 57.

24. See Gatta, *The Pastoral Art of the English Mystics*, 59–62, for her response to these questions.

25. Julian of Norwich, *Revelation of Love*, chap. 49, 86.

26. In chap. 33 of the Long Text Julian admits that she herself saw no person who would not be saved. She admits intellectually through her faith in the church's teachings that not all would be saved, but she does say that she saw no sight either of hell or purgatory. She

does admit to having seen a sight of the devil, however, as one who is reproved and condemned by God.

27. Julian of Norwich, *Revelation of Love,* chap. 5, 8.

28. Ibid., chap. 32, 54.

29. Ibid., chap. 15, 30.

30. Ibid., chap. 35, 60.

31. Ibid., chap. 11, 23.

32. Rom. 8:28 (NRSV).

33. Julian of Norwich, *Revelation of Love,* chap. 11, 23.

34. Ibid., chap. 27, 48.

35. Ibid., chap. 53, 106.

36. Jantzen, *Julian of Norwich,* 142.

37. Ibid., 143. Julian experienced this twofold aspect of human nature in the eighth showing when she refused to look away from the cross. She expresses this in chap. 55 of the Long Text. This experience provides the foundation for the development of her anthropology.

38. Julian of Norwich, *Revelation of Love,* chap. 29, 50–51. Julian used the term "Adam's sin" to represent humankind's fall or "first sin." In the Parable of the Lord and Servant, Julian described this fall literally and metaphorically. In attempting to do the Lord's will, the servant stumbles and falls. This fall is not a deliberate turning away from God; instead, it appears to be a consequence of human vulnerability. The servant stumbles because of his undue haste in attempting to satisfy the Lord's request. Thus, the fall comes about not through disobedience, but through a desire to please that results in imprudent haste. Julian also described Adam's fall as a movement from life to death. Birth into the world, therefore, is a form of fall. The saving nature of Christ's birth compensates for the pain of Adam's birth. See chap. 52 of the Long Text for a discussion of Adam's fall.

39. Ibid., chap. 29, 51.

40. Ibid.

41. Ibid. Julian also contrasted the efficacy of God's action in creation and redemption with the activity of "the fiend." The fiend has the misfortune of seeing souls escape him continually "for all that God allows him to do turns to our joy, yet to him it is a constant source of shame and woe." See chap. 13, 26.

42. Ibid., chap. 40, 69.

43. Ibid., chap. 52, 103.

44. Baker, *Julian of Norwich's Showings,* 68.

45. Julian of Norwich, *Revelation of Love,* chap. 27, 48.

46. Ibid., chap. 52, 104.

47. Julian described this understanding of the rewards of heaven in chap. 38 in the Long Text. The purpose of these rewards is "to make us glad and happy in love." The theology provides a concrete example of the power of rightfulness of God's creative work which matches evil and its attendant suffering with a corresponding and equal power for goodness and joy.

48. Ibid., chap. 51, 98.

49. Ibid., chap. 52,103.

50. Ibid., chap. 53, 105.

51. Ibid., chap. 57, 114–15.

52. Ibid., chap. 62, 126.

53. Ibid., chap. 60, 121.

54. It is also possible, however, that Julian was drawing on the writing of other medieval theologians, including Anselm, who develops this same image. Jennifer Heimmel, for example, notes that Marguerite d'Oingt compares Christ's cross to a bed of labor and also speaks of his life and death in terms of a mother's labor. See Jennifer P. Heimmel, *"God Is Our Mother": Julian of Norwich and the Medieval Image of Christian Feminine Divinity*, Salzburg Studies in English Literature 92:5 (Salzburg, Austria: Institut für Anglistik und Amerikanistik Universität Salzburg, 1982), 27–29.

55. This image may also have provided Julian with a means of finding meaning in suffering. Childbirth certainly required much suffering; nevertheless, most often it yields new life. I wonder if Julian may have used the metaphor as an interpretive framework for plague-related suffering. Might she have asked what new life emerged from the pain of loss?

56. Julian of Norwich, *Revelation of Love*, chap. 60, 120.

57. Ibid., chap. 55, 110.

58. Heimmel, "God Is Our Mother," 54–55.

59. Julian of Norwich, *Revelation of Love*, chap. 32, 55.

60. Ibid., chap. 32, 56.

61. Ibid., chap. 32, 55.

62. A third issue that may also arise for survivors is that of justice, that is, survivors may struggle with why they are suffering whereas others are not. Or, alternatively, when suffering is clearly unjust, they may develop a survivor mission focused on restoring justice. For a discussion of this issue in the context of AIDS survivors, see p. 135 below.

63. Gatta, *The Pastoral Art of the English Mystics*, 69.

64. Colledge and Walsh, *Showings*, chap. 21, Long Text, 214–15. This scene also calls to mind the experience of childbirth when, at the

moment of birth, the pain of labor is forgotten as the mother rejoices in the child's birth.

65. Jane F. Maynard, *Finding Religious and Spiritual Meaning in AIDS-Related Multiple Loss* (Ann Arbor, Mich.: Proquest, UMI Microform 3123956, 1994).

66. Kenneth L. Schmidt, interview by author, October 20, 1999, San Francisco. Tape recording.

67. The notion of "overshadowing death" was introduced by Gregory Neil Shrader in his 1992 dissertation focused on gay male survivors of AIDS-related losses. Shrader used this term to describe one significant death that seemed to overshadow all the other losses the survivors had experienced. This death was usually the death that had the single greatest impact on the survivor. See Gregory Neil Schrader, *A Descriptive Study of the Effects of Continuous Multiple AIDS-Related Losses among Gay Male Survivors* (Ann Arbor, Mich.: University of Michigan Press, 1992), 87.

68. Schmidt, interview.

69. Ibid.

70. Colledge and Walsh, *Showings,* chap. 77, Long Text, 331.

71. Ibid.

72. Gatta, *The Pastoral Art of the English Mystics,* 72.

73. Maynard, *Finding Religious and Spiritual Meaning,* 50–59.

74. Lucinda Grey, interview by author, August 29, 1999, San Francisco, tape recording. The name is a pseudonym for the sake of privacy.

75. Ibid.

76. Krister Stendahl, "Immortality Is Too Much and Too Little," in *Meanings: The Bible as Document and as Guide* (Philadelphia: Fortress, 1984), 197.

77. William Katz, interview by author, August 24, 1999, San Francisco, tape recording. The name is a pseudonym for the sake of privacy.

78. Rosemary Radford Ruether, *Sexism and God-Talk: Toward a Feminist Theology* (Boston: Beacon, 1983), 294.

79. Ibid., 258.

80. Colledge and Walsh, *Showings,* 309.

Chapter Five: Julian's Spirituality of Trust and Longing

1. Julian of Norwich, *Revelation of Love,* chap. 33, 76.

2. Gatta, *The Pastoral Art of the English Mystics,* 76.

3. Julian of Norwich, *Revelation of Love,* chap. 8, 16.

4. Ibid., chap. 72, 144.

5. Ibid., chap. 86, 162.

6. Ibid., chap. 43, 77.

7. Ibid.

8. Ibid., chap. 51, 93.

9. Ibid., chap. 42, 73.

10. Ibid., chap. 47, 83.

11. Ibid.

12. Ibid., chap. 72, 143.

13. Ibid., chap. 77, 152.

14. Ibid., chap. 63, 128.

15. Ibid., chap. 78, 153.

16. Ibid., chap. 70, 140.

17. Jerome Washington, interview by author, October 12, 1999, San Francisco, tape recording. The name is a pseudonym given for the sake of privacy.

18. Michael Wallace, interview by author, August 27, 1999, San Francisco, tape recording. The name is a pseudonym given to protect privacy.

19. Tom Morris, interview by author, September 28, 1999, San Francisco, tape recording. The name is a pseudonym given to protect privacy.

20. Ibid.

21. Jan Herzog, interview by author, August 19, 1999, San Francisco, tape recording. The name is a pseudonym given to protect privacy.

22. Leona Stark, interview by author, September 10, 1999, San Francisco, tape recording. The name is a pseudonym given to protect privacy.

23. Silas Manning, interview by author, October 14, 1999, Berkeley, tape recording. The name is a pseudonym given to protect privacy.

24. Ibid.

25. Michael Wallace, interview.

26. Julian of Norwich, *Revelation of Love,* chap. 80, 156. Note that these correspond to Julian's oft-cited distinctions between nature, mercy, and grace. Common sense resides in our nature, the church's teachings are an expression of Christ's mercy, and grace is the action of the Holy Spirit.

27. Ibid.

28. Ibid., chap. 52, 102–3.

29. Ibid., chap. 64, 131.

30. Ibid, chaps. 47 and 70.
31. Ibid., chap. 31, 53.
32. Ibid., chap. 10, 21.
33. Ibid., chap. 81, 158.
34. Ibid., chap. 56, 112.
35. Ibid., chap. 43, 75.
36. Ibid., 75–76.
37. Ibid., chap. 42, 74.
38. Ibid., chap. 39, 67.
39. Washington interview, October 12, 1999.
40. Ibid.
41. Ibid.
42. Manning interview.
43. Wallace interview.
44. Washington, group interview by author, April 25, 2000, San Francisco, tape recording.
45. Ibid.
46. Isaac Watts (1674–1748), "I'll praise my Maker while I've breath," Hymn 429, *The Hymnal 1982*, alt. by John Wesley (1703–1791); alt. based on Psalm 146 (New York: Church Hymnal Corporation, 1982).
47. Julian of Norwich, *Revelation of Love*, chap. 82, 158.
48. Ibid.
49. Ibid.
50. Ibid., chap. 85, 161.
51. Ibid., chap. 86, 163.
52. Ibid., chap. 85, 162.

Chapter Six: Exploring Traumatic Loss through Terrorism, Tremors, Wind, and Waves

1. Julian of Norwich, *Revelation of Love*, chap. 86, 163.
2. Bernard J. Lee, "Practical Theology as Phronetic: A Working Paper from/for those in Ministry Education," *APT Occasional Papers* 1 (winter 1998): 11.
3. Conservative Rabbi Irwin Kula in "Act II: The Face of God," *Faith and Doubt at Ground Zero* (Boston: WGBG Educational Foundation, PBS Home Video, 2002).
4. "Executive Summary," *The 9/11 Commission Report: Final Report of the National Commission on Terrorist Attacks upon the United States*, July 2004, *www.9-11commission.gov/report/911Report _Exec.pdf.*

5. Wikipedia contributors, "Non-American Casualties of the September 11, 2001 Attacks," *www.en.wikipedia.org/w/index.php?title= Non-American_casualties_of_the_September_11,_2001_ Attacks& oldid=38491505* (accessed February 28, 2006).

6. Wikipedia contributors, "September 11, 2001 Attacks," online at *www.en.wikipedia.org/w/index.php?title=September_11,_2001_ attacks&oldid=41549192* (accessed February 28, 2006).

7. "Executive Summary," *9/11 Commission Report*, 2–3.

8. *The 9/11 Commission Report: Final Report of the National Commission on Terrorist Attacks upon the United States*, Authorized Edition (New York: W. W. Norton, 2004), 47.

9. "Act IV: The Face of Religion," *Faith and Doubt at Ground Zero*.

10. Lifton, *Superpower Syndrome*, 137.

11. Richard Bernstein and the staff of the *New York Times, Out of the Blue: The Story of September 11, 2001, from Jihad to Ground Zero* (New York: Times Books, 2002), 8.

12. Ibid., 4.

13. *Wikipedia*, "September 11, 2001 Attacks."

14. Steve Fisherman, "The Miracle Survivors," *New York*, September 11, 2003, *www.newyorkmetro.com/nymetro/news/sept11/2003/n _9189//index.html* (accessed February 28, 2006).

15. Ibid.

16. See Lifton, "Americans as Survivors" in *Superpower Syndrome*, 137–58. For the anthrax scare, see 159–63.

17. See Charles Strozier, "The World Trade Center Disaster and the Apocalyptic," *Psychoanalytic Dialogues* 12 (2002): 361–80.

18. Fisherman, "The Miracle Survivors," *New York*.

19. Lifton, *Superpower Syndrome*, 154–58.

20. Robert Lifton, interview by Bill Moyers, *NOW, PBS*, October 18, 2002. Transcript: *www.pbs.org/now/transcript/transcript_lifton.html*.

21. *9/11 Commission Report*, 51.

22. Ibid., 50–51.

23. Ibid., 52.

24. Rabbi Irwin Kula, "Act II: Face of God," *Faith and Doubt at Ground Zero*.

25. Professor Khaled Abou El-Fadl, "Act IV: The Face of Religion," *Faith and Doubt at Ground Zero*.

26. Lifton, *Superpower Syndrome*, 199.

27. Ibid., 193–94.

28. Lifton, *Superpower Syndrome*, 149, emphasis his.

29. Monsignor Lorenzo Albacete, "Epilogue," *Faith and Doubt at Ground Zero.*

30. Earthquake Hazards Program, U.S. Department of the Interior, U.S. Geological Survey, "FAQ Everything You Want to Know about This Earthquake and Tsunami," *www.earthquake.usgs.gov/ eqcenter/eqinthenews/2004/usslav/neic_slav_faq.html* (accessed February 28, 2006).

31. U.S. Department of the Interior, U.S. Geological Survey, Earthquake Hazards Program, "Tectonic Summary: Magnitude 9.0 Off the West Coast of Northern Sumatra," *www.earthquake.usgs.gov/ eqcenter/eqinthenews/2004/usslav/#summary* (accessed March 3, 2006).

32. Wikipedia contributors, "2004 Indian Ocean Earthquake," accessed online at *www.en.wikipedia.org/w/index.php?title=2004_ Indian_Ocean_earthquake&oldid=42037577* (accessed on March 3, 2006).

33. Ibid.

34. U.S. Department of Interior, "Tectonic Summary."

35. Barry Bearak, "The Day the Sea Came," *New York Times*, November 27, 2005, *www.select.nytimes.com/* (accessed January 16, 2006).

36. Wikipedia contributors, "Countries affected by the 2004 Indian Ocean Earthquake," online at *www.en.wikipedia.org/w/index.php?title =Countries_affected_by_the_2004_Indian_Ocean_earthquake& oldid=40793474* (accessed March 3, 2006).

37. Editorial Desk, "Tsunami Afterward: The One Face of Grief," *New York Times*, December 30, 2004, *www.select.nytimes.com/* (accessed January 16, 2006).

38. Erich Krauss, *Wave of Destruction: The Stories of Four Families and History's Deadliest Tsunami* (Emmaus, Pa.: Rodale, 2006), 161–62.

39. Ibid., 163.

40. David Rohde, "Asia's Deadliest Waves: Grieving Parents; Tsunami's Cruelest Toll: Sons and Daughters Lost," *New York Times*, January 7, 2005, *www.select.nytimes.com/* (accessed January 16, 2006).

41. Ian Fisher, "Asia's Deadly Waves: Damage. On Indonesia's West Coast, Those Who Kept Their Lives Cope with Losing Everything Else," *New York Times*, January 12, 2005, *www.select.nytimes .com/* (accessed January 16, 2006).

42. Rohde, "Asia's Deadliest Wave: Grieving Parents."

43. Wikipedia contributors, "2004 Indian Ocean Earthquake."

44. Erich Krauss, "Respect Your Elders," *New York Times*, December 26, 2005, *www.select.nytimes.com/* (accessed January 16, 2006).

45. Bearak, "The Day the Sea Came."

46. Ibid.

47. U.S. Department of the Interior, U.S. Geological Survey, "Magnitude 8.7 Northern Sumatra Indonesia," *www.earthquake.usgs.gov/ /eqcenter/eqinthenews/2005/usweax/* (accessed January 16, 2006).

48. Seth Mydans, "Indonesian Tsunami Survivors Fearful of New Disasters," *New York Times*, July 9, 2005, *www.select.nytimes.com/* (accessed January 16, 2006).

49. Krauss, *Wave of Destruction*, 178.

50. Ibid., 184–85.

51. Ibid., 207–9.

52. Ibid., 213–19.

53. Amy Waldman, Evelyn Rusli, and Hari Kumar, "Asia's Deadliest Waves: Religions; Faith Divides the Survivors and It Unites Them, Too," *New York Times*, January 12, 2005, *www.select.nytimes.com/* (accessed January 16, 2006).

54. Asoka Bandarage, interview by Neil Conan, "Analysis: Reconciling Religion and Disaster," *Talk of the Nation*, National Public Radio, January 5, 2005, *www.nl.newsbank.com/* (accessed January 23, 2006).

55. *CNN Reports: Katrina — State of Emergency* (Kansas City, Mo.: Andrews McMeel Publishing, 2005), 38.

56. Ibid., 12.

57. Ibid., 10

58. Ivor van Heerden, "Introduction," *CNN Reports: Katrina*, 7.

59. *CNN Reports: Katrina*, 10–11.

60. Eric Lipton, "Republicans' Report on Katrina Assails Administration Response," *New York Times*, February 13, 2006, *www.select .nytimes.com/* (accessed March 3, 2006).

61. Ibid.

62. *CNN Reports: Katrina*, 168.

63. Shaila Dewan, "For Want of Money, Remains of Some Hurricane Victims Are Not Collected," *New York Times*, February 17, 2006, *www.select.nytimes.com/* (accessed February 18, 2006).

64. Ibid.

65. John Grisham, "Silent Nights on the Gulf Coast," *New York Times*, December 25, 2005, *www.select.nytimes.com/* (accessed February 18, 2006).

66. Shaila Dewan, "Hotel Aid Ends; Katrina Evacuees Seek Housing Again," *New York Times*, February 14, 2006, *www.select.nytimes .com/* (accessed February 18, 2006).

67. Adam Nossiter, "Hurricane Takes a Further Toll: Suicides Up in New Orleans," *New York Times*, December 27, 2005, *www.select .nytimes.com/* (accessed February 18, 2006).

68. Ibid.

69. Ibid.

70. Jane E. Brody, "After the Hurricanes, the Inner Storm for Children," *New York Times*, September 27, 2005, *www.select/nytimes .com/* (accessed February 18, 2006).

71. Jennifer Medina, "Storm and Crisis: Returnees, in Those Largely Spared, a Stubborn Sense of Guilt," *New York Times*, October 18, 2005, *www.select/nytimes.com/* (accessed February 18, 2006).

72. American Red Cross, "2005–2006 Disaster Relief Fund Donors Help Red Cross Respond," online at *www.redcross.org/sponsors/drf/ FY06_recognition.html* (accessed March 3, 2006).

73. Thomas Frank, "Katrina Inspires Record Charity," *USA Today*, November 30, 2005, *www.redcross.org/sponsors/drf/FY06_recognition .html* (accessed March 3, 2006).

74. Elisabeth Bumiller and Anne E. Kornblut, "Storm and Crisis: Political Memo; Black Leaders Say Storm Forced Bush to Confront Issues of Race and Poverty," *New York Times*, September 18, 2005, *www.select/nytimes.com/* (accessed February 18, 2006).

75. Ibid.

76. *CNN Reports: Katrina*, 173.

Chapter Seven: A Pastoral Theology and Praxis for Survivors of Traumatic Loss

1. Bonnie J. Miller-McLemore and Herbert Anderson, "Gender and Pastoral Care," in *Pastoral Care and Social Conflict*, ed. Pamela D. Couture and Rodney J. Hunter (Nashville: Abingdon, 1995), 111. The reference to brokenheartedness is drawn from Rita Nakashima Brock, *Journeys by Heart: A Christology of Erotic Power* (New York: Crossroad Publishing, 1988). The reference to the voice of God is from Charles Gerkin, "On the Art of Caring," *Journal of Pastoral Care* 45 (Winter): 406.

2. See chap. 6, n. 14.

3. Lifton, *Superpower Syndrome*, 138.

4. See chap. 6, n. 24.

5. Julian of Norwich, *Revelation of Love,* chap. 77, 152.

6. Stendahl, "Immortality Is Too Much," 197.

7. See the notes to chap. 1 for references to the work of these experts.

8. EMDR refers to eye movement desensitization and reprocessing. This is a specialized psychotherapeutic technique used for treating post-traumatic stress disorder that combines elements of cognitive behavioral therapy, exposure therapy, and attention to eye movements. See "American Psychiatric Association Practice Guidelines. Practice Guidelines for the Treatment of Patients with Acute Stress Disorder and Posttraumatic Stress Disorder," accessed August 12, 2006, at *www.psych.org/psych-prac/treat/pg/PTSD-PG-PartsA-B-C-New.pdf.*

9. See, for example, World Health Organization, *Mental Health in Emergencies: Mental and Social Aspects of Health of Populations Exposed to Extreme Stressors,* 2003, *www.who.int/mental_health/media/en/640.pdf,* 4 (accessed March 3, 2006).

10. Andrew J. Weaver, Laura T. Flannelly and John D. Preston, "Making a Referral to a Mental Health Specialist," in Weaver, Flannelly, and Preston, *Counseling Survivors of Traumatic Events,* 191–95.

11. Andrew D. Lester, *Hope in Pastoral Care and Counseling* (Louisville: Westminster John Knox, 1995).

12. Camille B. Wortman and Roxanne Cohen Silver, "The Myths of Coping with Loss," *Journal of Consulting and Clinical Psychology* 57, no. 3 (1989): 349–57.

13. James W. Pennebaker, *Opening Up: The Healing Power of Confiding in Others* (New York: W. Morrow, 1990).

14. Lifton, *Superpower Syndrome,* 192.

15. Washington, interview, October 12, 1999.

16. John Donne, "Meditation 17," in *England in Literature,* ed. Robert C. Pooley, George K. Anderson, Paul Farmer, and Helen Thornton (Glenview, Ill.: Scott, Foresman, 1968), 184–85.

17. Robert Llewelyn, "Julian and Her Cell Today," in *With Pity Not with Blame* (1982; repr. London: Darton, Longman & Todd, 2003), 1.

For Further Reading

Julian of Norwich: Primary Sources

Julian of Norwich. *Revelations of Divine Love.* Trans. Grace Warrack. London: Methuen, 1907.

———. *A Shewing of God's Love.* Ed. Anna Maria Reynolds. London: Sheed & Ward, 1974.

———. *Showings.* Trans. Edmund Colledge and James Walsh. New York: Paulist, 1978.

———. *Revelation of Love: Julian of Norwich.* Ed. and trans. John Skinner. Image Books. New York: Doubleday, 1997.

———. *Revelations of Divine Love.* Trans. Elizabeth Spearing. London: Penguin, 1998.

Julian of Norwich: Secondary Sources

Theology and Spirituality

Baker, Denise Nowakowski. *Julian of Norwich's Showings: From Vision to Book.* Princeton, N.J.: Princeton University Press, 1994.

Bradley, Ritamary. *Julian's Way: A Practical Commentary on Julian of Norwich.* London: HarperCollinsReligious, 1992.

Heimmel, Jennifer P. *"God Is Our Mother": Julian of Norwich and the Medieval Image of Christian Feminine Divinity.* Salzburg Studies in English Literature, 92:5. Salzburg, Austria: Institut für Anglistik und Amerikanistik, Universität Salzburg, 1982.

Jantzen, Grace. *Julian of Norwich: Mystic and Theologian.* London: SPCK, 1987.

———. *Power, Gender and Christian Mysticism.* Cambridge: Cambridge University Press, 1995.

Llewelyn, Robert. *With Pity Not with Blame: The Spirituality of Julian of Norwich and the Cloud of Unknowing for Today.* London: Darton, Longman & Todd, 1982.

———, ed. *Julian, Woman of Our Day.* London: Darton, Longman & Todd, 1985.

Pelphrey, Brant. *Love Was His Meaning: The Theology and Mysticism of Julian of Norwich.* Salzburg, Austria: Institut für Anglistik und Amerikanistik, Universität Salzburg, 1982.

Julian's Times

Aberth, John. *From the Brink of Apocalypse: Confronting Famine, War, Plague and Death in the Later Middle Ages.* New York: Routledge, 2001.

Gatta, Julia. *The Pastoral Art of the English Mystics: Julian of Norwich, The Cloud of Unknowing, Walter Hilton.* Eugene, Ore.: Wipf & Stock, 2004.

Gilchrist, Roberta, and Marilyn Oliva. *Religious Women in Medieval East Anglia: History and Archaeology.* Studies in East Anglian History, 1. Norwich, England: Centre of East Anglian Studies, University of East Anglia, 1993.

Kempe, Margery. *The Book of Margery Kempe.* Trans. B. A. Windeatt. Rev. ed. New York: Penguin, 1994.

Nuth, Joan M. *God's Lovers in an Age of Anxiety: The Medieval English Mystics.* London: Darton, Longman & Todd, 2001.

Tanner, Norman P. *The Church in Late Medieval Norwich, 1370–1532.* Toronto: Pontifical Institute of Medieval Studies, 1984.

Tuchman, Barbara W. *A Distant Mirror: The Calamitous 14th Century.* New York: Ballantine Books, 1978.

Black Death

Cantor, Norman F. *In the Wake of the Plague: The Black Death and the World It Made.* New York: Free Press, 2001.

Friedman, John B. "'He hath a thousand slayn this pestilence': The Iconography of the Plague in the Late Middle Ages." In *Social Unrest in the Late Middle Ages: Papers of the Fifteenth Annual Conference of the Center for Medieval and Early Renaissance Studies,* ed. Francis X. Newman, 75–112. Binghamton, N.Y.: Medieval and Renaissance Texts and Studies, 1986.

Horrox, Rosemary, ed. and trans. *The Black Death.* Manchester Medieval Series. Manchester: Manchester University Press, 1994.

Ormrod, Mark, and Phillip Lindley, eds. *The Black Death in England.* Stamford, Lincolnshire, England: Paul Watkins, 1996.

Literature on Traumatic Loss

Psychological Analyses of Traumatic Loss

Erikson, Kai T. *Everything in Its Path: Destruction of Community in the Buffalo Creek Flood.* New York: Simon & Schuster, 1976.

Goldblum, Peter, and Sarah Erickson. *Working with AIDS Bereavement: A Comprehensive Approach for Mental Health Providers.* UCSF AIDS Health Project, Monograph Series, 3. San Francisco: University of California San Francisco, 1999.

Lifton, Robert Jay. *The Broken Connection: On Death and the Continuity of Life.* New York: Simon & Schuster, 1979.

————. *Death in Life: Survivors of Hiroshima.* New York: Random House, 1967.

————. *The Future of Immortality and Other Essays for a Nuclear Age.* New York: Basic Books, 1987.

Zinner, Ellen, ed. *When a Community Weeps: Case Studies in Group Survivorship.* Philadelphia: Brunner/Mazel, 1999.

Contemporary Experiences of Traumatic Loss

Bernstein, Richard, and the staff of the *New York Times. Out of the Blue: The Story of September 11, 2001, from Jihad to Ground Zero.* New York: Times Books, 2002.

CNN Reports. *Katrina: State of Emergency.* Kansas City, Mo.: Andrew McMeel Publishing, 2005.

Editors of *TIME. Hurricane Katrina: The Storm That Changed America.* New York: TIME Books, 2005.

Garfield, Charles A., with Cindy Springer and Doris Ober. *Sometimes My Heart Goes Numb: Love and Caregiving in a Time of AIDS.* San Francisco: Jossey-Bass, 1995.

Johnson, Fenton. *Geography of the Heart: A Memoir.* New York: Scribner, 1996.

Krauss, Erich. *Wave of Destruction: The Stories of Four Families and History's Deadliest Tsunami.* Emmaus, Pa.: Rodale, 2005.

Lifton, Robert. *Superpower Syndrome: America's Apocalyptic Confrontation with the World.* New York: Thunder's Mouth Press, 2003.

Mann, Jonathan, and Daniel Tarantola, eds. *AIDS in the World II: Global Dimensions, Social Roots and Responses.* Global AIDS Policy Commission. New York: Oxford University Press, 1996.

The 9/11 Commission Report. Final Report of the National Commission on Terrorist Acts upon the United States. Authorized edition. New York: W. W. Norton, 2004.

Nord, David. *Multiple AIDS-Related Loss: A Handbook for Understanding and Surviving a Perpetual Fall.* Washington, D.C.: Taylor & Francis, 1997.

Shepard, Benjamin Heim, ed. *White Nights and Ascending Shadows: An Oral History of the San Francisco AIDS Epidemic.* London: Cassell, 1997.

Shrader, Gregory Neil. "A Descriptive Study of the Effects of Continuous Multiple AIDS-Related Losses among Gay Male Survivors." Ph.D. diss., California School of Professional Psychology, Los Angeles, 1992.

Wortman, Camille B., and Roxanne Cohen Silver. "The Myths of Coping with Loss." *Journal of Consulting and Clinical Psychology* 57, no. 3 (1989): 349–57.

Pastoral Literature Helpful to Caregivers

Graham, Larry Kent. *Care of Persons, Care of Worlds: A Psychosystems Approach to Pastoral Care and Counseling.* Nashville: Abingdon, 1992.

————. *Discovering Images of God: Narratives of Care among Lesbians and Gays.* Louisville: Westminster John Knox, 1997.

Hardy, Richard P. *Knowing the God of Compassion: Spirituality and Persons Living with AIDS.* Inner Journey Series. Ottawa: Novalis, 1993.

————. *Loving Men: Gay Partners, Spirituality and AIDS.* New York: Continuum, 1998.

Lester, Andrew. *Hope in Pastoral Care and Counseling.* Louisville: Westminster John Knox, 1999.

Sunderland, Ron. *Getting through Grief: Caregiving by Congregations.* Nashville: Abingdon, 1993.

Weatherford, Ronald Jeffrey, and Carole Boston Weatherford. *Somebody's Knocking at Your Door: AIDS and the African-American Church.* Binghamton, N.Y.: Haworth Pastoral Press, 1999.

Weaver, Andrew J., Laura T. Flannelly, and John D. Preston, *Counseling Survivors of Traumatic Events: A Handbook for Pastors and Other Helping Professionals.* Nashville: Abingdon, 2003.

Woodward, James, ed. *Embracing the Chaos: Theological Responses to AIDS.* London: SPCK, 1990.

Printed in the United States
62745LVS00005B/124-249